2007
Moon Sign Book

THIS BOOK BELONGS TO

WENDY LEE

613-774-5460

THIS BOOK BELONGS to

Editor/Designer: Sharon Leah
Cover Design & Art: Gavin Dayton Duffy
Cover Photo © age fotostock/SuperStock
ISBN 0-7387-0325-7

You can order Llewellyn annuals and books from *New Worlds*, Llewellyn's
magazine catalog. To request _____ 1-877-
NEW-WRLD, or visit our We_____

Llewellyn is a registered trade_____
2134 Wooddale Drive, Wood_____
Printed in the U.S.A.

NS
A ST.
METCALFE, ONTARIO
WWW.LUVDRAGONS.CA

D0967708

Table of Contents

". . . the times, they are a changing."

—BOB DYLAN

To Readers

A lot has changed in this country and around the world since 1905, when pizza was introduced in New York City by Gennaro Lombardi, and the Pennsylvania Railroad's "fastest train in the world" made the trip between New York and Chicago in eighteen hours. The *Moon Sign Book* was published for the first time in Portland, Oregon, that same year.

Today, a space shuttle can fly around Earth in ninety minutes at an altitude of about 190 miles, pizza is as close as the nearest store, and the *Moon Sign Book*, now in its 102nd year, is published in Woodbury, Minnesota.

Back in 1905, the *Moon Sign Book* was 4" X 5.75" in size, it contained about 150 pages, and sold for $1. Readers wanted to know the best times to plant their gardens and harvest their crops, when to travel, roof a building, and sell their livestock, among other things. Today, more people live in urban areas than ever before, but we still love to garden and plan our lives in sync with natural cycles. So, the daily information you expect—the

Moon's sign, phase, void-of-course times, and planetary aspects, the tables of favorable and unfavorable days, and activity timing aids—are still in this almanac. For the gardeners among you, we've created a new gardening guide and forecast section that begins on page 7. There you'll find the best dates to plant, fertilize, weed, and harvest your crops in weekly tables for easy use. Be sure and check Kris Brandt Riske's weather forecasts for eight zones when you need information about short- and long-range weather trends, and Dorothy Kovach's insights on the economic trends we can expect in 2007 may put you on track toward a better financial future.

And back, due to popular demand, is the Astro Almanac! This at-a-glance timing guide, which begins on page 94, shows the best times to begin activities, from the simple things, like getting a haircut, to the complex, like buying or selling a home.

If you want to choose your own times to begin projects, plan meetings, etc., you'll find a convenient how to guide beginning on page 106.

Why Our Almanac Is Different

Readers have asked why the *Moon Sign Book* says that the Moon is in Taurus and some almanacs indicate that the Moon is in the previous sign of Aries on the same date. It's because there are two different zodiac systems in use today: the tropical and the sidereal. The *Moon Sign Book* is based on the tropical zodiac.

The tropical zodiac takes 0 degrees of Aries to be the Spring Equinox in the Northern Hemisphere. This is the time and date when the Sun is directly overhead at noon along the equator, usually about March 20–21. The rest of the signs are positioned at 30 degree intervals from this point.

The sidereal zodiac, which is based on the location of fixed stars, uses the positions of the fixed stars to determine the starting point of 0 degrees of Aries. In the sidereal system, 0 degrees of Aries always begins at the same point. This does create a problem though, because the positions of the fixed stars, as seen from Earth, have changed since the constellations were named. The term "precession of the equinoxes" is used to describe the change.

Precession of the equinoxes describes an astronomical phenomenon brought about by the Earth's wobble as it rotates and orbits the Sun. The Earth's axis is inclined toward the Sun at an angle of about 23½ degrees, which creates our seasonal weather changes. Although the change is slight, because one complete circle of the Earth's axis takes 25,800 years to complete, we can actually see that the positions of the fixed stars seem to shift. The result is that each year, in the tropical system, the Spring Equinox occurs at a slightly different time.

Does Precession Matter?

There is an accumulative difference of about 23 degrees between the Spring Equinox (0 degrees Aries in the tropical zodiac and 0 degrees Aries in the sidereal zodiac) so that 0 degrees Aries at Spring Equinox in the tropical zodiac actually occurs at about 7 degrees Pisces in the sidereal zodiac system. You can readily see that those who use the other almanacs may be planting seeds (in the garden and in their individual lives) based on the belief that it is occurring in a fruitful sign, such as Taurus, when in fact it would be occurring in Gemini, one of the most barren signs of the zodiac. So, if you wish to plant and plan activities by the Moon, it is helpful to follow the *Moon Sign Book*. Before we go on, there are important things to understand about the Moon, her cycles, and their correlation with everyday living. For more information about gardening by the Moon, see page 60.

Gardening Guide & Forecasts

Your Guide to Lunar Gardening, Weather, and the Economy for 2007

I think having land and not ruining it is the most beautiful art anyone could want to own.

— ANDY WARHOL

January

Week of January 1–6

Be not afraid of greatness; some men are born great, some achieve greatness, and some have greatness thrust upon them.

—WILLIAM SHAKESPEARE

Jan 2, 10:14 am– Jan 3, 8:57 am	2nd	Cancer	Plant grains, leafy annuals. Fertilize (chemical). Graft or bud plants. Irrigate. Trim to increase growth.
Jan 3, 8:57 am– Jan 4, 4:14 pm	3rd	Cancer	Plant biennials, perennials, bulbs, and roots. Prune. Irrigate. Fertilize (organic).
Jan 4, 4:14 pm– Jan 7, 1:18 am	3rd	Leo	Cultivate. Destroy weeds and pests. Harvest fruits and root crops for food. Trim to retard growth.

Blueberries are considered one of the world's healthiest foods and scientists have confirmed that they protect against an array of common disorders from inflammation to tired eyes to brain aging! They have the highest antioxidant capacity of all fruits and vegetables, and adding just ½ cup a day to your diet is enough to provide health benefits.

JANUARY

S	M	T	W	T	F	S
	1	2	3	4	5	6
7	8	9	10	11	12	13
14	15	16	17	18	19	20
21	22	23	24	25	26	27
28	29	30	31			

Jan 7, 1:18 am– Jan 9, 1:15 pm	3rd	Virgo	Cultivate, especially medicinal plants. Destroy weeds and pests. Trim to retard growth.
Jan 12, 2:08 am– Jan 14, 1:11 pm	4th	Scorpio	Plant biennials, perennials, bulbs, and roots. Prune. Irrigate. Fertilize (organic).

Capricorn (December 21–January 20) and its ruler, Saturn, are associated with structure and limitation, which can also be thought about as "containment." Capricorn rules the knees, bone structure, and skin, architects, builders, and a building's framework. Your garden's structure is under Capricorn's influence as well. So as the Sun travels through Capricorn, take advantage of the planetary energy and plan the structure of the gardens you'll plant in a few months.

Herbs known to be ruled by Capricorn are:

- Wintergreen, used to remedy rheumatism in the joints
- Comfrey root, an excellent remedy for skin problems that can be applied as an ointment
- Slippery elm, a cooling and soothing digestive aid that also strengthens the bone structure

_____

_____

_____

_____

_____

_____

Jan 14, 1:11 pm– Jan 16, 8:49 pm	4th	Sagittarius	Cultivate. Destroy weeds and pests. Harvest fruits and root crops for food. Trim to retard growth.
Jan 16, 8:49 pm– Jan 18, 11:01 pm	4th	Capricorn	Plant potatoes and tubers. Trim to retard growth.
Jan 18, 11:01 pm– Jan 19, 1:15 am	1st	Capricorn	Graft or bud plants. Trim to increase growth.

Birds are finicky about the company they keep, or as the saying goes: "Birds of a feather flock together." They're finicky about the food they eat, too. For example:

- Mourning doves prefer red and white millet or cracked corn
- Blue jays prefer black sunflower seeds, peanut kernels, or suet
- Chickadees prefer black sunflower seeds or suet
- Wrens prefer suet
- House finches prefer white millet, and black or hulled sunflower seeds

_____

_____

_____

JANUARY

S	M	T	W	T	F	S
		1	2	3	4	5	6
7	8	9	10	11	12	13
14	15	16	17	18	19	20
21	22	23	24	25	26	27
28	29	30	31			

Jan 21, 3:48 am– Jan 23, 5:52 am	1st	Pisces	Plant grains, leafy annuals. Fertilize (chemical). Graft or bud plants. Irrigate. Trim to increase growth.
Jan 25, 8:28 am– Jan 25, 6:01 pm	1st	Taurus	Plant annuals for hardiness. Trim to increase growth.
Jan 25, 6:01 pm– Jan 27, 12:10 pm	2nd	Taurus	Plant annuals for hardiness. Trim to increase growth.

The Sun will be in Aquarius from January 20 to February 18. After the limitation we experienced in many ways during the past month, the desire to break free is strong. Perhaps it is the energy of Aquarius and Uranus, its ruler, that moves so many of us to take vacations in foreign destinations at this time of year. Aquarius opposes Leo, the Sun's home, and we are drawn, like bees are to honey, to the nurturing warmth of places where the Sun reigns supreme.

In southern areas of the U.S., it's time to plant cool-season annuals. Some of these include balsam, calendula, hollyhocks, coneflower, annual phlox, and larkspur.

Be sure to provide protection—heavy mulch or a temporary cover—and sufficient water to protect your plants from serious freezing. Watering is especially important for bare-root plants and trees.

February

Week of January 28–February 3

I'm fat, but I'm thin inside. Has it ever struck you that there's a thin man inside every fat man, just as they say there is a statue inside every block of stone?

— GEORGE ORWELL, *COMING UP FOR AIR*

Jan 29, 5:16 pm– Feb 1, 12:14 am	2nd	Cancer	Plant grains, leafy annuals. Fertilize (chemical). Graft or bud plants. Irrigate. Trim to increase growth.

At this time of year, not so long ago, gardeners—especially those of us who live in northern climates—watched and waited for seed catalogs to arrive in our mailboxes. Once those wonderful messengers of spring arrived, we spent hours poring over the pages and planning what to plant when the ground warmed enough. Today, we can log onto the Internet and visit the Web sites of favorite suppliers to satisfy the impulse to shop for seeds. Next time you're browsing the Internet, check out Web sites like Seed Savers Exchange at www.seedsavers.org.

_____

_____

_____

_____

FEBRUARY

S	M	T	W	T	F	S
				1	2	3
4	5	6	7	8	9	10
11	12	13	14	15	16	17
18	19	20	21	22	23	24
25	26	27	28			

Feb 5, 9:15 pm– Feb 8, 10:09 am	3rd	Libra	Plant annuals for fragrance and beauty. Trim to increase growth.
Feb 8, 10:09 am– Feb 10, 4:51 am	3rd	Scorpio	Plant grains, leafy annuals. Fertilize (chemical). Graft or bud plants. Irrigate. Trim to increase growth .
Feb 10, 4:51 am– Feb 10, 10:01 pm	4th	Scorpio	Plant biennials, perennials, bulbs and roots. Prune. Irrigate. Fertilize (organic).

Now is the time to plant roses if you live where the ground is not frozen and covered with snow. Libra is the zodiac sign associated with beauty and fragrance, and Libra-ruled roses embody both qualities. Your roses will be happiest if you locate them in places that get morning or midday sunlight.

"Elle," a 2005 All-American Rose Selection winner, is a hybrid tea that produces pink flowers tipped with gold on 10-inch stems. With blooms that don't fade, and its spicy-citrus fragrance, this rose may be perfect in your garden.

If romance is high on your list, you may want to consider the beautiful white "Bolero." It's fragrant and lush, and it can be trained to grow up an arbor or trellis.

Feb 10, 10:01 pm–Feb 13, 6:42 am	4th	Sagittarius	Cultivate. Destroy weeds and pests. Harvest fruits and root crops for food. Trim to retard growth.
Feb 13, 6:42 am–Feb 15, 11:34 am	4th	Capricorn	Plant potatoes and tubers. Trim to retard growth.
Feb 15, 11:34 am–Feb 17, 11:14 am	4th	Aquarius	Cultivate. Destroy weeds and pests. Harvest fruits and root crops for food. Trim to retard growth.
Feb 17, 1:30 pm–Feb 19, 2:06 pm	1st	Pisces	Plant grains, leafy annuals. Fertilize (chemical). Graft or bud plants. Irrigate. Trim to increase growth.

Crocus, narcissus, and daffodil bulbs planted now will produce blooms in early April. Bigger bulbs will usually produce larger blooms, so if you're planting in indoor pots, size should be a consideration when you select your bulbs. Buy bulbs that have been stored in a cool area—60 degrees Fahrenheit or cooler. Look for plump bulbs with no bruises or cuts. If you're planting outside, choose a sunny location and well-drained soil. Add compost or peat moss to your soil if needed to improve drainage.

FEBRUARY

S	M	T	W	T	F	S
				1	2	3
4	5	6	7	8	9	10
11	12	13	14	15	16	17
18	19	20	21	22	23	24
25	26	27	28			

Feb 21, 3:03 pm– Feb 23, 5:42 pm	1st	Taurus	Plant annuals for hardiness. Trim to increase growth.

Common complaints at this time of year include sore throats, coughs from colds, and depression. The energy is "yin" (damp, cold, withdrawn), and to balance it, or alleviate the symptoms, we need to introduce "yang" (active, outgoing) energy through activity and what we eat or drink. Activities that get you out of the house—classes, walking, skating, or running—are yang activities.

Use bee balm or coltsfoot for colds and to relieve coughing. Garlic helps your heart stay healthy and keeps colds away. Nasturtium is considered a stimulant (try it in tea), and its peppery taste makes it a good addition to salads.

Other stimulants include mint, cloves, parsley, rosemary, cinnamon, and cayenne pepper. Try to include them in your food dishes whenever possible.

Rose hips added to teas or fruit juices will provide extra vitamin C to your diet. Add 2 teaspoons of chopped rose hips to boiling water, cover and steep for 15 minutes, sweeten, and enjoy!

March

Week of February 25–March 3

Let us not forget that the cultivation of the Earth is the most important labor of man. When tillage begins, other arts will follow. The farmers, therefore, are the founders of civilization.

—DANIEL WEBSTER

Feb 25, 10:47 pm–Feb 28, 6:29 am	2nd	Cancer	Plant grains, leafy annuals. Fertilize (chemical). Graft or bud plants. Irrigate. Trim to increase growth.

Some evidence suggests an eclipse will have a negative effect on things that are planted or harvested on an eclipse day because the energy of the more distant planet is interrupted or altered by the energy of the closer planet, or the Moon if it's a lunar eclipse. There will be a lunar eclipse on March 3 and again on August 28, and a solar eclipse on March 18 and again on September 11 of this year.

MARCH

S	M	T	W	T	F	S
				1	2	3
4	5	6	7	8	9	10
11	12	13	14	15	16	17
18	19	20	21	22	23	24
25	26	27	28	29	30	31

Mar 3, 6:17 pm– Mar 5, 4:25 am	3rd	Virgo	Cultivate, especially medicinal plants. Destroy weeds and pests. Trim to retard growth.
Mar 7, 5:16 pm– Mar 10, 5:37 am	3rd	Scorpio	Plant biennials, perennials, bulbs, and roots. Prune. Irrigate. Fertilize (organic).
Mar 10, 5:37 am– Mar 11, 11:54 pm	3rd	Sagittarius	Cultivate. Destroy weeds and pests. Harvest fruits and root crops for food. Trim to retard growth.

Temperature fluctuations—typical of spring weather—are vital to the flow of sap in maple trees. On warm days, pressure develops in the trees and causes the sap to flow out through a wound or tap hole. When temperatures fall below freezing, water is pulled into the tree through the roots, replenishing sap that was lost. Only healthy trees should be tapped, and damage doesn't occur to the tree when guidelines are followed, because only about 10 percent of the available sap is removed during a typical "sap season."

Mar 11, 11:54 pm– Mar 12, 4:34 pm	4th	Sagittarius	Cultivate. Destroy weeds and pests. Harvest fruits and root crops for food. Trim to retard growth.
Mar 12, 4:34 pm– Mar 14, 10:52 pm	4th	Capricorn	Plant potatoes and tubers. Trim to retard growth.
Mar 14, 10:52 pm– Mar 17, 1:30 am	4th	Aquarius	Cultivate. Destroy weeds and pests. Harvest fruits and root crops for food. Trim to retard growth.
Mar 17, 1:30 am– Mar 18, 10:42 pm	4th	Pisces	Plant biennials, perennials, bulbs, and roots. Prune. Irrigate. Fertilize (organic).

Many gardeners will agree that experience and results are wonderful teachers, and experiments can be fun. The "rules" for gardening by the Moon's sign and phase had a trial-and-error beginning, and the results of those early experiments benefit us today. Early gardeners learned that it is as important to choose the best times to hoe as it is to plant. You might try your own experiments, like hoeing lettuce during the fourth quarter (diminishing), while the Moon is in Pisces (water sign), and comparing the results you get if you hoe lettuce while the Moon is in Aquarius (air sign). If you need some motivation, see page 89.

MARCH

S	M	T	W	T	F	S
				1	2	3
4	5	6	7	8	9	10
11	12	13	14	15	16	17
18	19	20	21	22	23	24
25	26	27	28	29	30	31

Mar 18, 10:42 pm–Mar 19, 1:41 am	1st	Pisces	Plant grains, leafy annuals. Fertilize (chemical). Graft or bud plants. Irrigate. Trim to increase growth.
Mar 21, 1:15 am–Mar 23, 2:06 am	1st	Taurus	Plant annuals for hardiness. Trim to increase growth.

Take cuttings from plants you want to propagate when the Moon is waxing and in the sign related to the plant "type." Plants with soft, watery stems (like African violets) will do best when cuttings are taken when the Moon is in a water sign (Pisces, Cancer, or Scorpio), and plants or bushes with woody stems will do best when cuttings are taken in earth signs (Taurus and Capricorn). Wrap the cuttings in moistened paper and plant them after the Full Moon (in a sign related to the plant) to promote root growth. After the Full Moon, the energy is descending and root growth will be more vigorous.

Mar 25, 5:49 am– Mar 25, 2:16 pm	1st	Cancer	Plant grains, leafy annuals. Fertilize (chemical). Graft or bud plants. Irrigate. Trim to increase growth.
Mar 25, 2:16 pm– Mar 27, 1:04 pm	2nd	Cancer	Plant grains, leafy annuals. Fertilize (chemical). Graft or bud plants. Irrigate. Trim to increase growth.

Crop rotation is very important if you want to grow healthy plants and minimize insect pests. Rotating crops is as important for backyard gardeners as it is for farmers. It may seem too challenging to rotate crops in a small garden, but when you consider the limited space you have to work with, it becomes even more important to protect the integrity of your soil. Planting different crop families, and following the "root, leaf, blossom, and fruit" model, is recommended. For example, in year one, plant carrots (root), followed by peas (leaf) in year two, flowers (blossom) in year three, and tomatoes (fruit) in year four. Then, start over again. Plan your garden ahead of time, write it down so you don't forget, and enjoy the variety your small spaces can provide.

_____

_____

_____

_____

MARCH

S	M	T	W	T	F	S
				1	2	3
4	5	6	7	8	9	10
11	12	13	14	15	16	17
18	19	20	21	22	23	24
25	26	27	28	29	30	31

 # April

Week of April 1–7

Whatever you do, stamp out abuses and love those who love you.
—VOLTAIRE, *LETTER TO M. D'ALEMBERT,*
11/28/1762

Apr 1, 11:43 am–Apr 2, 1:15 pm	2nd	Libra	Plant annuals for fragrance and beauty. Trim to increase growth.
Apr 4, 12:35 am–Apr 6, 12:56 pm	3rd	Scorpio	Plant biennials, perennials, bulbs and roots. Prune. Irrigate. Fertilize (organic).
Apr 6, 12:56 pm–Apr 8, 11:36 pm	3rd	Sagittarius	Cultivate. Destroy weeds and pests. Harvest fruits and root crops for food. Trim to retard growth.

Bird watching is a fascinating hobby, and easy to do from your own backyard or balcony. Providing wild birds with food, water, and a place to live adds to the fun, but when it comes to birdhouses, location is very important. Bluebirds like nesting boxes that are at the edge of a field or lawn. Chickadees like their houses about five feet from the ground and hanging from a tree branch (the hole should be 1⅛ inch in diameter). Flycatchers want their nests to be up high. Place their houses in an orchard, or at the edge of a field, about 10 feet off the ground.

	APRIL					
S	M	T	W	T	F	S
1	2	3	4	5	6	7
8	9	10	11	12	13	14
15	16	17	18	19	20	21
22	23	24	25	26	27	28
29	30					

Apr 8, 11:36 pm–Apr 10, 2:04 pm	3rd	Capricorn	Plant potatoes and tubers. Trim to retard growth.
Apr 10, 2:04 pm–Apr 11, 7:23 am	4th	Capricorn	Plant potatoes and tubers. Trim to retard growth.
Apr 11, 7:23 am–Apr 13, 11:38 am	4th	Aquarius	Cultivate. Destroy weeds and pests. Harvest fruits and root crops for food. Trim to retard growth.
Apr 13, 11:38 am–Apr 15, 12:46 pm	4th	Pisces	Plant biennials, perennials, bulbs, and roots. Prune. Irrigate. Fertilize (organic).

Aries (March 20–April 20) is associated with the head and face, and after a long winter, a facial may be just what you and your skin need. You can give yourself an easy facial by adding peppermint leaves to boiling water. Use a bath-size towel to make a tent over your head as you lean over the steaming water. To tighten the pores of your skin after steaming, mix fresh or dried lavender flowers and a little warm milk into an egg white. Apply the egg white–lavender paste to your face and let it dry. Rinse your face with cool water and pat dry.

APRIL

S	M	T	W	T	F	S
	1	2	3	4	5	6	7
8	9	10	11	12	13	14
15	16	17	18	19	20	21
22	23	24	25	26	27	28
29	30					

Apr 15, 12:46 pm– Apr 17, 7:36 am	4th	Aries	Cultivate. Destroy weeds and pests. Harvest fruits and root crops for food. Trim to retard growth.
Apr 17, 12:11 pm– Apr 19, 11:51 am	1st	Taurus	Plant annuals for hardiness. Trim to increase growth.
Apr 21, 1:50 pm– Apr 23, 7:38 pm	1st	Cancer	Plant grains, leafy annuals. Fertilize (chemical). Graft or bud plants. Irrigate. Trim to increase growth.

Gardeners often plant marigolds with tomatoes to control nematodes, but research has shown that planting a bed of marigolds in the same location you plan to grow tomatoes, and then turning the ground over, burying the marigolds and planting the tomatoes over them, is a better deterrent.

_____

_____

_____

_____

_____

_____

_____

Apr 21, 1:50 pm– Apr 23, 7:38 pm	1st	Cancer	Plant grains, leafy annuals. Fertilize (chemical). Graft or bud plants. Irrigate. Trim to increase growth.
Apr 28, 5:44 pm– May 1, 6:41 am	2nd	Libra	Plant annuals for fragrance and beauty. Trim to increase growth.

To grow strawberries on your deck or balcony this summer, you'll need a growing bag, a container that is approximately the same size and shape (usually available at garden centers), and several strawberry plants. Lay the bag in the container, cut open the top of the bag to expose the planting mixture, remove plants from starter pots, make planting holes (plant in two rows close to container edges), set the plants in the holes, cover roots with planting mix. Water. Don't overwater after planting as there are no drainage holes in the growing bag.

APRIL

S	M	T	W	T	F	S
1	2	3	4	5	6	7
8	9	10	11	12	13	14
15	16	17	18	19	20	21
22	23	24	25	26	27	28
29	30					

May

Week of April 29–May 5

Beautiful young people are accidents of nature,
But beautiful old people are works of art.

—ELEANOR ROOSEVELT

May 1, 6:41 am– May 2, 6:09 am	2nd	Scorpio	Plant grains, leafy annuals. Fertilize (chemical). Graft or bud plants. Irrigate. Trim to increase growth.
May 2, 6:09 am– May 3, 6:47 pm	3rd	Scorpio	Plant biennials, perennials, bulbs and roots. Prune. Irrigate. Fertilize (organic).
May 3, 6:47 pm– May 6, 5:21 am	3rd	Sagittarius	Cultivate. Destroy weeds and pests. Harvest fruits and root crops for food. Trim to retard growth.

According to a recent report in the *American Journal for Clinical Nutrition*, the folate found in leafy vegetables may help protect against cognitive decline in older adults.

<table>
<tr><th colspan="7">MAY</th></tr>
<tr><th>S</th><th>M</th><th>T</th><th>W</th><th>T</th><th>F</th><th>S</th></tr>
<tr><td></td><td></td><td>1</td><td>2</td><td>3</td><td>4</td><td>5</td></tr>
<tr><td>6</td><td>7</td><td>8</td><td>9</td><td>10</td><td>11</td><td>12</td></tr>
<tr><td>13</td><td>14</td><td>15</td><td>16</td><td>17</td><td>18</td><td>19</td></tr>
<tr><td>20</td><td>21</td><td>22</td><td>23</td><td>24</td><td>25</td><td>26</td></tr>
<tr><td>27</td><td>28</td><td>29</td><td>30</td><td>31</td><td></td><td></td></tr>
</table>

May 6, 5:21 am–May 8, 1:48 pm	3rd	Capricorn	Plant potatoes and tubers. Trim to retard growth.
May 8, 1:48 pm–May 10, 12:27 am	3rd	Aquarius	Cultivate. Destroy weeds and pests. Harvest fruits and root crops for food. Trim to retard growth.
May 10, 12:27 am–May 10, 7:31 pm	4th	Aquarius	Cultivate. Destroy weeds and pests. Harvest fruits and root crops for food. Trim to retard growth.
May 10, 7:31 pm–May 12, 10:19 pm	4th	Pisces	Plant biennials, perennials, bulbs and roots. Prune. Irrigate. Fertilize (organic).

Morel mushrooms are also called May mushrooms because, unlike most mushrooms that appear in late summer and fall, morels can be found in May. Morels have a very distinctive look, but they can be confused with another called the false morel. To avoid getting them confused, remember that the true morel mushroom grows in May and the false morel appears in the fall.

MAY

S	M	T	W	T	F	S
		1	2	3	4	5
6	7	8	9	10	11	12
13	14	15	16	17	18	19
20	21	22	23	24	25	26
27	28	29	30	31		

May 12, 10:19 pm–May 14, 10:48 pm	4th	Aries	Cultivate. Destroy weeds and pests. Harvest fruits and root crops for food. Trim to retard growth.
May 14, 10:48 pm–May 16, 3:27 pm	4th	Taurus	Plant potatoes and tubers. Trim to retard growth.
May 16, 3:27 pm–May 16, 10:34 pm	1st	Taurus	Plant annuals for hardiness. Trim to increase growth.
May 18, 11:38 pm–May 21, 3:56 am	1st	Cancer	Plant grains, leafy annuals. Fertilize (chemical). Graft or bud plants. Irrigate. Trim to increase growth.

Interesting color combinations can add a lot of pizzazz to a garden space. The soft, golden branches of false cypress provide a beautiful background for the magenta flowers that appear on creeping phlox, for example. A fun way to develop your color skills is to take hints from the flowers themselves. Pansies come in a wide range of colors and the blossoms often have a second color. Try to find other flowers that match the colors you see in the pansy you like—purple and yellow, for example, or violet and orange. Be sure to take plant size into consideration, too. Mixing a too-tall plant with a short one may not give you the look you're after. This technique works particularly well for container gardens.

May 18, 11:38 pm– May 21, 3:56 am	1st	Cancer	Plant grains, leafy annuals. Fertilize (chemical). Graft or bud plants. Irrigate. Trim to increase growth.
May 26, 12:16 am– May 28, 1:11 pm	2nd	Libra	Plant annuals for fragrance and beauty. Trim to increase growth.

Gemini (May 21–June 21) and its ruler, Mercury, are associated with arms and hands, gentle breezes, butterflies, small birds, paths, weather vanes, and a variety of plants.

A gardener's hands get a lot of abuse that even wearing gloves may only minimize. Mother Nature offers help, though. To treat a cut on your hand, apply aloe vera to prevent infection. You can also bruise a handful of fresh oak leaves and apply directly to the wound. Covering the leaves with a damp cloth (warm, if possible) will assist the leaves in fighting infection.

To make a moisturizing lotion that is good for combating skin irritation, place flowers collected from mullein and crushed up with a small amount of water (added to soften) in an earthenware bowl. Cover with almond oil and let stand for about a week. Strain and bottle.

_____

_____

_____

_____

MAY

S	M	T	W	T	F	S
		1	2	3	4	5
6	7	8	9	10	11	12
13	14	15	16	17	18	19
20	21	22	23	24	25	26
27	28	29	30	31		

June

Week of May 27–June 2

Cheerfulness keeps up a kind of daylight in the mind,
and fills it with a steady and perpetual serenity.

—Joseph Addison

May 28, 1:11 pm– May 31, 1:06 am	2nd	Scorpio	Plant grains, leafy annuals. Fertilize (chemical). Graft or bud plants. Irrigate. Trim to increase growth.
May 31, 9:04 pm– Jun 2, 11:09 am	3rd	Sagittarius	Cultivate. Destroy weeds and pests. Harvest fruits and root crops for food. Trim to retard growth.
Jun 2, 11:09 am– Jun 4, 7:15 pm	3rd	Capricorn	Plant potatoes and tubers. Trim to retard growth.

Butterflies are welcome visitors in yards and gardens, and inviting them to stay for an hour or a day is as easy as planting flowers that will entice them. Some butterfly favorites are Queen Anne's lace, yarrow, shasta daisy, blanket flowers, bee balm, English lavender, columbine, and butterfly weed.

JUNE

S	M	T	W	T	F	S
					1	2
3	4	5	6	7	8	9
10	11	12	13	14	15	16
17	18	19	20	21	22	23
24	25	26	27	28	29	30

Jun 2, 11:09 am–Jun 4, 7:15 pm	3rd	Capricorn	Plant potatoes and tubers. Trim to retard growth.
Jun 4, 7:15 pm–Jun 7, 1:24 am	3rd	Aquarius	Cultivate. Destroy weeds and pests. Harvest fruits and root crops for food. Trim to retard growth.
Jun 7, 1:24 am–Jun 8, 7:43 am	3rd	Pisces	Plant biennials, perennials, bulbs, and roots. Prune. Irrigate. Fertilize (organic).
Jun 8, 7:43 am–Jun 9, 5:26 am	4th	Pisces	Plant biennials, perennials, bulbs and roots. Prune. Irrigate. Fertilize (organic).
Jun 9, 5:26 am–Jun 11, 7:29 am	4th	Aries	Cultivate. Destroy weeds and pests. Harvest fruits and root crops for food. Trim to retard growth.

Honeybees are among the few insects that stay active all winter. Their constant movement keeps the hive warm and a cache of stored honey is their food supply for several months. Now, with summer in full bloom, the honeybees are busy collecting nectar. They prefer single flowers and clusters of compact florets, like those found on large sedums. Daffodils, forsythia, witch hazel, asters, lavender, clover, and sunflowers will also attract bees. They love lush dandelions, too, and they'll love you for leaving some in your yard (even if the neighbors won't).

		JUNE				
S	M	T	W	T	F	S
					1	2
3	4	5	6	7	8	9
10	11	12	13	14	15	16
17	18	19	20	21	22	23
24	25	26	27	28	29	30

Jun 11, 7:29 am–Jun 13, 8:24 am	4th	Taurus	Plant potatoes and tubers. Trim to retard growth.
Jun 13, 8:24 am–Jun 14, 11:13 pm	4th	Gemini	Cultivate. Destroy weeds and pests. Harvest fruits and root crops for food. Trim to retard growth.
Jun 15, 9:45 am–Jun 17, 1:25 pm	1st	Cancer	Plant grains, leafy annuals. Fertilize (chemical). Graft or bud plants. Irrigate. Trim to increase growth.

Trees grow in three ways—down at the roots, up through the branches, and wider in the trunk. We notice new growth (*meristem*) on the branches because it is usually a lighter or brighter green than the rest of the branch. On pine trees the new growth is called candles.

One thing that really stresses trees is pruning, and a tree that is pruned during the summer will experience even more stress because the tree is deprived of leaves that provide shade and allow food production. Trees are often pruned for the wrong reason. If you prune a tree because it is too large, perhaps you planted the wrong tree in your yard. You might be overwatering or overfertilizing the tree, too. Consider the tree's needs as well as your own before you bring it home and plant it.

Jun 22, 7:43 am– Jun 22, 9:15 am	1st	Libra	Plant annuals for fragrance and beauty. Trim to increase growth.
Jun 22, 9:15 am– Jun 24, 8:26 pm	2nd	Libra	Plant annuals for fragrance and beauty. Trim to increase growth.

Mosquitoes are most abundant in June, and it is the female mosquito that bites humans. Males feed on plant sap, but the female needs blood protein for her developing eggs. Mosquitoes don't see very well, but they are attracted, like heat-seeking missiles, by carbon dioxide and the warmth that is emitted by warm-blooded animals, including humans.

Citronella will repel mosquitoes, but you have to stay in the smoke from the burning candle or coil for it to be effective. Zappers are not the best solution either, because they kill beneficial bugs along with the mosquitoes. If you like the smell of citronella, you could use citronella soap when bathing. The soaps (a product of the Bahamas and Belize) are made with olive oil and aloe vera.

Planting marigolds around your yard will keep some mosquitoes away because don't like the smell. And don't forget frogs; they love to eat mosquitoes!

JUNE

S	M	T	W	T	F	S
					1	2
3	4	5	6	7	8	9
10	11	12	13	14	15	16
17	18	19	20	21	22	23
24	25	26	27	28	29	30

Jun 24, 8:26 pm– Jun 27, 8:23 am	2nd	Scorpio	Plant grains, leafy annuals. Fertilize (chemical). Graft or bud plants. Irrigate. Trim to increase growth.
Jun 29, 6:05 pm– Jun 30, 9:49 am	2nd	Capricorn	Graft or bud plants. Trim to increase growth.
Jun 30, 9:49 am– Jul 2, 1:24 am	3rd	Capricorn	Plant potatoes and tubers. Trim to retard growth.

The best kind of frog, in many people's opinions, may be the hollow metal variety that sits on a conveniently located rock at the edge of an artificial pond and spouts water from its mouth. But frogs are an important part of the ecosystem. They are part of the food chain, eating insects and providing food for birds, snakes, and some animals. They often show us that something is wrong in our environment, too. Where frogs are born deformed, or die in unusual numbers, we may find toxins that are harmful to humans.

♋ July

Week of July 1–7

*We are an arrogant species, full of terrible potential,
but we also have a great capacity for love, friendship, generosity, kindness, faith, hope, and joy.*

—DEAN KOONTZ

Jul 2, 1:24 am– Jul 4, 6:52 am	3rd	Aquarius	Cultivate. Destroy weeds and pests. Harvest fruits and root crops for food. Trim to retard growth.
Jul 4, 6:52 am– Jul 6, 10:56 am	3rd	Pisces	Plant biennials, perennials, bulbs, and roots. Prune. Irrigate. Fertilize (organic).
Jul 6, 10:56 am– Jul 7, 12:53 pm	3rd	Aries	Cultivate. Destroy weeds and pests. Harvest fruits and root crops for food. Trim to retard growth.
Jul 7, 12:53 pm– Jul 8, 1:54 pm	4th	Aries	Cultivate. Destroy weeds and pests. Harvest fruits and root crops for food. Trim to retard growth.

Organic fertilizers made from animal and plant products are slower to release because micro-organisms in the soil have to break them down before plants can use them. It is best to alternate between chemical and organic fertilizers unless you are committed to completely natural gardening.

JULY

S	M	T	W	T	F	S
1	2	3	4	5	6	7
8	9	10	11	12	13	14
15	16	17	18	19	20	21
22	23	24	25	26	27	28
29	30	31				

Jul 8, 1:54 pm– Jul 10, 4:10 pm	4th	Taurus	Plant potatoes and tubers. Trim to retard growth.
Jul 10, 4:10 pm– Jul 12, 6:39 pm	4th	Gemini	Cultivate. Destroy weeds and pests. Harvest fruits and root crops for food. Trim to retard growth.
Jul 12, 6:39 pm– Jul 14, 8:04 am	4th	Cancer	Plant biennials, perennials, bulbs, and roots. Prune. Irrigate. Fertilize (organic).
Jul 14, 8:04 am– Jul 14, 10:43 pm	1st	Cancer	Plant grains, leafy annuals. Fertilize (chemical). Graft or bud plants. Irrigate. Trim to increase growth.

Certified organic products have a paper trail—a series of documents—that provide proof the producer of the product is following the rules. Only companies that meet all the criteria can be certified organic, and the certificate is available to consumers upon request. But in addition to the certificate, which is issued by a certifying agency, other documents report the field history, harvest and storage records, weigh tickets, clean-truck affidavits, inventory purchase records, packaging reports, maintenance and sanitation reports, and more. All of this paperwork takes time, and time equals money, which is only one of the reasons we pay more for certified organic products.

Jul 19, 3:53 pm– Jul 22, 2:29 am	1st	Libra	Plant annuals for fragrance and beauty. Trim to increase growth.
Jul 22, 2:29 am– Jul 22, 4:18 am	2nd	Libra	Plant annuals for fragrance and beauty. Trim to increase growth.

Fragrance, sensual texture, and beauty are in Venus' domain. When you walk through your gardens, try to identify the flowers, trees, and shrubs that Venus and Libra rule. For more information about planting and plants in this sign, see Janice Sharkey's article, "Venus, Goddess of Gardens," on page 266.

_____

_____

_____

_____

JULY

S	M	T	W	T	F	S
1	2	3	4	5	6	7
8	9	10	11	12	13	14
15	16	17	18	19	20	21
22	23	24	25	26	27	28
29	30	31				

Jul 22, 4:18 am– Jul 24, 4:29 pm	2nd	Scorpio	Plant grains, leafy annuals. Fertilize (chemical). Graft or bud plants. Irrigate. Trim to increase growth.
Jul 27, 2:21 am– Jul 29, 9:13 am	2nd	Capricorn	Graft or bud plants. Trim to increase growth.

Leo (July 22–August 23) and its ruler, the Sun, are associated with your personal will and life force. Leo rules the heart, spine, and upper back, as well as royalty, games of chance, poppies, and yellow or orange lilies. The flowers that fall within Leo's domain are big and showy. If you want to make an even bigger impression at your next dinner party or celebration (also Leo-ruled), add a bold stroke of color to your table with sunflowers or peonies in gold-colored vases. Your guests will feel important and appreciate your efforts. To read more about planning celebrations, see Lynn Gordon Sellon's article, "Entertaining by the Signs," on page 332.

August

Week of July 29–August 4

There is nothing wrong with America that cannot be cured by what is right with America.

—Bill Clinton

Jul 29, 8:48 pm– Jul 31, 1:40 pm	3rd	Aquarius	Cultivate. Destroy weeds and pests. Harvest fruits and root crops for food. Trim to retard growth.
Jul 31, 1:40 pm– Aug 2, 4:43 pm	3rd	Pisces	Plant biennials, perennials, bulbs, and roots. Prune. Irrigate. Fertilize (organic).
Aug 2, 4:43 pm– Aug 4, 7:16 pm	3rd	Aries	Cultivate. Destroy weeds and pests. Harvest fruits and root crops for food. Trim to retard growth.

Even your most adored pet may not be welcome in your gardens. Dogs are indiscriminate about where they dig or flop down for a nap, and cats don't discriminate between a litter box and soft garden soil. Sprinkle ginger around your flower beds to keep cats away. They hate the smell. A whiff of cayenne pepper will send dogs into less hostile territory, and a smart dog won't return.

July

S	M	T	W	T	F	S
1	2	3	4	5	6	7
8	9	10	11	12	13	14
15	16	17	18	19	20	21
22	23	24	25	26	27	28
29	30	31				

Aug 4, 7:16 pm– Aug 5, 5:19 pm	3rd	Taurus	Plant potatoes and tubers. Trim to retard growth.
Aug 5, 5:19 pm– Aug 6, 10:01 pm	4th	Taurus	Plant potatoes and tubers. Trim to retard growth.
Aug 6, 10:01 pm– Aug 9, 1:36 am	4th	Gemini	Cultivate. Destroy weeds and pests. Harvest fruits and root crops for food. Trim to retard growth.
Aug 9, 1:36 am– Aug 11, 6:42 am	4th	Cancer	Plant biennials, perennials, bulbs, and roots. Prune. Irrigate. Fertilize (organic).
Aug 11, 6:42 am– Aug 12, 7:02 pm	4th	Leo	Cultivate. Destroy weeds and pests. Harvest fruits and root crops for food. Trim to retard growth.

Using herbs (and flowers) to tone up your body is just one of the ways you can keep your body in good working order. Tonics and teas made from natural products can aid in strengthening your body and immune system. To help your heart, try this heart strengthening honey tonic. To make the tonic, put 1 tablespoon of chopped ginseng and 1 tablespoon of cinnamon in 2 cups of honey. Simmer 30 minutes. Strain and take by the tablespoon several times a day. This tonic will increase blood circulation. You can read more about the uses of herbs and flower in Sally Cragin's article, "A Potpourri of Herbal Goodies," beginning on page 256.

AUGUST

S	M	T	W	T	F	S
			1	2	3	4
5	6	7	8	9	10	11
12	13	14	15	16	17	18
19	20	21	22	23	24	25
26	27	28	29	30	31	

Aug 16, 12:04 am– Aug 18, 12:13 pm	1st	Libra	Plant annuals for fragrance and beauty. Trim to increase growth.
Aug 18, 12:13 pm– Aug 20, 7:54 pm	1st	Scorpio	Plant grains, leafy annuals. Fertilize (chemical). Graft or bud plants. Irrigate. Trim to increase growth.

Hydro-cooling is a common method that commercial growers use to cool produce. When combined with a chlorinated wash, hydro-cooling also sanitizes the product. The amount of chlorine used to prevent contamination of fruits and vegetables from salmonella and E. coli bacteria varies. Alfalfa sprouts, which can harbor E. coli within the seed itself, must be treated in water containing 20,000 ppm of chlorine, while some produce can be processed with as low as 4 ppm.

AUGUST

S	M	T	W	T	F	S
			1	2	3	4
5	6	7	8	9	10	11
12	13	14	15	16	17	18
19	20	21	22	23	24	25
26	27	28	29	30	31	

♍ Week of August 19–25

Aug 20, 7:54 pm–Aug 21, 12:44 am	2nd	Scorpio	Plant grains, leafy annuals. Fertilize (chemical). Graft or bud plants. Irrigate. Trim to increase growth.
Aug 23, 11:20 am–Aug 25, 6:35 pm	2nd	Capricorn	Graft or bud plants. Trim to increase growth.

Put your garden to work fighting crime. There are things you can do when you design your gardens to enhance their protective qualities, and perhaps most important is not giving intruders places to hide. You can also include spiny shrubs like berberis, roses, or ornamental currant, and cover any paths with gravel. The scrunching sound provides a warning that will help to deter unwanted visitors.

Aug 27, 10:34 pm–Aug 28, 6:35 am	2nd	Pisces	Plant grains, leafy annuals. Fertilize (chemical). Graft or bud plants. Irrigate. Trim to increase growth.
Aug 28, 6:35 am–Aug 30, 12:24 am	3rd	Pisces	Plant biennials, perennials, bulbs, and roots. Prune. Irrigate. Fertilize (organic).
Aug 30, 12:24 am–Sep 1, 1:35 am	3rd	Aries	Cultivate. Destroy weeds and pests. Harvest fruits and root crops for food. Trim to retard growth.
Sep 1, 1:35 am–Sep 3, 3:30 am	3rd	Taurus	Plant potatoes and tubers. Trim to retard growth.

What would summer be without a fair? In 1818 the people in Topsfield, Massachusetts, sponsored a fair. Today, it is this country's longest consecutive-running fair. The Biscuit Booth at the Mississippi State Fair (est. 1849) serves over 50,000 biscuits drizzled in maple syrup every year, making it one of the most popular "go to" places at the fair, and the Southern Texas State Fair features a Spam recipe contest. Every fair has its claim to fame, but mostly they're a really great place to get together with friends and family.

AUGUST

S	M	T	W	T	F	S
				1	2	3	4
5	6	7	8	9	10	11
12	13	14	15	16	17	18
19	20	21	22	23	24	25
26	27	28	29	30	31	

♍ September

Week of September 2–8

Nowadays most people die of a sort of creeping common sense, and discover when it is too late that the only things one never regrets are one's mistakes.

—OSCAR WILDE, THE PICTURE OF DORIAN GRAY

Sep 3, 10:32 pm– Sep 5, 7:08 am	4th	Gemini	Cultivate. Destroy weeds and pests. Harvest fruits and root crops for food. Trim to retard growth.
Sep 5, 7:08 am– Sep 7, 12:59 pm	4th	Cancer	Plant biennials, perennials, bulbs, and roots. Prune. Irrigate. Fertilize (organic).
Sep 7, 12:59 pm– Sep 9, 9:10 pm	4th	Leo	Cultivate. Destroy weeds and pests. Harvest fruits and root crops for food. Trim to retard growth.

A 1,129-pound Atlantic Giant pumpkin took first place in the 2005 pumpkin weigh-off held in Half Moon Bay, California. First prize was $5 per pound, which put $6,145 in prize money in the winner's pocket. Lots of water, fertilizer, and hand-pollination were the key elements to this pumpkin's success.

SEPTEMBER

S	M	T	W	T	F	S
						1
2	3	4	5	6	7	8
9	10	11	12	13	14	15
16	17	18	19	20	21	22
23	24	25	26	27	28	29
30						

43

Sep 9, 9:10 pm– Sep 11, 8:44 am	4th	Virgo	Cultivate, especially medicinal plants. Destroy weeds and pests. Trim to retard growth.
Sep 12, 7:31 am– Sep 14, 7:37 pm	1st	Libra	Plant annuals for fragrance and beauty. Trim to increase growth.
Sep 14, 7:37 pm– Sep 17, 8:21 am	1st	Scorpio	Plant grains, leafy annuals. Fertilize (chemical). Graft or bud plants. Irrigate. Trim to increase growth.

Commodities trading is a big gamble, and if you're going to invest, you'd better know something about hedge funds and the beans you're trading. Soybean futures were up 12.1 percent and sugar was up 22.1 percent in 2005, and the lure of quick payouts can be tempting. Dorothy Kovach, our economic forecaster, urges investors to use caution. ". . . [September] has always proven to be the toughest month on the market and this year is no exception. Caution is the watch-word," she says in her article, "2007 Economic Forecast." You can read more of Dorothy's forecasts beginning on page 212.

SEPTEMBER						
S	M	T	W	T	F	S
						1
2	3	4	5	6	7	8
9	10	11	12	13	14	15
16	17	18	19	20	21	22
23	24	25	26	27	28	29
30						

Sep 19, 7:51 pm– Sep 22, 4:18 am	2nd	Capricorn	Graft or bud plants. Trim to increase growth.

The phrase "poetic justice" might have been coined by a Libra soul. Rewarding virtue and punishing vice is the balance and justice that defines Libra (September 23–October 23), an intellectual air sign. These usually courteous, pleasant, peace-loving people would want to both punish and reward with modesty, but above all, with taste and sensitivity. Libra rules relationships and equality, and it corresponds to the lower back and kidneys.

On September 22, the Sun moves from the northern hemisphere to the southern hemisphere, and for a brief time, day and night are equal in length.

Sep 24, 8:55 am–Sep 26, 10:22 am	2nd	Pisces	Plant grains, leafy annuals. Fertilize (chemical). Graft or bud plants. Irrigate. Trim to increase growth.
Sep 26, 3:45 pm–Sep 28, 10:17 am	3rd	Aries	Cultivate. Destroy weeds and pests. Harvest fruits and root crops for food. Trim to retard growth.
Sep 28, 10:17 am–Sep 30, 10:34 am	3rd	Taurus	Plant potatoes and tubers. Trim to retard growth.

A compost pile can be started anytime, although decomposition will be much slower in colder temperatures. *Psychronphiles*—the first wave of aerobic bacteria to work in raw organic material—are most efficient at about 55 degrees Fahrenheit, but they'll work at much colder temperatures, too. Did you know that the bacteria count in ice cream that is stored in a deep freeze will actually increase over time? The bacteria that grows in ice cream is the same kind that starts the decomposing process in organic matter. Mesophile bacteria begin to take over when the compost's temperature is above 40 degrees Fahrenheit, and mesophiles are replaced by thermophiles when the composting matter reaches about 110 degrees.

SEPTEMBER

S	M	T	W	T	F	S
						1
2	3	4	5	6	7	8
9	10	11	12	13	14	15
16	17	18	19	20	21	22
23	24	25	26	27	28	29
30						

 # October

Week of September 30–October 6

Rumor travels faster, but it don't stay put as long as truth.

> —WILL ROGERS, "POLITICS GETTING READY TO JELL," *THE ILLITERATE DIGEST*, 1924

Sep 30, 10:34 am–Oct 2, 12:57 pm	3rd	Gemini	Cultivate. Destroy weeds and pests. Harvest fruits and root crops for food. Trim to retard growth.
Oct 2, 12:57 pm–Oct 3, 6:06 am	3rd	Cancer	Plant biennials, perennials, bulbs, and roots. Prune. Irrigate. Fertilize (organic).
Oct 3, 6:06 am–Oct 4, 6:27 pm	4th	Cancer	Plant biennials, perennials, bulbs, and roots. Prune. Irrigate. Fertilize (organic).
Oct 4, 6:27 pm–Oct 7, 3:03 am	4th	Leo	Cultivate. Destroy weeds and pests. Harvest fruits and root crops for food. Trim to retard growth.

Every community could grow more jobs and more food at the same time if unused urban lands were planted into gardens. That's the vision of a handful of professional farmers. These farmers are challenging the misconception that food must be grown far from where the people live. Imagine how it might look and feel in your community if gardens, orchards, and public markets filled now vacant, littered lots. Farming and food create community and encourage awareness of the natural cycles in life.

OCTOBER

S	M	T	W	T	F	S
	1	2	3	4	5	6
7	8	9	10	11	12	13
14	15	16	17	18	19	20
21	22	23	24	25	26	27
28	29	30	31			

47

♎ Week of October 7–13

Oct 7, 3:03 am– Oct 9, 1:57 pm	4th	Virgo	Cultivate, especially medicinal plants. Destroy weeds and pests. Trim to retard growth.
Oct 12, 2:13 am– Oct 14, 2:58 pm	1st	Scorpio	Plant biennials, perennials, bulbs, and roots. Prune. Irrigate. Fertilize (organic).

Chickadees form small flocks and survive the cold northern winters by eating a diet of seeds, acorns, and insects. In urban areas, they are often the first sign of life on frosty mornings. They love sunflower seeds, suet, and peanut butter. To maintain a daytime body temperature of 104 degrees, these little birds will eat at backyard feeders from dawn until dusk, and store extra seeds in trees for security.

OCTOBER

S	M	T	W	T	F	S
	1	2	3	4	5	6
7	8	9	10	11	12	13
14	15	16	17	18	19	20
21	22	23	24	25	26	27
28	29	30	31			

Oct 14, 2:58 pm–Oct 17, 3:03 am	1st	Sagittarius	Cultivate. Destroy weeds and pests. Harvest fruits and root crops for food. Trim to retard growth.
Oct 17, 3:03 am–Oct 19, 4:33 am	1st	Capricorn	Plant potatoes and tubers. Trim to retard growth.
Oct 19, 4:33 am–Oct 19, 12:52 pm	2nd	Capricorn	Graft or bud plants. Trim to increase growth.

Ever wondered how apples are kept "fresh" for several months after they are picked and before they appear in grocery stores, which can be up to nine months?

Growers use "controlled storage." After the apples are picked, they are stored in boxes, loaded onto pallets, and placed in very large refrigerators (football field size!). Then all the air is sucked out and replaced with carbon dioxide and oxygen. The doors are sealed and the temperature inside the refrigerator is maintained at 33 degrees Fahrenheit.

_____

_____

_____

_____

_____

_____

_____

Oct 21, 7:02 pm– Oct 23, 9:24 pm	2nd	Pisces	Plant grains, leafy annuals. Fertilize (chemical). Graft or bud plants. Irrigate. Trim to increase growth.
Oct 25, 9:07 pm– Oct 26, 12:51 am	2nd	Taurus	Plant annuals for hardiness. Trim to increase growth.
Oct 26, 12:51 am– Oct 27, 8:11 pm	3rd	Taurus	Plant potatoes and tubers. Trim to retard growth.

Scorpio (October 23–November 22) and its ruler Pluto are associated with regeneration, the natural follow-up to acts of destruction. Autumn's cold and frost, on the heels of the passing summer's heat, will kill fragile vegetation and start the decomposing process. Then, the soil will compost and absorb the vines and foliage left on fields to replenish itself for the next growing season.

Some astrologers place mushrooms under Scorpio's rulership, particularly the poisonous varieties. There are several thousand different kinds of mushrooms growing in the U.S. and Canada, and while there are no general rules to tell an edible fungus from a poisonous one, caution is advised. It's always best to know what you're eating before you take a bite.

OCTOBER

S	M	T	W	T	F	S
	1	2	3	4	5	6
7	8	9	10	11	12	13
14	15	16	17	18	19	20
21	22	23	24	25	26	27
28	29	30	31			

♏ November

Week of October 28–November 3

The best measure of a man's honesty isn't his income tax return. It's the zero adjust on his bathroom scale.
—ARTHUR C. CLARKE

Oct 29, 8:49 pm–Nov 1, 12:48 pm	3rd	Cancer	Plant grains, leafy annuals. Fertilize (chemical). Graft or bud plants. Irrigate. Trim to increase growth.
Nov 1, 12:48 am–Nov 3, 8:44 am	4th	Leo	Cultivate. Destroy weeds and pests. Harvest fruits and root crops for food. Trim to retard growth.
Nov 3, 8:44 am–Nov 5, 6:47 pm	4th	Virgo	Cultivate, especially medicinal plants. Destroy weeds and pests. Trim to retard growth.

If you decide to collect mushrooms, keep the species separate in order not to confuse the different kinds. A useful item to take along when you're mushroom picking is waxed paper. It can be used to keep them separate and to protect their delicate flesh. The old saying that a silver coin will turn black if placed with poisonous mushrooms that are cooking is false, and just because a mushroom shows signs of having been eaten by an animal doesn't make it safe.

NOVEMBER						
S	M	T	W	T	F	S
					1	2	3
4	5	6	7	8	9	10
11	12	13	14	15	16	17
18	19	20	21	22	23	24
25	26	27	28	29	30	

Nov 3, 8:44 am– Nov 5, 6:47 pm	4th	Virgo	Cultivate, especially medicinal plants. Destroy weeds and pests. Trim to retard growth.
Nov 8, 7:18 am– Nov 9, 6:03 pm	4th	Scorpio	Plant biennials, perennials, bulbs, and roots. Prune. Irrigate. Fertilize (organic).
Nov 9, 6:03 pm– Nov 10, 7:59 pm	1st	Scorpio	Plant grains, leafy annuals. Fertilize (chemical). Graft or bud plants. Irrigate. Trim to increase growth.

Any permanent pond in the Midwest is apt to have muskrats living in it—even ponds in urban areas. Pond muskrats dig holes in the mud along the edge of the pond, and that is what pond owners dislike most about the furry little critters. If you own a pond, one way to avoid muskrat tenants is to make your pond less hospitable to them, and the best way to send them packing is to eliminate, or at least minimize, the kind of food they like to eat. Starchy cattails are one of their favorite foods. Planting spike rush, leafy bulrush, and water willow is recommended.

_____

_____

_____

_____

_____

NOVEMBER

S	M	T	W	T	F	S
					1	2	3
4	5	6	7	8	9	10
11	12	13	14	15	16	17
18	19	20	21	22	23	24
25	26	27	28	29	30	

| Nov 13, 8:00 am–
Nov 15, 6:30 pm | 1st | Capricorn | Graft or bud plants. Trim to increase growth. |
| Nov 18, 2:14 am–
Nov 20, 6:24 am | 2nd | Pisces | Plant grains, leafy annuals. Fertilize (chemical). Graft or bud plants. Irrigate. Trim to increase growth. |

Healthy soil is crucial to healthy gardens, crops, and lawns. Even window boxes and patio containers need to contain healthy soil. Plants will adapt themselves to particular types of soils and climates, and they in turn feed the soil they live in. The soil is also fed by the remains of animals, bugs, worms, and bacteria.

If even one species or micro-organism leaves, or is destroyed, it sets off a chain reaction through the support system that can have far-reaching implications. The disappearance of plants can cause the disappearance of animals, and so on. If you put back into the soil what you take away, the balance is maintained.

Nov 18, 2:14 am– Nov 20, 6:24 am	2nd	Pisces	Plant grains, leafy annuals. Fertilize (chemical). Graft or bud plants. Irrigate. Trim to increase growth.
Nov 22, 7:18 am– Nov 24, 6:29 am	2nd	Taurus	Plant annuals for hardiness. Trim to increase growth.
Nov 24, 9:30 am– Nov 26, 6:07 am	3rd	Gemini	Cultivate. Destroy weeds and pests. Harvest fruits and root crops for food. Trim to retard growth.

Sagittarius (November 22–December 21) is associated with generosity, joy, frivolity, hope, and charitable qualities. Jupiter, this sign's ruler, is in its own sign (Sagittarius) until December 18. This tends to bring good fortune, in general, and it's particularly favorable for matters connected with sports, horses, publishing, and religious organizations. Be joyful and generous with others whenever an opportunity to do so presents itself.

_____

_____

NOVEMBER

S	M	T	W	T	F	S
				1	2	3
4	5	6	7	8	9	10
11	12	13	14	15	16	17
18	19	20	21	22	23	24
25	26	27	28	29	30	

December

Week of November 25–December 1

I can never remember if it snowed for six days and six nights when I was twelve or whether it snowed for twelve days and twelve nights when I was six.
—DYLAN THOMAS, *A CHILD'S CHRISTMAS IN WALES*

Nov 26, 6:07 am– Nov 28, 8:23 am	3rd	Cancer	Plant biennials, perennials, bulbs, and roots. Prune. Irrigate. Fertilize (organic).
Nov 28, 8:23 am– Nov 30, 2:44 pm	3rd	Leo	Cultivate. Destroy weeds and pests. Harvest fruits and root crops for food. Trim to retard growth.
Nov 30, 2:44 pm– Dec 1, 7:44 am	3rd	Virgo	Cultivate, especially medicinal plants. Destroy weeds and pests. Trim to retard growth.
Dec 1, 7:44 am– Dec 3, 1:01 am	4th	Virgo	Cultivate, especially medicinal plants. Destroy weeds and pests. Trim to retard growth.

Place a pile of wood ashes in the chicken yard for the chickens to take a dust bath in. They love to use it, and the wood ash keeps them lice free. For more information on growing your own poultry, see Tammy Sullivan's article, "Raising Poultry," on page 294.

page 294.

DECEMBER						
S	M	T	W	T	F	S
					1	2	3
4	5	6	7	8	9	10
11	12	13	14	15	16	17
18	19	20	21	22	23	24
25	26	27	28	29	30	

Dec 1, 7:44 am– Dec 3, 1:01 am	4th	Virgo	Cultivate, especially medicinal plants. Destroy weeds and pests. Trim to retard growth.
Dec 5, 1:31 pm– Dec 8, 2:11 am	4th	Scorpio	Plant biennials, perennials, bulbs, and roots. Prune. Irrigate. Fertilize (organic).
Dec 8, 2:11 am– Dec 9, 12:40 pm	4th	Sagittarius	Cultivate. Destroy weeds and pests. Harvest fruits and root crops for food. Trim to retard growth.

If you're looking for a unique holiday gift, look no farther than the grocery story. The number of beautifully packaged, gourmet products—olive oils, specialty cheeses, trendy sauces and vinegars, luscious chocolates, and more—is growing every day. Pack your food gifts in a box or basket, and your shopping is done! The Internet is a terrific source for hard to find food items. If you've enjoyed fabulous cookies courtesy of a hotel where you stayed, for example, check their Web site. You'll most likely be able to order them.

DECEMBER

S	M	T	W	T	F	S
						1
2	3	4	5	6	7	8
9	10	11	12	13	14	15
16	17	18	19	20	21	22
23	24	25	26	27	28	29
30	31					

Week of December 9–15

| Dec 10, 1:50 pm–
Dec 13, 12:01 am | 1st | Capricorn | Graft or bud plants. Trim to increase growth. |
| Dec 15, 8:15 am–
Dec 17, 5:17 am | 1st | Pisces | Plant grains, leafy annuals. Fertilize (chemical). Graft or bud plants. Irrigate. Trim to increase growth. |

Winter is barely upon us, and already thoughts of a vacation in sunnier locales are as common as snow flakes. You can give yourself a little trip insurance, though.

- Prevent dehydration by drinking water during flights
- Drink herbal teas instead of alcohol and caffeine drinks
- Eat yogurt and take organic garlic capsules to replace and fortify friendly intestinal bacteria
- Add a few drops of pure peppermint to tea or water to control internal digestive spasms
- If you react to climate changes, different water, or different foods, you may want to pack some herbal laxative tablets.
- Drink chamomile or linden tea to combat insomnia brought on by overexcitement
- Use Bach flower Rescue Remedy during a stressful day

Dec 15, 8:15 am– Dec 17, 5:17 am	1st	Pisces	Plant grains, leafy annuals. Fertilize (chemical). Graft or bud plants. Irrigate. Trim to increase growth.
Dec 17, 5:17 am– Dec 17, 1:52 pm	2nd	Pisces	Plant grains, leafy annuals. Fertilize (chemical). Graft or bud plants. Irrigate. Trim to increase growth.
Dec 19, 4:38 pm– Dec 21, 5:14 pm	2nd	Taurus	Plant annuals for hardiness. Trim to increase growth.

The practice of feng shui has been used for thousands of years to direct beneficial chi around homes and yards. You can tell a lot about your yard and the flow of chi by observing what is growing there. For example, lilacs do very well in alkaline soil, and elder trees can indicate geopathic stress. Dogs will avoid the stressed areas, but cats love them and will sit along lines of difficulty for hours. For more information on feng shui and gardening, see Christine Ayres article, "Feng Shui for the Garden," on page 244.

DECEMBER

S	M	T	W	T	F	S
						1
2	3	4	5	6	7	8
9	10	11	12	13	14	15
16	17	18	19	20	21	22
23	24	25	26	27	28	29
30	31					

Dec 23, 5:18 pm– Dec 23, 8:15 pm	2nd	Cancer	Plant grains, leafy annuals. Fertilize (chemical). Graft or bud plants. Irrigate. Trim to increase growth.
Dec 23, 8:15 pm– Dec 25, 6:52 pm	3rd	Cancer	Plant biennials, perennials, bulbs, and roots. Prune. Irrigate. Fertilize (organic).
Dec 25, 6:52 pm– Dec 27, 11:44 pm	3rd	Leo	Cultivate. Destroy weeds and pests. Harvest fruits and root crops for food. Trim to retard growth.
Dec 27, 11:44 pm– Dec 30, 8:37 am	3rd	Virgo	Cultivate, especially medicinal plants. Destroy weeds and pests. Trim to retard growth.

The day the Sun moves into Capricorn (December 22–January 22), marking the Winter Solstice (sometimes called the grave), is the shortest day of the year. The Sun remains at this low point of southern declination for three days. On December 25, it begins to move toward the northern hemisphere again—ascending—and heralding the return of longer days.

_____

_____

_____

_____

_____

_____

Gardening by the Moon

Today, people often reject the notion of gardening according to the Moon's phase and sign. The usual nonbeliever is not a scientist but the city dweller who has never had any real contact with nature and little experience of natural rhythms.

Camille Flammarian, the French astronomer, testifies to the success of Moon planting, though:

"Cucumbers increase at Full Moon, as well as radishes, turnips, leeks, lilies, horseradish, and saffron; onions, on the contrary, are much larger and better nourished during the decline and old age of the Moon than at its increase, during its youth and fullness, which is the reason the Egyptians abstained from onions, on account of their antipathy to the Moon. Herbs gathered while the Moon increases are of great efficiency. If the vines are trimmed at night when the Moon is in the sign of the Lion, Sagittarius, the Scorpion, or the Bull, it will save them from field rats, moles, snails, flies, and other animals."

Dr. Clark Timmins is one of the few modern scientists to have conducted tests in Moon planting. Following is a summary of his experiments:

Beets: When sown with the Moon in Scorpio, the germination rate was 71 percent; when sown in Sagittarius, the germination rate was 58 percent.

Scotch marigold: When sown with the Moon in Cancer, the germination rate was 90 percent; when sown in Leo, the rate was 32 percent.

Carrots: When sown with the Moon in Scorpio, the germination rate was 64 percent; when sown in Sagittarius, the germination rate was 47 percent.

Tomatoes: When sown with the Moon in Cancer, the germination rate was 90 percent; but when sown with the Moon in Leo, the germination rate was 58 percent.

Two things should be emphasized. First, remember that this is only a summary of the results of the experiments; the experiments themselves were conducted in a scientific manner to eliminate any variation in soil, temperature, moisture, and so on, so that only the Moon sign is varied. Second, note that these astonishing results were obtained without regard to the phase of the Moon—the other factor we use in Moon planting, and which presumably would have increased the differential in germination rates.

Dr. Timmins also tried transplanting Cancer- and Leo-planted tomato seedlings while the Cancer Moon was waxing. The result was 100 percent survival. When transplanting was done with the waning Sagittarius Moon, there was 0 percent survival. Dr. Timmins' tests show that the Cancer-planted tomatoes had blossoms twelve days earlier than those planted under Leo; the Cancer-planted tomatoes had an average height of twenty inches at that time compared to fifteen inches for the Leo-planted; the first ripe tomatoes were gathered from the Cancer plantings eleven days ahead of the Leo plantings; and a count of the hanging fruit and its size and weight shows an advantage to the Cancer plants over the Leo plants of 45 percent.

Dr. Timmins also observed that there have been similar tests that did not indicate results favorable to the Moon planting theory. As a scientist, he asked why one set of experiments indicated a positive verification of Moon planting, and others did not. He checked these other tests and found that the experimenters had not followed the geocentric system for determining the Moon sign positions, but the heliocentric. When the times used in these other tests were converted to the geocentric system, the dates chosen often were found to be in barren, rather than fertile, signs. Without going into a technical explanation, it is sufficient to point out that geocentric and heliocentric positions often vary by as much as four days. This is a large enough differential to place the Moon in Cancer, for example, in the heliocentric system, and at the same time in Leo by the geocentric system.

Most almanacs and calendars show the Moon's signs heliocentrically—and thus incorrectly for Moon planting—while the *Moon Sign Book* is calculated correctly for planting purposes, using the geocentric system. Some readers are confused because the *Moon Sign Book* talks about first, second, third, and fourth quarters, while other almanacs refer to these same divisions as New Moon, first quarter, Full Moon, and fourth quarter. Thus the almanacs say first quarter when the *Moon Sign Book* says second quarter.

There is nothing complicated about using astrology in agriculture and horticulture in order to increase both pleasure and profit, but there is one very important rule that is often neglected—use common sense! Of course this is one rule that should be remembered in every activity we undertake, but in the case of gardening and farming by the Moon, if it is not possible to use the best dates for planting or harvesting, we must select the next best and just try to do the best we can.

This brings up the matter of the other factors to consider in your gardening work. The dates we give as best for a certain activity apply to the entire country (with slight time correction), but in your section of the country you may be buried under three feet of snow on a date we say is good to plant your flowers. So we have factors of weather, season, temperature and moisture variations, soil conditions, your own available time and opportunity, and so forth. Some astrologers like to think it is all a matter of science, but gardening is also an art. In art, you develop an instinctive identification with your work and influence it with your feelings and wishes.

The *Moon Sign Book* gives you the place of the Moon for every day of the year so that you can select the best times once you have become familiar with the rules and practices of lunar agriculture. We give you specific, easy-to-follow directions so that you can get right down to work.

We give you the best dates for planting, and also for various related activities, including cultivation, fertilizing, harvesting, irrigation, and getting rid of weeds and pests. But we cannot tell you exactly when it's good to plant. Many of these rules were learned by observation and experience; as the body of experience grew we could see various patterns emerging that allowed us to make judgments about new things. That's what you should do, too. After you have worked with lunar agriculture for a while and have gained a working knowledge, you will probably begin to try new things—and we hope you will share your experiments and findings with us. That's how the science grows.

Here's an example of what we mean. Years ago Llewellyn George suggested that we try to combine our bits of knowledge about what to expect in planting under each of the Moon signs in order to gain benefit from several lunar factors in one plant. From this came our rule for developing "thoroughbred seed." To develop thoroughbred seed, save the seed for three successive years from plants grown by the correct Moon sign and phase. You can plant in the first quarter phase and in the sign of Cancer for fruitfulness; the second year, plant seeds from the first year plants in Libra for beauty; and in the third year, plant the seeds from the second year plants in Taurus to produce hardiness. In a similar manner you can combine the fruitfulness of Cancer, the good root growth of Pisces, and the sturdiness and good vine growth of Scorpio. And don't forget the characteristics of Capricorn: hardy like Taurus, but drier and perhaps more resistant to drought and disease.

Unlike common almanacs, we consider both the Moon's phase and the Moon's sign in making our calculations for the proper timing of our work. It is perhaps a little easier to understand this if we remind you that we are all living in the center of a vast electromagnetic field that is the Earth and its environment in space. Everything that occurs within this electromagnetic field has an effect on everything else within the field. The Moon and the Sun are the most important of the factors affecting the life of the Earth, and it is their relative positions to the Earth that we project for each day of the year.

Many people claim that not only do they achieve larger crops gardening by the Moon, but that their fruits and vegetables are much tastier. A number of organic gardeners have also become lunar gardeners using the natural rhythm of life forces that we experience through the relative movements of the Sun and Moon. We provide a few basic rules and then give you day-by-day guidance for your gardening work. You will be able to choose the best dates to meet your own needs and opportunities.

Planting by the Moon's Phases

During the increasing or waxing light—from New Moon to Full Moon—plant annuals that produce their yield above the ground. An annual is a plant that completes its entire life cycle within one growing season and has to be seeded each year. During the decreasing or waning light—from Full Moon to New Moon—plant biennials, perennials, and bulb and root plants. Biennials include crops that are planted one season to winter over and produce crops the next, such as winter wheat. Perennials and bulb and root plants include all plants that grow from the same root each year.

A simpler, less-accurate rule is to plant crops that produce above the ground during the waxing Moon, and to plant crops that produce below the ground during the waning Moon. Thus the old adage, "Plant potatoes during the dark of the Moon." Llewellyn George's system divided the lunar month into quarters. The first two from New Moon to Full Moon are the first and second quarters, and the last two from Full Moon to New Moon the third and fourth quarters. Using these divisions, we can increase our accuracy in timing our efforts to coincide with natural forces.

First Quarter

Plant annuals producing their yield above the ground, which are generally of the leafy kind that produce their seed outside the fruit. Some examples are asparagus, broccoli, brussels sprouts, cabbage, cauliflower, celery, cress, endive, kohlrabi, lettuce, parsley, and spinach. Cucumbers are an exception, as they do best in the first quarter rather than the second, even though the seeds are inside the fruit. Also plant cereals and grains.

Second Quarter

Plant annuals producing their yield above the ground, which are generally of the viney kind that produce their seed inside the fruit. Some examples include beans, eggplant, melons, peas, peppers, pumpkins, squash, tomatoes, etc. These are not hard-and-fast divisions. If you can't plant during the first quarter, plant during the second, and vice versa. There are many plants that seem to do equally well planted in either quarter, such as watermelon, hay, and cereals and grains.

Third Quarter

Plant biennials, perennials, bulbs, root plants, trees, shrubs, berries, grapes, strawberries, beets, carrots, onions, parsnips, rutabagas, potatoes, radishes, peanuts, rhubarb, turnips, winter wheat, etc.

Fourth Quarter

This is the best time to cultivate, turn sod, pull weeds, and destroy pests of all kinds, especially when the Moon is in Aries, Leo, Virgo, Gemini, Aquarius, and Sagittarius.

The Moon in the Signs

Moon in Aries

Barren, dry, fiery, and masculine. Use for destroying noxious weeds.

Moon in Taurus

Productive, moist, earthy, and feminine. Use for planting many crops when hardiness is important, particularly root crops. Also used for lettuce, cabbage, and similar leafy vegetables.

Moon in Gemini

Barren and dry, airy and masculine. Use for destroying noxious growths, weeds, and pests, and for cultivation.

Moon in Cancer

Fruitful, moist, feminine. Use for planting and irrigation.

Moon in Leo

Barren, dry, fiery, masculine. Use for killing weeds or cultivation.

Moon in Virgo

Barren, moist, earthy, and feminine. Use for cultivation and destroying weeds and pests.

Moon in Libra

Semi-fruitful, moist, and airy. Use for planting crops that need good pulp growth. A very good sign for flowers and vines. Also used for seeding hay, corn fodder, and the like.

Moon in Scorpio

Very fruitful and moist, watery and feminine. Nearly as productive as Cancer; use for the same purposes. Especially good for vine growth and sturdiness.

Moon in Sagittarius

Barren and dry, fiery and masculine. Use for planting onions, seeding hay, and for cultivation.

Moon in Capricorn

Productive and dry, earthy and feminine. Use for planting potatoes and other tubers.

Moon in Aquarius

Barren, dry, airy, and masculine. Use for cultivation and destroying noxious growths and pests.

Moon in Pisces

Very fruitful, moist, watery, and feminine. Especially good for root growth.

Companion Planting Guide

Plant	Companions	Hindered by
Asparagus	Tomatoes, parsley, basil	None known
Beans	Tomatoes, carrots, cucumbers, garlic, cabbage, beets, corn	Onions, gladiolas
Beets	Onions, cabbage, lettuce, mint, catnip	Pole beans
Broccoli	Beans, celery, potatoes, onions	Tomatoes
Cabbage	Peppermint, sage, thyme, tomatoes	Strawberries, grapes
Carrots	Peas, lettuce, chives, radishes, leeks, onions, sage	Dill, anise
Citrus trees	Guava, live oak, rubber trees, peppers	None known
Corn	Potatoes, beans, peas, melon, squash, pumpkin, sunflowers, soybeans	Quack grass, wheat straw mulch
Cucumbers	Beans, cabbage, radishes, sunflowers, lettuce, broccoli, squash	Aromatic herbs
Eggplant	Green beans, lettuce, kale	None known
Grapes	Peas, beans, blackberries	Cabbage, radishes
Melons	Corn, peas	Potatoes, gourds
Onions, leeks	Beets, chamomile, carrots, lettuce	Peas, beans, sage
Parsnip	Peas	None known
Peas	Radishes, carrots, corn, cucumbers, beans, tomatoes, spinach, turnips	Onion, garlic
Potatoes	Beans, corn, peas, cabbage, hemp, cucumbers, eggplant, catnip	Raspberries, pumpkins, tomatoes, sunflowers
Radishes	Peas, lettuce, nasturtiums, cucumbers	Hyssop
Spinach	Strawberries	None known
Squash/Pumpkin	Nasturtiums, corn, mint, catnip	Potatoes
Tomatoes	Asparagus, parsley, chives, onions, carrots, marigolds, nasturtiums, dill	Black walnut roots, fennel, potatoes
Turnips	Peas, beans, brussels sprouts	Potatoes

Plant	Companions	Uses
Anise	Coriander	Flavor candy, pastry, cheeses, cookies
Basil	Tomatoes	Dislikes rue; repels flies and mosquitoes
Borage	Tomatoes, squash	Use in teas
Buttercup	Clover	Hinders delphinium, peonies, monkshood, columbine

Plant	Companions	Uses
Catnip		Repels flea beetles
Chamomile	Peppermint, wheat, onions, cabbage	Roman chamomile may control damping-off disease; use in herbal sprays
Chervil	Radishes	Good in soups and other dishes
Chives	Carrots	Use in spray to deter black spot on roses
Coriander	Plant anywhere	Hinders seed formation in fennel
Cosmos		Repels corn earworms
Dill	Cabbage	Hinders carrots and tomatoes
Fennel	Plant in borders away from garden	Disliked by all garden plants
Horseradish		Repels potato bugs
Horsetail		Makes fungicide spray
Hyssop		Attracts cabbage fly away from cabbage; harmful to radishes
Lavender	Plant anywhere	Use in spray to control insects on cotton, repels clothes moths
Lovage		Lures horn worms away from tomatoes
Marigolds		Pest repellent; use against Mexican bean beetles and nematodes
Mint	Cabbage, tomatoes	Repels ants, flea beetles, and cabbage worm butterflies
Morning glory	Corn	Helps melon germination
Nasturtiums	Cabbage, cucumbers	Deters aphids, squash bugs, and pumpkin beetles
Okra	Eggplant	Will attract leafhopper (use to trap insects away from other plants)
Parsley	Tomatoes, asparagus	Freeze chopped up leaves to flavor foods
Purslane		Good ground cover
Rosemary		Repels cabbage moths, bean beetles, and carrot flies
Savory		Plant with onions to give them added sweetness
Tansy		Deters Japanese beetles, striped cucumber beetles, and squash bugs
Thyme		Repels cabbage worms
Yarrow		Increases essential oils of neighbors

2007 Dates to Destroy Weeds and Pests

From		To		Sign	Qtr.
Jan 4	4:14 pm	Jan 7	1:18 am	Leo	3rd
Jan 7	1:18 am	Jan 9	1:15 pm	Virgo	3rd
Jan 14	1:11 pm	Jan 16	8:49 pm	Sagittarius	4th
Feb 3	9:34 am	Feb 5	9:15 pm	Virgo	3rd
Feb 10	10:01 pm	Feb 13	6:42 am	Sagittarius	4th
Feb 15	11:34 am	Feb 17	11:14 am	Aquarius	4th
Mar 3	6:17 pm	Mar 5	4:25 am	Virgo	3rd
Mar 10	5:37 am	Mar 11	11:54 pm	Sagittarius	3rd
Mar 11	11:54 pm	Mar 12	4:34 pm	Sagittarius	4th
Mar 14	10:52 pm	Mar 17	1:30 am	Aquarius	4th
Apr 6	12:56 pm	Apr 8	11:36 pm	Sagittarius	3rd
Apr 11	7:23 am	Apr 13	11:38 am	Aquarius	4th
Apr 15	12:46 pm	Apr 17	7:36 am	Aries	4th
May 3	6:47 pm	May 6	5:21 am	Sagittarius	3rd
May 8	1:48 pm	May 10	12:27 am	Aquarius	3rd
May 10	12:27 am	May 10	7:31 pm	Aquarius	4th
May 12	10:19 pm	May 14	10:48 pm	Aries	4th
May 31	9:04 pm	Jun 2	11:09 am	Sagittarius	3rd
Jun 4	7:15 pm	Jun 7	1:24 am	Aquarius	3rd
Jun 9	5:26 am	Jun 11	7:29 am	Aries	4th
Jun 13	8:24 am	Jun 14	11:13 pm	Gemini	4th
Jul 2	1:24 am	Jul 4	6:52 am	Aquarius	3rd
Jul 6	10:56 am	Jul 7	12:53 pm	Aries	3rd
Jul 7	12:53 pm	Jul 8	1:54 pm	Aries	4th

From		To		Sign	Qtr.
Jul 10	4:10 pm	Jul 12	6:39 pm	Gemini	4th
Jul 29	8:48 pm	Jul 31	1:40 pm	Aquarius	3rd
Aug 2	4:43 pm	Aug 4	7:16 pm	Aries	3rd
Aug 6	10:01 pm	Aug 9	1:36 am	Gemini	4th
Aug 11	6:42 am	Aug 12	7:02 pm	Leo	4th
Aug 30	12:24 am	Sep 1	1:35 am	Aries	3rd
Sep 3	3:30 am	Sep 3	10:32 pm	Gemini	3rd
Sep 3	10:32 pm	Sep 5	7:08 am	Gemini	4th
Sep 7	12:59 pm	Sep 9	9:10 pm	Leo	4th
Sep 9	9:10 pm	Sep 11	8:44 am	Virgo	4th
Sep 26	3:45 pm	Sep 28	10:17 am	Aries	3rd
Sep 30	10:34 am	Oct 2	12:57 pm	Gemini	3rd
Oct 4	6:27 pm	Oct 7	3:03 am	Leo	4th
Oct 7	3:03 am	Oct 9	1:57 pm	Virgo	4th
Oct 14	2:58 pm	Oct 17	3:03 am	Sagittarius	4th
Nov 1	12:48 am	Nov 3	8:44 am	Leo	4th
Nov 3	8:44 am	Nov 5	6:47 pm	Virgo	4th
Nov 24	9:30 am	Nov 26	6:07 am	Gemini	3rd
Nov 28	8:23 am	Nov 30	2:44 pm	Leo	3rd
Nov 30	2:44 pm	Dec 1	7:44 am	Virgo	3rd
Dec 1	7:44 am	Dec 3	1:01 am	Virgo	4th
Dec 8	2:11 am	Dec 9	12:40 pm	Sagittarius	4th
Dec 25	6:52 pm	Dec 27	11:44 pm	Leo	3rd
Dec 27	11:44 pm	Dec 30	8:37 am	Virgo	3rd

Moon Void-of-Course

by Kim Rogers-Gallagher

The Moon circles the Earth in about twenty-eight days, moving through each zodiac sign in two-and-a-half days. As she passes through the thirty degrees of each sign, she "visits" with the planets in numerical order, forming aspects with them. Because she moves one degree in just two to two-and-a-half hours, her influence on each planet lasts only a few hours. She eventually reaches the planet that's in the highest degree of any sign, and forms what will be her final aspect before leaving the sign. From this point until she enters the next sign, she is referred to as void-of-course.

Think of it this way: the Moon is the emotional "tone" of the day, carrying feelings with her particular to the sign she's "wearing" at the moment. After she has contacted each of the planets, she symbolically "rests" before changing her costume, so her instinct is temporarily on hold. It's during this time that many people feel "fuzzy" or "vague." Plans or decisions made now often do not pan out. Without the instinctual "knowing" the Moon provides as she touches each planet, we tend to be unrealistic or exercise poor judgment. The traditional definition of the void Moon is that "nothing will come of this." Actions initiated under a void Moon are often wasted, irrelevant, or incorrect—usually because information is hidden, missing, or has been overlooked.

Although it's not a good time to initiate plans, routine tasks seem to go along just fine. This period is ideal for reflection. On the lighter side, remember there are good uses for the void Moon. It is the period when the universe seems to be most open to loopholes. It's a great time to make plans you don't want to fulfill or schedule things you don't want to do. See the table on pages 73–78 for a schedule of the Moon's void-of-course times in 2007.

Moon Void-of-Course Dates

Last Aspect		Moon Enters New Sign		
		January		
2	5:06 am	2	Cancer	10:14 am
3	8:57 am	4	Leo	4:14 pm
6	7:55 pm	7	Virgo	1:18 am
9	7:51 am	9	Libra	1:15 pm
11	8:56 pm	12	Scorpio	2:08 am
14	10:49 am	14	Sagittarius	1:11 pm
16	4:28 pm	16	Capricorn	8:49 pm
18	8:01 pm	19	Aquarius	1:15 am
21	12:00 am	21	Pisces	3:48 am
23	2:11 am	23	Aries	5:52 am
25	4:50 am	25	Taurus	8:28 am
27	11:08 am	27	Gemini	12:10 pm
29	1:40 pm	29	Cancer	5:16 pm
30	4:30 pm	Feb 1	Leo	12:14 am
		February		
3	5:55 am	3	Virgo	9:34 am
5	5:37 pm	5	Libra	9:15 pm
8	6:38 am	8	Scorpio	10:09 am
10	5:39 am	10	Sagittarius	10:01 pm
13	3:45 am	13	Capricorn	6:42 am
14	10:24 pm	15	Aquarius	11:34 am
17	11:14 am	17	Pisces	1:30 pm
19	11:43 am	19	Aries	2:06 pm
21	12:42 pm	21	Taurus	3:03 pm
23	2:46 pm	23	Gemini	5:42 pm
25	8:21 pm	25	Cancer	10:47 pm
27	1:03 am	28	Leo	6:29 am

Last Aspect · Moon Enters New Sign

March				
2	2:02 am	2	Virgo	4:32 pm
5	1:56 am	5	Libra	4:25 am
7	2:51 pm	7	Scorpio	5:16 pm
9	8:51 pm	10	Sagittarius	5:37 am
12	2:27 pm	12	Capricorn	4:34 pm
14	4:21 pm	14	Aquarius	10:52 pm
17	12:01 pm	17	Pisces	1:30 am
18	11:59 pm	19	Aries	1:41 am
20	11:33 pm	21	Taurus	1:15 am
22	11:12 am	23	Gemini	2:06 am
25	3:57 am	25	Cancer	5:49 am
26	10:36 am	27	Leo	1:04 pm
29	9:24 pm	29	Virgo	11:27 pm
April				
1	9:37 am	1	Libra	11:43 am
3	10:30 pm	4	Scorpio	12:35 am
5	10:54 pm	6	Sagittarius	12:56 pm
8	9:35 pm	8	Capricorn	11:36 pm
11	5:57 am	11	Aquarius	7:23 am
13	9:50 am	13	Pisces	11:38 am
15	11:02 am	15	Aries	12:46 pm
17	7:26 am	17	Taurus	12:11 pm
18	10:29 pm	19	Gemini	11:51 am
21	11:52 am	21	Cancer	1:50 pm
23	5:10 am	23	Leo	7:38 pm
26	3:01 am	26	Virgo	5:24 am
28	3:14 pm	28	Libra	5:44 pm

Last Aspect		Moon Enters New Sign		
		May		
1	4:07 am	1	Scorpio	6:41 am
3	2:42 am	3	Sagittarius	6:47 pm
6	2:45 am	6	Capricorn	5:21 am
8	3:34 am	8	Aquarius	1:48 pm
10	5:47 pm	10	Pisces	7:31 pm
12	7:53 pm	12	Aries	10:19 pm
14	8:24 pm	14	Taurus	10:48 pm
16	3:27 pm	16	Gemini	10:34 pm
18	8:57 pm	18	Cancer	11:38 pm
21	3:46 am	21	Leo	3:56 am
23	9:08 am	23	Virgo	12:26 pm
25	8:43 pm	26	Libra	12:16 am
28	12:17 pm	28	Scorpio	1:11 pm
30	1:11 pm	31	Sagittarius	1:06 am
		June		
2	7:29 am	2	Capricorn	11:09 am
4	5:43 pm	4	Aquarius	7:15 pm
6	9:47 pm	7	Pisces	1:24 am
9	1:52 am	9	Aries	5:26 am
11	3:57 am	11	Taurus	7:29 am
12	7:17 pm	13	Gemini	8:24 am
15	5:59 am	15	Cancer	9:45 am
17	3:39 am	17	Leo	1:25 pm
19	5:22 pm	19	Virgo	8:45 pm
22	2:50 am	22	Libra	7:43 am
24	3:22 pm	24	Scorpio	8:26 pm
26	4:23 pm	27	Sagittarius	8:23 am
29	1:08 pm	29	Capricorn	6:05 pm

Last Aspect   Moon Enters New Sign

		July		
1	4:45 am	2	Aquarius	1:24 am
4	2:02 am	4	Pisces	6:52 am
6	6:08 am	6	Aries	10:56 am
8	9:06 am	8	Taurus	1:54 pm
10	12:54 pm	10	Gemini	4:10 pm
12	5:12 pm	12	Cancer	6:39 pm
14	8:04 am	14	Leo	10:43 pm
16	11:55 pm	17	Virgo	5:39 am
19	9:44 am	19	Libra	3:53 pm
22	2:29 am	22	Scorpio	4:18 am
24	6:30 am	24	Sagittarius	4:29 pm
26	8:13 pm	27	Capricorn	2:21 am
28	10:23 pm	29	Aquarius	9:13 am
31	7:55 am	31	Pisces	1:40 pm
		August		
2	11:36 am	2	Aries	4:43 pm
4	1:31 pm	4	Taurus	7:16 pm
6	9:50 pm	6	Gemini	10:01 pm
9	1:27 am	9	Cancer	1:36 am
10	8:57 am	11	Leo	6:42 am
13	9:34 am	13	Virgo	2:03 pm
15	5:02 pm	16	Libra	12:04 am
18	8:21 am	18	Scorpio	12:13 pm
20	9:34 pm	21	Sagittarius	12:44 am
23	8:54 am	23	Capricorn	11:20 am
24	7:41 pm	25	Aquarius	6:35 pm
27	9:23 pm	27	Pisces	10:34 pm
29	6:22 pm	30	Aries	12:24 am

Last Aspect   **Moon Enters New Sign**

		September			
1	1:18 am	1	Taurus		1:35 am
2	8:47 pm	3	Gemini		3:30 am
5	7:00 am	5	Cancer		7:08 am
6	1:04 pm	7	Leo		12:59 pm
9	2:07 pm	9	Virgo		9:10 pm
12	12:14 am	12	Libra		7:31 am
14	12:10 pm	14	Scorpio		7:37 pm
16	7:40 pm	17	Sagittarius		8:21 am
19	12:48 pm	19	Capricorn		7:51 pm
22	2:15 am	22	Aquarius		4:18 am
24	5:14 am	24	Pisces		8:55 am
26	8:31 am	26	Aries		10:22 am
28	9:58 am	28	Taurus		10:17 am
30	1:10 am	30	Gemini		10:34 am
		October			
2	6:51 am	2	Cancer		12:57 pm
3	4:41 pm	4	Leo		6:27 pm
7	1:28 am	7	Virgo		3:03 am
9	7:08 am	9	Libra		1:57 pm
11	7:22 pm	12	Scorpio		2:13 am
13	5:23 pm	14	Sagittarius		2:58 pm
16	8:32 pm	17	Capricorn		3:03 am
19	4:33 am	19	Aquarius		12:52 pm
21	3:36 pm	21	Pisces		7:02 pm
23	4:17 pm	23	Aries		9:24 pm
25	5:46 pm	25	Taurus		9:07 pm
27	3:15 am	27	Gemini		8:11 pm
29	3:50 pm	29	Cancer		8:49 pm
31	1:13 am	Nov 1	Leo		12:48 am

		November			
3	3:13 am	3		Virgo	8:44 am
5	1:10 pm	5		Libra	6:47 pm
8	1:46 am	8		Scorpio	7:18 am
9	10:19 pm	10		Sagittarius	7:59 pm
13	2:53 am	13		Capricorn	8:00 am
15	4:19 am	15		Aquarius	6:30 pm
17	9:51 pm	18		Pisces	2:14 am
20	2:26 am	20		Aries	6:24 am
22	3:40 am	22		Taurus	7:18 am
23	1:53 pm	24		Gemini	6:29 am
26	2:37 am	26		Cancer	6:07 am
27	11:22 pm	28		Leo	8:23 am
30	12:25 pm	30		Virgo	2:44 pm
		December			
2	9:12 pm	3		Libra	1:01 am
5	9:48 am	5		Scorpio	1:31 pm
7	5:16 am	8		Sagittarius	2:11 am
10	10:36 am	10		Capricorn	1:50 pm
11	6:57 pm	13		Aquarius	12:01 am
15	6:50 am	15		Pisces	8:15 am
17	1:27 pm	17		Aries	1:52 pm
19	2:33 pm	19		Taurus	4:38 pm
21	1:06 am	21		Gemini	5:14 pm
23	3:25 pm	23		Cancer	5:18 pm
25	8:17 am	25		Leo	6:52 pm
27	9:54 pm	27		Virgo	11:44 pm
30	8:08 am	30		Libra	8:37 am

The Moon's Rhythm

The Moon journeys around Earth in an elliptical orbit that takes about 27.33 days, which is known as a sidereal month (period of revolution of one body about another). She can move up to 15 degrees or as few as 11 degrees in a day, with the fastest motion occurring when the Moon is at perigee (closest approach to Earth). The Moon is never retrograde, but when her motion is slow, the effect is similar to a retrograde period.

Astrologers have observed that people born on a day when the Moon is fast will process information differently from those who are born when the Moon is slow in motion. People born when the Moon is fast process information quickly and tend to react quickly, while those born during a slow Moon will be more deliberate.

The time from New Moon to New Moon is called the synodic month (involving a conjunction), and the average time span between this Sun-Moon alignment is 29.53 days. Since 29.53 won't divide into 365 evenly, we can have a month with two Full Moons (May 2007) or two New Moons (December 2005).

Moon Aspects

The aspects the Moon will make during the times you are considering are also important. A trine or sextile, and sometimes a conjunction, are considered favorable aspects. A trine or sextile between the Sun and Moon is an excellent foundation for success. Whether or not a conjunction is considered favorable depends upon the planet the Moon is making a conjunction to. If it's joining the Sun, Venus, Mercury, Jupiter, or even Saturn, the aspect is favorable. If the Moon joins Pluto or Mars, however, that would not be considered favorable. There may be exceptions, but it would depend on what you are electing to do. For example, a trine to Pluto might hasten the end of a relationship you want to be free of.

It is important to avoid times when the Moon makes an aspect to or is conjoining any retrograde planet, unless, of course, you want the thing started to end in failure.

After the Moon has completed an aspect to a planet, that planetary energy has passed. For example, if the Moon squares Saturn at 10:00 am, you can disregard Saturn's influence on your activity if it will occur after that time. You should always look ahead at aspects the Moon will make on the day in question, though, because if the Moon opposes Mars at 11:30 pm on that day, you can expect events that stretch into the evening to be affected by the Moon-Mars aspect. A testy conversation might lead to an argument, or more.

Moon Signs

Much agricultural work is ruled by earth signs—Virgo, Capricorn, and Taurus; and the air signs—Gemini, Aquarius, and Libra—rule flying and intellectual pursuits.

Each planet has one or two signs in which its characteristics are enhanced or "dignified," and the planet is said to "rule" that sign. The Sun rules Leo and the Moon rules Cancer, for example. The ruling planet for each sign is listed below. These should not be considered complete lists. We recommend that you purchase a book of planetary rulerships for more complete information.

Aries Moon

The energy of an Aries Moon is masculine, dry, barren, and fiery. Aries provides great start-up energy, but things started at this time may be the result of impulsive action that lacks research or necessary support. Aries lacks staying power.

Use this assertive, outgoing Moon sign to initiate change, but have a plan in place for someone to pick up the reins when you're impatient to move on to the next thing. Work that requires skillful, but not necessarily patient, use of tools—hammering, cutting down trees, etc.—is appropriate in Aries. Expect things to occur rapidly but to also quickly pass. If you are prone to injury or accidents, exercise caution and good judgment in Aries-related activities.

RULER: Mars
IMPULSE: Action
RULES: Head and face

Taurus Moon

A Taurus Moon's energy is feminine, semi-fruitful, and earthy. The Moon is exalted—very strong—in Taurus. Taurus is known as the farmer's sign because of its associations with farmland and precipitation that is the typical day-long "soaker" variety. Taurus energy is good to incorporate into your plans when patience, practicality, and perseverance are needed. Be aware, though, that you may also experience stubbornness in this sign.

Things started in Taurus tend to be long lasting and to increase in value. This can be very supportive energy in a marriage election. On the downside, the fixed energy of this sign resists change or the letting go of even the most difficult situations. A divorce following a marriage that occurred during a Taurus Moon may be difficult and costly to end. Things begun now tend to become habitual and hard to alter. If you want to make changes in something you start, it would be better to wait for Gemini. This is a good time to get a loan, but expect the people in charge of money to be cautious and slow to make decisions.

RULER: Venus

IMPULSE Stability

RULES: Neck, throat, and voice

Gemini Moon

A Gemini Moon's energy is masculine, dry, barren, and airy. People are more changeable than usual and may prefer to follow intellectual pursuits and play mental games rather than apply themselves to practical concerns.

This sign is not favored for agricultural matters, but it is an excellent time to prepare for activities, to run errands, and write letters. Plan to use a Gemini Moon to exchange ideas, meet people, go on vacations that include walking or biking, or be in situations that require versatility and quick thinking on your feet.

RULER: Mercury

IMPULSE: Versatility

RULES: Shoulders, hands, arms, lungs, and nervous system

Cancer Moon

A Cancer Moon's energy is feminine, fruitful, moist, and very strong. Use this sign when you want to grow things—flowers, fruits, vegetables, commodities, stocks, or collections—for example. This sensitive sign stimulates rapport between people. Considered the most fertile of the signs, it is often associated with mothering. You can use this moontime to build personal friendships that support mutual growth.

Cancer is associated with emotions and feelings. Prominent Cancer energy promotes growth, but it can also turn people pouty and prone to withdrawing into their shells.

RULER: The Moon

IMPULSE Tenacity

RULES: Chest area, breasts, and stomach

Leo Moon

A Leo Moon's energy is masculine, hot, dry, fiery, and barren. Use it whenever you need to put on a show, make a presentation, or entertain colleagues or guests. This is a proud yet playful energy that exudes self-confidence and is often associated with romance.

This is an excellent time for fund-raisers and ceremonies, or to be straight forward, frank, and honest about something. It is advisable not to put yourself in a position of needing public approval or where you might have to cope with underhandedness, as trouble in these areas can bring out the worst Leo traits. There is a tendency in this sign to become arrogant or self-centered.

RULER: The Sun

IMPULSE: I am

RULES: Heart and upper back

Virgo Moon

A Virgo Moon is feminine, dry, barren, earthy energy. It is favorable for anything that needs painstaking attention—especially those things where exactness rather than innovation is preferred.

Use this sign for activities when you must analyze information, or when you must determine the value of something. Virgo is the sign of bargain hunting. It's friendly toward agricultural matters with an emphasis on animals and harvesting vegetables. It is an excellent time to care for animals, especially training them and veterinary work.

This sign is most beneficial when decisions have already been made and now need to be carried out. The inclination here is to see details rather than the bigger picture.

There is a tendency in this sign to overdo. Precautions should be taken to avoid becoming too dull from all work and no play. Build a little relaxation and pleasure into your routine from the beginning.

RULER: Mercury
IMPULSE: Discriminating
RULES: Abdomen and intestines

Libra Moon

A Libra Moon's energy is masculine, semi-fruitful, and airy. This energy will benefit any attempt to bring beauty to a place or thing. Libra is considered good energy for starting things of an intellectual nature. Libra is the sign of partnership and unions, which make it an excellent time to form partnerships of any kind, to make agreements, and to negotiate. Even though this sign is good for initiating things, it is crucial to work with a partner who will provide incentive and encouragement, however. A Libra Moon accentuates teamwork (particularly teams of two) and artistic work (especially work that involves color). Make use of this sign when you are decorating your home or shopping for better quality clothing.

RULER: Venus
IMPULSE: Balance
RULES: Lower back, kidneys, and buttocks

Scorpio Moon

The Scorpio Moon is feminine, fruitful, cold, and moist. It is useful when intensity (that sometimes borders on obsession) is needed. Scorpio is considered a very psychic sign. Use this Moon sign when you must back up something you strongly believe in, such as union or employer relations. There is strong group loyalty here, but a Scorpio Moon is also a good time to end connections thoroughly. This is also a good time to conduct research.

The desire nature is so strong here that there is a tendency to manipulate situations to get what one wants, or to not see one's responsibility in an act.

RULER: Pluto, Mars (traditional)
IMPULSE: Transformation
RULES: Reproductive organs, genitals, groin, and pelvis

Sagittarius Moon

The Moon's energy is masculine, dry, barren, and fiery in Sagittarius, encouraging flights of imagination and confidence in the flow of life. Sagittarius is the most philosophical sign. Candor and honesty are enhanced when the Moon is here. This is an excellent time to "get things off your chest," and to deal with institutions of higher learning, publishing companies, and the law. It's also a good time for sport and adventure.

Sagittarians are the crusaders of this world. This is a good time to tackle things that need improvement, but don't try to be the diplomat while influenced by this energy. Opinions can run strong and the tendency to proselytize is increased.

RULER: Jupiter

IMPULSE: Expansion

RULES: Thighs and hips

Capricorn Moon

In Capricorn the Moon's energy is feminine, semi-fruitful, and earthy. Because Cancer and Capricorn are polar opposites, the Moon's energy is thought to be weakened here. This energy encourages the need for structure, discipline, and organization. This is a good time to set goals and plan for the future, tend to family business, and to take care of details requiring patience or a businesslike manner. Institutional activities are favored. This sign should be avoided if you're seeking favors, as those in authority can be insensitive under this influence.

RULER: Saturn

IMPULSE: Ambitious

RULES: Bones, skin, and knees

Aquarius Moon

An Aquarius Moon's energy is masculine, barren, dry, and airy. Activities that are unique, individualistic, concerned with humanitarian issues, society as a whole, and making improvements are favored under this Moon. It is this quality of making improvements that has caused this sign to be associated with inventors and new inventions.

An Aquarius Moon promotes the gathering of social groups for friendly exchanges. People tend to react and speak from an intellectual rather than emotional viewpoint when the Moon is in this sign.

RULER: Uranus and Saturn

IMPULSE: Reformer

RULES: Calves and ankles

Pisces Moon

A Pisces Moon is feminine, fruitful, cool, and moist. This is an excellent time to retreat, meditate, sleep, pray, or make that dreamed-of escape into a fantasy vacation. However, things are not always what they seem to be with the Moon in Pisces. Personal boundaries tend to be fuzzy, and you may not be seeing things clearly. People tend to be idealistic under this sign, which can prevent them from seeing reality.

There is a live and let live philosophy attached to this sign, which in the idealistic world may work well enough, but chaos is frequently the result. That's why this sign is also associated with alcohol and drug abuse, drug trafficking, and counterfeiting. On the lighter side, many musicians and artists are ruled by Pisces. It's only when they move too far away from reality that the dark side of substance abuse, suicide, or crime takes away life.

RULER: Jupiter and Neptune

IMPULSE: Empathetic

RULES: Feet

More About Zodiac Signs

Element (Triplicity)

Each of the zodiac signs is classified as belonging to an element, and these are the four basic elements:

Fire Signs

Aries, Sagittarius, and Leo are action-oriented, outgoing, energetic, and spontaneous.

Earth Signs

Taurus, Capricorn, and Virgo are stable, conservative, practical, and oriented to the physical and material realm.

Air Signs

Gemini, Aquarius, and Libra are sociable and critical, and they tend to represent intellectual responses rather than feelings.

Water Signs

Cancer, Scorpio, and Pisces are emotional, receptive, intuitive, and can be very sensitive.

Quality (Quadruplicity)

Each zodiac sign is further classified as being cardinal, mutable, or fixed. There are four signs in each quadruplicity, one sign from each element.

Cardinal Signs

Aries, Cancer, Libra, and Capricorn represent beginnings and initiate new action. They initiate each new season in the cycle of the year.

Fixed Signs

Taurus, Leo, Scorpio, and Aquarius want to maintain the status quo through stubbornness and persistence; they represent that "between" time. For example, Leo is the month when summer really feels like summer.

Mutable Signs

Pisces, Gemini, Virgo, and Sagittarius adapt to change and tolerate situations. They represent the last month of each season, when things are changing in preparation for the coming season.

Nature and Fertility

In addition to a sign's element and quality, each sign is further classified as either fruitful, semi-fruitful, or barren. This classification is the most important for readers who use the gardening information in the *Moon Sign Book* because the timing of most events depends on the fertility of the sign occupied by the Moon. The water signs of Cancer, Scorpio, and Pisces are the most fruitful. The semi-fruitful signs are the earth signs Taurus and Capricorn, and the air sign Libra. The barren signs correspond to the fire signs Aries, Leo, and Sagittarius; the air signs Gemini and Aquarius; and earth-sign Virgo.

Lunar Gardening Works: the Proof Is in the Pumpkin

Years ago Llewellyn's *Moon Sign Book* sponsored a gardening contest based on planting by the Moon. Readers were asked to note the Moon's sign and phase on the day of planting, and then to keep track of the size and yield of their fruits and vegetables. They could also keep track of results obtained from deliberately planting seeds in the incorrect signs or quarters. Lunar planting is an invitation to each gardener to be his or her own scientist, to experiment with finding the best ways to align with the forces of nature rather than working against them.

Results of experiments were reported in the next year's *Moon Sign Book*, and some of the results were astounding—like the cauliflower that was one-foot across and weighed eight pounds, and a butternut squash that weighed twenty pounds.

Every year places like Half Moon Bay in California sponsor contests for the largest pumpkin, the tallest corn, the biggest sunflowers, and so on. We're not sponsoring a contest with prizes, but if you want to send us a photo and the record of extraordinary results you achieve by following lunar gardening practices, we'd like to hear from you. Submitting your photo and gardening record will be considered permission by you to use them in our *Moon Sign Book* the following year. Photos will not be returned. Please send to Moon Sign Book Editor, 2143 Wooddale Drive, Woodbury, MN 55125-2989. Happy gardening!

Key Agricultural Events During Last 50 Years

The most important change in agriculture in the past fifty years was the hybridization and improvement of crops, according to members of North American Agricultural Journalists. A list of forty important events was released in April 2003. Also on the list in order of importance were:

1. Genetically modified crops that have been engineered to kill insect pests and tolerate herbicides, starting in the 1990s.

2. The discovery of DNA, the chemical building block of heredity, 1953.

3. Norman Borlaug's "Green Revolution." Borlaug won the Nobel Peace Prize in 1970. He developed a high-yield dwarf wheat that helped turn Third World countries into food exporters.

4. Agricultural debt crisis of the 1980s, which started when the Federal Reserve Bank encouraged higher interest rates to slow inflation. This forced many small farmers out of business.

5. Publication of Rachel Carson's book *Silent Spring* in 1962, which documented how DDT accumulates in the environment and harms mammals and birds. Her book helped start the environmental movement.

6. Use of antibiotics for livestock and poultry, approved by the FDA nearly fifty years ago.

7. Adoption of no-till farming, which avoids plowing and slows soil erosion, tied with the fact that the farm population dropped below 2 percent of the U.S. population during the 1990s.

8. Adoption of anhydrous ammonia fertilizer in the 1950s.

9. Integration of the poultry business in the 1960s.

This information was used with permission from the Texas A&M University System Agricultural Program. Contact: Kathleen Phillips.

Good Timing

By Sharon Leah

Electional astrology is the art of electing times to begin any undertaking. Say, for example, you want to start a business. That business will experience ups and downs, as well as reach its potential, according to the promise held in the universe at the time the business was started—its birth time. The horoscope (birth chart) set for the date, time, and place that a business starts would indicate the outcome—its potential to succeed.

So, you might ask yourself the question: If the horoscope for a business start can show success or failure, why not begin at a time that is more favorable to the venture? Well, you can.

While no time is perfect, there are better times and better days to undertake specific activities. There are thousands of examples that prove electional astrology is not only practical, but that it can make a difference in our lives. There are rules for electing times to begin various activities—even shopping. You'll find detailed instructions about how to make elections beginning on page 106.

Personalizing Elections

The election rules in this almanac are based upon the planetary positions at the time for which the election is made. They do not depend on any type of birth chart. However, a birth chart based upon the time, date, and birthplace of an event has advantages. No election is effective for every person. For example, you may leave home to begin a trip at the same time as a friend, but each of you will have a different experience according to whether or not your birth chart favors the trip.

Not all elections require a birth chart, but the timing of very important events—business starts, marriages, etc.—would benefit from the additional accuracy a birth chart provides. To order a birth chart for yourself or a planned event, visit our Web site at www.llewellyn.com.

Some Things to Consider

You've probably experienced good timing in your life. Maybe you were at the right place at the right time to meet a friend whom you hadn't seen in years. Frequently, when something like that happens, it is the result of following an intuitive impulse—that "gut instinct." Consider for a moment that you were actually responding to planetary energies. Electional astrology is a tool that can help you to align with energies, present and future, that are available to us through planetary placements.

Significators

Decide upon the important significators (planet, sign, and house ruling the matter) for which the election is being made. The Moon is the most important significator in any election, so the

Moon should always be fortified (strong by sign, and making favorable aspects to other planets). The Moon's aspects to other planets are more important than the sign the Moon is in.

Other important considerations are the significators of the Ascendant and Midheaven—the house ruling the election matter, and the ruler of the sign on that house cusp. Finally, any planet or sign that has a general rulership over the matter in question should be taken into consideration.

Nature and Fertility

Determine the general nature of the sign that is appropriate for your election. For example, much agricultural work is ruled by the earth signs of Virgo, Capricorn, and Taurus; while the air signs—Gemini, Aquarius, and Libra—rule intellectual pursuits.

One Final Comment

Use common sense. If you must do something, like plant your garden or take an airplane trip on a day that doesn't have the best aspects, proceed anyway, but try to minimize problems. For example, leave early for the airport to avoid being left behind due to delays in the security lanes. When you have no other choice, do the best that you can under the circumstances at the time.

If you want to personalize your elections, please turn to page 106 for more information. If you want a quick and easy answer, you can refer to Llewellyn's Astro Almanac.

Llewellyn's Astro Almanac

The Astro Almanac tables, beginning on the next page, can help you find the dates best suited to particular activities. The dates provided are determined from the Moon's sign, phase, and aspects to other planets. Please note that the Astro Almanac does not take personal factors, such as your Sun and Moon sign, into account. The dates are general, and they will apply for everyone. Some activities will not have suitable dates during a particular month, so no dates will be shown.

Astro Almanac Tables

Activity	January
Advertise in Print	8, 10, 15, 23, 29
Automobile (Buy)	19
Animals (Neuter or spay)	15, 16, 17
Animals (Sell or buy)	28, 29, 31
Build (Start excavation)	20
Business (Start new)	23
Can Fruits and Vegetables	
Concrete (Pour)	5, 6
Consultants (Begin work with)	5, 8, 29
Contracts (Bid on)	19, 29
Copyrights/Patents (Apply for)	4, 8, 14, 19, 31
Cultivate	5, 6, 7, 8, 15, 16
Cut Wood	7, 8
Entertain Guests	5, 6, 11, 12
Employee (Hire)	7, 8, 9, 25, 26
Fertilize and Compost (Chemical)	2, 30, 31
Fertilize and Compost (Organic)	12, 13
Grafting or Budding (See p. 115)	2, 3, 21, 22
Habits (Break)	
Hair (Cut)	15, 16, 17, 22, 25, 26, 27
Harvest (Crops to dry)	5, 6
Harvest (Grain or root crops)	5, 6
Job (Start new)	2, 3, 4, 6, 23, 24, 31
Legal (To gain damages, start)	24, 25
Loan (Ask for)	
Massage (Relaxing)	9, 12, 26, 27
Mushrooms (Pick)	2, 3, 4
Promotion (Ask for)	19, 22, 24, 29
Prune to Promote Healing	17, 18
Prune to Retard Growth	12, 13, 14
Sauerkraut (Make)	
Spray Pests and Weeds	
Wean Children	1, 15, 16, 17
Weight (Reduce)	7, 8

Activity	February
Advertise in Print	7, 9
Automobile (Buy)	
Animals (Neuter or spay)	11, 12, 13, 14
Animals (Sell or buy)	25, 26, 27
Build (Start excavation)	22, 23
Business (Start new)	21, 22, 23
Can Fruits and Vegetables	
Concrete (Pour)	
Consultants (Begin work with)	
Contracts (Bid on)	
Copyrights/Patents (Apply for)	2, 3
Cultivate	2, 3, 4, 5, 11, 12
Cut Wood	3, 4, 5, 13, 14
Entertain Guests	7
Employee (Hire)	5, 22, 23
Fertilize and Compost (Chemical)	26, 27
Fertilize and Compost (Organic)	8, 9, 10
Grafting or Budding (See p. 115)	18, 19, 26, 27
Habits (Break)	15, 16
Hair (Cut)	11, 12, 13, 22, 23, 24
Harvest (Crops to dry)	
Harvest (Grain or root crops)	10, 11, 12, 15, 16
Job (Start new)	1, 2, 3, 20, 21, 22
Legal (To gain damages, start)	20
Loan (Ask for)	1, 2, 23
Massage (Relaxing)	9, 22, 23
Mushrooms (Pick)	1, 2, 3
Promotion (Ask for)	23
Prune to Promote Healing	13, 14
Prune to Retard Growth	8, 9
Sauerkraut (Make)	
Spray Pests and Weeds	15, 16, 17
Wean Children	11, 12, 13, 14, 15
Weight (Reduce)	3, 4, 5

Activity	March
Advertise in Print	16, 21, 25
Automobile (Buy)	13
Animals (Neuter or spay)	10, 11, 12, 13, 14
Animals (Sell or buy)	26, 27, 28
Build (Start excavation)	21, 22
Business (Start new)	
Can Fruits and Vegetables	17
Concrete (Pour)	
Consultants (Begin work with)	12, 21
Contracts (Bid on)	12, 23
Copyrights/Patents (Apply for)	1, 2, 20, 25
Cultivate	4, 10, 11
Cut Wood	4, 13, 14
Entertain Guests	5, 6
Employee (Hire)	5, 21, 22
Fertilize and Compost (Chemical)	18, 19, 25, 26
Fertilize and Compost (Organic)	8, 9
Grafting or Budding (See p. 115)	25, 26, 27
Habits (Break)	15, 16
Hair (Cut)	10, 11, 13, 14, 22, 24
Harvest (Crops to dry)	10, 11
Harvest (Grain or root crops)	10, 11, 12, 15, 16
Job (Start new)	20, 26, 28, 29
Legal (To gain damages, start)	1, 2, 20
Loan (Ask for)	1, 2
Massage (Relaxing)	1, 2, 16, 21, 22, 29
Mushrooms (Pick)	2, 3, 4
Promotion (Ask for)	12, 16, 21
Prune to Promote Healing	13, 14
Prune to Retard Growth	8, 9
Sauerkraut (Make)	
Spray Pests and Weeds	15, 16
Wean Children	10, 11, 12, 13, 14
Weight (Reduce)	4

Activity	April
Advertise in Print	7, 11, 15, 21, 26, 30
Automobile (Buy)	10, 21
Animals (Neuter or spay)	8, 9, 10, 11
Animals (Sell or buy)	25, 26
Build (Start excavation)	18, 19
Business (Start new)	
Can Fruits and Vegetables	13, 14, 15
Concrete (Pour)	
Consultants (Begin work with)	9, 20, 21
Contracts (Bid on)	9, 10, 11, 21
Copyrights/Patents (Apply for)	9, 11, 12, 15, 25, 26
Cultivate	7, 8, 11, 12
Cut Wood	
Entertain Guests	1, 2, 25
Employee (Hire)	17, 18, 19, 26, 27
Fertilize and Compost (Chemical)	21, 22, 23
Fertilize and Compost (Organic)	4, 5, 6, 13, 14
Grafting or Budding (See p. 115)	21, 22, 23
Habits (Break)	11, 12
Hair (Cut)	7, 9, 10, 13, 14, 18, 19, 20
Harvest (Crops to dry)	7, 8
Harvest (Grain or root crops)	6, 7, 8, 11, 12, 15, 16
Job (Start new)	16, 17, 21, 24, 25
Legal (To gain damages, start)	21
Loan (Ask for)	25
Massage (Relaxing)	15, 17, 18, 24
Mushrooms (Pick)	1, 2, 3
Promotion (Ask for)	11, 20, 25
Prune to Promote Healing	8, 9
Prune to Retard Growth	4, 5, 6
Sauerkraut (Make)	4, 5, 6
Spray Pests and Weeds	11, 12
Wean Children	7, 8, 9, 10, 11
Weight (Reduce)	

Activity	May
Advertise in Print	21, 28, 30
Automobile (Buy)	7, 8, 18
Animals (Neuter or spay)	8, 9, 10
Animals (Sell or buy)	27, 28, 30
Build (Start excavation)	22, 23
Business (Start new)	
Can Fruits and Vegetables	11, 12
Concrete (Pour)	8, 9
Consultants (Begin work with)	14, 21
Contracts (Bid on)	8
Copyrights/Patents (Apply for)	13, 14, 21, 22
Cultivate	4, 5, 8, 9, 13, 14
Cut Wood	15
Entertain Guests	21, 22, 23, 27
Employee (Hire)	15, 16
Fertilize and Compost (Chemical)	1, 2, 19, 20, 29, 30
Fertilize and Compost (Organic)	11, 12
Grafting or Budding (See p. 115)	1, 2, 19, 20, 29, 30
Habits (Break)	
Hair (Cut)	4, 5, 7, 11, 12, 15, 16, 17, 18
Harvest (Crops to dry)	4, 5
Harvest (Grain or root crops)	4, 5, 7, 8, 13, 14
Job (Start new)	13, 14, 15, 21, 22, 23
Legal (To gain damages, start)	21, 22
Loan (Ask for)	22
Massage (Relaxing)	15, 16, 19
Mushrooms (Pick)	1, 2, 3, 30
Promotion (Ask for)	7, 14, 17, 22, 28
Prune to Promote Healing	6, 7, 8
Prune to Retard Growth	1, 2, 3
Sauerkraut (Make)	3
Spray Pests and Weeds	8, 9, 10
Wean Children	4, 5, 6, 7, 8
Weight (Reduce)	

Activity	June
Advertise in Print	7, 9
Automobile (Buy)	4, 13, 14
Animals (Neuter or spay)	1, 2, 3, 4
Animals (Sell or buy)	23, 25, 26, 28
Build (Start excavation)	18, 19
Business (Start new)	
Can Fruits and Vegetables	7, 8
Concrete (Pour)	5, 6
Consultants (Begin work with)	5, 7
Contracts (Bid on)	4
Copyrights/Patents (Apply for)	5, 6
Cultivate	1, 5, 6, 9, 10
Cut Wood	11, 12
Entertain Guests	18, 19, 23
Employee (Hire)	11, 13, 20, 21
Fertilize and Compost (Chemical)	15, 16, 17, 25, 26
Fertilize and Compost (Organic)	7, 8
Grafting or Budding (See p. 115)	15, 16, 25, 26
Habits (Break)	
Hair (Cut)	1, 2, 3, 7, 8, 11, 12, 13, 27, 28
Harvest (Crops to dry)	1
Harvest (Grain or root crops)	1, 5, 6, 9, 10
Job (Start new)	11
Legal (To gain damages, start)	
Loan (Ask for)	18, 19
Massage (Relaxing)	11, 12, 18, 19
Mushrooms (Pick)	1, 29, 30
Promotion (Ask for)	7
Prune to Promote Healing	2, 3, 4
Prune to Retard Growth	
Sauerkraut (Make)	
Spray Pests and Weeds	5, 6
Wean Children	1, 2, 3, 4, 5, 6
Weight (Reduce)	

Activity	July
Advertise in Print	17, 27
Automobile (Buy)	12, 27, 28
Animals (Neuter or spay)	1, 2, 3, 4
Animals (Sell or buy)	24, 25, 26, 27
Build (Start excavation)	15, 16
Business (Start new)	
Can Fruits and Vegetables	9, 10
Concrete (Pour)	8, 9, 10
Consultants (Begin work with)	15, 17
Contracts (Bid on)	11, 12, 28
Copyrights/Patents (Apply for)	2, 3
Cultivate	2, 3, 6, 7, 11, 12
Cut Wood	
Entertain Guests	15, 16, 20, 21
Employee (Hire)	9, 10, 17, 18
Fertilize and Compost (Chemical)	22, 23
Fertilize and Compost (Organic)	4, 5, 13
Grafting or Budding (See p. 115)	22, 23, 28, 29
Habits (Break)	
Hair (Cut)	4, 5, 9, 10, 11, 12, 23, 26, 27, 28
Harvest (Crops to dry)	6, 7
Harvest (Grain or root crops)	2, 3, 6, 7, 11, 12
Job (Start new)	6, 7, 8, 13, 16, 30
Legal (To gain damages, start)	16
Loan (Ask for)	15
Massage (Relaxing)	8, 9, 10, 15
Mushrooms (Pick)	1, 28, 29, 30
Promotion (Ask for)	12, 17, 22
Prune to Promote Healing	1
Prune to Retard Growth	
Sauerkraut (Make)	4, 5, 31
Spray Pests and Weeds	
Wean Children	2, 3, 4, 5
Weight (Reduce)	

Activity	August
Advertise in Print	4, 15, 17, 18, 22
Automobile (Buy)	8, 23, 24
Animals (Neuter or spay)	
Animals (Sell or buy)	22, 23, 24
Build (Start excavation)	19, 20
Business (Start new)	
Can Fruits and Vegetables	5, 6, 9, 10
Concrete (Pour)	5, 6
Consultants (Begin work with)	1, 9, 16, 17, 18
Contracts (Bid on)	9
Copyrights/Patents (Apply for)	3, 4, 9, 10, 18
Cultivate	3, 4, 7, 8
Cut Wood	5, 6, 7, 8
Entertain Guests	11, 16, 17, 18
Employee (Hire)	
Fertilize and Compost (Chemical)	18, 19, 20, 27, 28
Fertilize and Compost (Organic)	1, 2, 9, 10, 29
Grafting or Budding (See p. 115)	18, 19, 20
Habits (Break)	11
Hair (Cut)	1, 6, 7, 8, 21, 22, 23, 24
Harvest (Crops to dry)	2, 3, 4, 30, 31
Harvest (Grain or root crops)	3, 4, 7, 8, 11
Job (Start new)	2, 3, 4, 6, 8, 12, 13, 30, 31
Legal (To gain damages, start)	16, 17, 18, 21
Loan (Ask for)	
Massage (Relaxing)	4, 8
Mushrooms (Pick)	27, 28, 29
Promotion (Ask for)	2, 6, 12, 18, 23
Prune to Promote Healing	
Prune to Retard Growth	
Sauerkraut (Make)	29, 30
Spray Pests and Weeds	11
Wean Children	1, 2, 21, 22, 23
Weight (Reduce)	

Activity	September
Advertise in Print	2, 7, 13, 17, 27
Automobile (Buy)	4, 20, 22
Animals (Neuter or spay)	
Animals (Sell or buy)	20, 22, 23, 24
Build (Start excavation)	15, 16
Business (Start new)	
Can Fruits and Vegetables	1, 2, 5, 6, 7
Concrete (Pour)	1, 2
Consultants (Begin work with)	1, 2, 13, 14
Contracts (Bid on)	
Copyrights/Patents (Apply for)	7, 8, 13, 27, 28
Cultivate	3, 4, 7, 8, 9, 10
Cut Wood	1, 2, 3, 4, 10
Entertain Guests	7, 8, 13, 14
Employee (Hire)	13, 14, 28
Fertilize and Compost (Chemical)	15, 16, 24, 25
Fertilize and Compost (Organic)	5, 6, 7
Grafting or Budding (See p. 115)	15, 16, 20, 21
Habits (Break)	7, 8, 9, 10
Hair (Cut)	1, 2, 3, 4, 17, 18, 20, 21
Harvest (Crops to dry)	27
Harvest (Grain or root crops)	3, 4, 7, 8, 9, 27
Job (Start new)	1, 2, 5, 6, 7, 27, 28
Legal (To gain damages, start)	13, 14, 20, 27, 28
Loan (Ask for)	
Massage (Relaxing)	1, 2, 7, 8
Mushrooms (Pick)	25, 26, 27
Promotion (Ask for)	13, 17, 18
Prune to Promote Healing	
Prune to Retard Growth	
Sauerkraut (Make)	
Spray Pests and Weeds	8, 9
Wean Children	24, 25, 26
Weight (Reduce)	10

Activity	October
Advertise in Print	2, 7
Automobile (Buy)	17, 18, 19
Animals (Neuter or spay)	15, 16, 17, 18
Animals (Sell or buy)	20, 21, 22
Build (Start excavation)	12, 13
Business (Start new)	20, 21
Can Fruits and Vegetables	2, 3, 4
Concrete (Pour)	
Consultants (Begin work with)	5, 6, 17
Contracts (Bid on)	2, 17, 18, 29
Copyrights/Patents (Apply for)	2, 3
Cultivate	1, 5, 6, 7, 8
Cut Wood	7, 8, 27, 28, 29
Entertain Guests	5, 6, 10, 11
Employee (Hire)	26
Fertilize and Compost (Chemical)	22, 23
Fertilize and Compost (Organic)	2, 3, 4, 12, 13, 30, 31
Grafting or Budding (See p. 115)	12, 13, 14
Habits (Break)	5, 6, 7, 8
Hair (Cut)	1, 15, 16, 17, 18, 22, 26, 27
Harvest (Crops to dry)	
Harvest (Grain or root crops)	1, 5, 6, 28, 29
Job (Start new)	2, 3, 5, 6
Legal (To gain damages, start)	
Loan (Ask for)	
Massage (Relaxing)	5, 6, 25, 26
Mushrooms (Pick)	25, 26, 27
Promotion (Ask for)	2
Prune to Promote Healing	
Prune to Retard Growth	
Sauerkraut (Make)	29, 30, 31
Spray Pests and Weeds	5, 6
Wean Children	20, 21, 22
Weight (Reduce)	7, 8

Activity	November
Advertise in Print	13, 16, 21
Automobile (Buy)	13, 14, 15
Animals (Neuter or spay)	11, 12, 13, 14
Animals (Sell or buy)	20, 21, 22
Build (Start excavation)	
Business (Start new)	13, 14
Can Fruits and Vegetables	26, 27
Concrete (Pour)	28, 29, 30
Consultants (Begin work with)	2, 3
Contracts (Bid on)	13, 27
Copyrights/Patents (Apply for)	2, 3, 7, 8, 13, 14
Cultivate	1, 2, 3, 4
Cut Wood	3, 4, 5, 22, 23
Entertain Guests	2, 7, 28
Employee (Hire)	
Fertilize and Compost (Chemical)	18, 19
Fertilize and Compost (Organic)	8, 9, 10, 26, 27
Grafting or Budding (See p. 115)	9, 10, 13, 14
Habits (Break)	2, 3, 4, 5
Hair (Cut)	11, 12, 13, 14, 18, 19, 22, 23, 24, 25
Harvest (Crops to dry)	28, 29, 30
Harvest (Grain or root crops)	1, 2, 25, 28, 29, 30
Job (Start new)	20, 21, 22, 26, 27, 28
Legal (To gain damages, start)	12, 21
Loan (Ask for)	12, 21, 30
Massage (Relaxing)	22, 23, 28, 29
Mushrooms (Pick)	23, 24, 25
Promotion (Ask for)	3, 7, 18
Prune to Promote Healing	
Prune to Retard Growth	
Sauerkraut (Make)	26, 27
Spray Pests and Weeds	2, 28, 29, 30
Wean Children	
Weight (Reduce)	3, 4, 5

Activity	December
Advertise in Print	3, 29, 30
Automobile (Buy)	11, 12
Animals (Neuter or spay)	11, 12, 13
Animals (Sell or buy)	18, 19, 20
Build (Start excavation)	13, 14
Business (Start new)	10, 11
Can Fruits and Vegetables	24, 25
Concrete (Pour)	26, 27
Consultants (Begin work with)	28, 29
Contracts (Bid on)	12
Copyrights/Patents (Apply for)	3, 4, 5, 14, 15
Cultivate	1, 2, 8, 26, 27, 28, 29
Cut Wood	1, 2, 28, 29
Entertain Guests	4
Employee (Hire)	28, 29
Fertilize and Compost (Chemical)	15, 16, 17
Fertilize and Compost (Organic)	5, 6, 25, 26
Grafting or Budding (See p. 115)	15, 16, 17
Habits (Break)	1, 2
Hair (Cut)	8, 9, 10, 11, 12, 15, 16, 20, 21, 22
Harvest (Crops to dry)	26, 27
Harvest (Grain or root crops)	8, 26, 27
Job (Start new)	24, 25, 27
Legal (To gain damages, start)	14
Loan (Ask for)	12
Massage (Relaxing)	3, 19
Mushrooms (Pick)	22, 23, 24
Promotion (Ask for)	11, 28
Prune to Promote Healing	
Prune to Retard Growth	5, 6
Sauerkraut (Make)	24, 25
Spray Pests and Weeds	
Wean Children	10, 11, 12, 13
Weight (Reduce)	1, 2, 28, 29

Choose the Best Time for Your Activities

When rules for elections refer to "favorable" and "unfavorable" aspects to your Sun or other planets, please refer to the Favorable and Unfavorable Days Tables and Lunar Aspectarian for more information. You'll find instructions beginning on page 127 and the tables beginning on page 134.

The material in this section came from several sources including: *The New A to Z Horoscope Maker and Delineator* by Llewellyn George (Llewellyn, 1999), *Moon Sign Book* (Llewellyn, 1945), and *Electional Astrology* by Vivian Robson (Slingshot Publishing, 2000). Robson's book was originally published in 1937.

Advertise (Internet)

The Moon should be conjunct, sextile, or trine Mercury or Uranus; and in the sign of Gemini, Capricorn, or Aquarius.

Advertise (Print)

Write ads on a day favorable to your Sun. The Moon should be conjunct, sextile, or trine Mercury or Venus. Avoid hard aspects to Mars and Saturn. Ad campaigns produce the best results when the Moon is well aspected in Gemini (to enhance communication) or Capricorn (to build business).

Animals

Take home new pets when the day is favorable to your Sun, or when the Moon is trine, sextile, or conjunct Mercury, Venus, or Jupiter, or in the sign of Virgo or Pisces. However, avoid days when the Moon is either square or opposing the Sun, Mars, Saturn, Uranus, Neptune, or Pluto. When selecting a pet, have the Moon well aspected by the planet that rules the animal. Cats are ruled by the Sun, dogs by Mercury, birds by Venus, horses by Jupiter, and fish by Neptune. Buy large animals when the Moon is in Sagittarius or Pisces, and making favorable aspects to Jupiter or Mercury. Buy animals smaller than sheep when the Moon is in Virgo with favorable aspects to Mercury or Venus.

Animals (Breed)

Animals are easiest to handle when the Moon is in Taurus, Cancer, Libra, or Pisces, but try to avoid the Full Moon. To encourage healthy births, animals should be mated so births occur when the Moon is increasing in Taurus, Cancer, Pisces, or Libra. Those born during a semi-fruitful sign (Taurus and Capricorn) will produce leaner meat. Libra yields beautiful animals for showing and racing.

Animals (Declaw)

Declaw cats in the dark of the Moon. Avoid the week before and after the Full Moon and the sign of Pisces.

Animals (Neuter or spay)

Have livestock and pets neutered or spayed when the Moon is in Sagittarius, Capricorn, or Pisces; after it has passed through Scorpio, the sign that rules reproductive organs. Avoid the week before and after the Full Moon.

Animals (Sell or buy)

In either buying or selling, it is important to keep the Moon and Mercury free from any aspect to Mars. Aspects to Mars will create discord and increase the likelihood of wrangling over price and quality. The Moon should be passing from the first quarter to full and sextile or trine Venus or Jupiter. When buying racehorses, let the Moon be in an air sign. The Moon should be in air signs when you buy birds. If the birds are to be pets, let the Moon be in good aspect to Venus.

Animals (Train)

Train pets when the Moon is in Virgo or when the Moon trines Mercury.

Animals (Train dogs to hunt)

Let the Moon be in Aries in conjunction with Mars, which makes them courageous and quick to learn. But let Jupiter also be in aspect to preserve them from danger in hunting.

Automobiles

When buying an automobile, select a time when the Moon is conjunct, sextile, or trine to Mercury, Saturn, or Uranus; and in the sign Gemini or Capricorn.

Baking Cakes

Your cakes will have a lighter texture if you see that the Moon is in Gemini, Libra, or Aquarius, and in good aspect to Venus or Mercury. If you are decorating a cake or confections are being made, have the Moon placed in Libra.

Beauty Treatments (Massage, etc.)

See that the Moon is in Taurus, Cancer, Leo, Libra, or Aquarius, and in favorable aspect to Venus. In the case of plastic surgery, aspects to Mars should be avoided, and the Moon should not be in the sign ruling the part to be operated on.

Borrow (Money or goods)

See that the Moon is not placed between 15 degrees Libra and 15 degrees Scorpio. Let the Moon be waning and in Leo, Scorpio (16 to 30 degrees), Sagittarius, or Pisces. Venus should be in good aspect to the Moon, and the Moon should not be square, opposing, or conjunct either Saturn or Mars.

Brewing

Start brewing during the third or fourth quarter, when the Moon is in Cancer, Scorpio, or Pisces

Build (Start foundation)

Turning the first sod for the foundation marks the beginning of the building. For best results, excavate the site when the Moon is in the first quarter of a fixed sign and making favorable aspects to Saturn.

Business (Start new)

When starting a business, have the Moon be in Taurus, Virgo, or Capricorn, and increasing. The Moon should be sextile or trine Jupiter or Saturn, but avoid oppositions or squares. The planet ruling the business should be well aspected, too.

Buy Goods

Buy during the third quarter, when the Moon is in Taurus for quality, or in a mutable sign (Gemini, Sagittarius, Virgo, or Pisces) for savings. Good aspects to Venus or the Sun are desirable. If you are buying for yourself, it is good if the day is favorable for your Sun sign. You may also apply rules for buying specific items.

Canning

Can fruits and vegetables when the Moon is in either the third or fourth quarter, and in the water sign Cancer or Pisces. Preserves and jellies use the same quarters and the signs Cancer, Pisces, or Taurus.

Clothing

Buy clothing on a day that is favorable for your Sun sign, and when Venus or Mercury is well aspected. Avoid aspects to Mars and Saturn. Buy your clothing when the Moon is in Taurus if you want to remain satisfied. Do not buy clothing or jewelry when the Moon is in Scorpio or Aries. See that the Moon is sextile or trine the Sun during the first or second quarters.

Collections

Try to make collections on days when your Sun is well aspected. Avoid days when the Moon is opposing or square Mars or Saturn. If possible, the Moon should be in a cardinal sign (Aries, Cancer, Libra, or Capricorn). It is more difficult to collect when the Moon is in Taurus or Scorpio.

Concrete

Pour concrete when the Moon is in the third quarter of the fixed sign Taurus, Leo, or Aquarius.

Construction (Begin new)

The Moon should be sextile or trine Jupiter. According to Hermes, no building should be begun when the Moon is in Scorpio or Pisces. The best time to begin building is when the Moon is in Aquarius.

Consultants (Work with)

The Moon should be conjunct, sextile, or trine Mercury or Jupiter.

Contracts (Bid on)

The Moon should be in Gemini or Capricorn, and either the Moon or Mercury should be conjunct, sextile, or trine Jupiter.

Copyrights/Patents

The Moon should be conjunct, trine, or sextile either Mercury or Jupiter.

Coronations and Installations

Let the Moon be in Leo and in favorable aspect to Venus, Jupiter, or Mercury. The Moon should be applying to these planets.

Cultivate

Cultivate when the Moon is in a barren sign and waning, ideally the fourth quarter in Aries, Gemini, Leo, Virgo, or Aquarius. The third quarter in the sign of Sagittarius will also work.

Cut Timber

Timber cut during the waning Moon does not become worm-eaten; it will season well, and not warp, decay, or snap during burning. Cut when the Moon is in Taurus, Gemini, Virgo, or Capricorn—especially in August. Avoid the water signs. Look for favorable aspects to Mars.

Decorating or Home Repairs

Have the Moon waxing, and in the sign of Libra, Gemini, or Aquarius. Avoid squares or oppositions to either Mars or Saturn. Venus in good aspect to Mars or Saturn is beneficial.

Demolition

Let the waning Moon be in Leo, Sagittarius, or Aries.

Dental and Dentists

Visit the dentist when the Moon is in Virgo, or pick a day marked favorable for your Sun sign. Mars should be marked sextile, conjunct, or trine; and avoid squares or oppositions to Saturn, Uranus, or Jupiter.

Teeth are best removed when the Moon is in Gemini, Virgo, Sagittarius, or Pisces, and during the first or second quarter. Avoid the Full Moon! The day should be favorable for your lunar cycle, and Mars and Saturn should be marked conjunct, trine, or sextile. Fillings should be done in the third or fourth quarters in the sign of Taurus, Leo, Scorpio, or Pisces. The same applies for dentures.

Dressmaking

William Lilly wrote in 1676: "Make no new clothes, or first put them on when the Moon is in Scorpio or afflicted by Mars, for they will be apt to be torn and quickly worn out." Design, repair, and sew clothes in the first and second quarters of Taurus, Leo, or Libra on a day marked favorable for your Sun sign. Venus, Jupiter, and Mercury should be favorably aspected, but avoid hard aspects to Mars or Saturn.

Egg-setting

Eggs should be set so chicks will hatch during fruitful signs. To set eggs, subtract the number of days given for incubation or gestation from the fruitful dates. Chickens incubate in twenty-one days, turkeys and geese in twenty-eight days.

A freshly laid egg loses quality rapidly if it is not handled properly. Use plenty of clean litter in the nests to reduce the number of dirty or cracked eggs. Gather eggs daily in mild weather and at least two times daily in hot or cold weather. The eggs should be placed in a cooler immediately after gathering and stored at 50 to 55 degrees Fahrenheit. Do not store eggs with foods or products that give off pungent odors since eggs may absorb the odors.

Eggs saved for hatching purposes should not be washed. Only clean and slightly soiled eggs should be saved for hatching. Dirty eggs should not be incubated. Eggs should be stored in a cool place with the large ends up. It is not advisable to store the eggs longer than one week before setting them in an incubator.

Electricity and Gas (Install)

The Moon should be in a fire sign, and there should be no squares, oppositions, or conjunctions with Uranus (ruler of electricity), Neptune (ruler of gas), Saturn, or Mars. Hard aspects to Mars can cause fires.

Electronics (Buying)

Choose a day when the Moon is in an air sign (Gemini, Libra, Aquarius) and well aspected by Mercury and/or Uranus when buying electronics.

Electronics (Repair)

The Moon should be sextile or trine Mars or Uranus, and in a fixed sign (Taurus, Leo, Scorpio, Aquarius).

Entertain Friends

Let the Moon be in Leo or Libra and making good aspects to Venus. Avoid squares or oppositions to either Mars or Saturn by the Moon or Venus.

Eyes and Eyeglasses

Have your eyes tested and glasses fitted on a day marked favorable for your Sun sign, and on a day that falls during your favorable lunar cycle. Mars should not be in aspect with the Moon. The same applies for any treatment of the eyes, which should also be started during the Moon's first or second quarter.

Fence Posts

Set posts when the Moon is in the third or fourth quarter of the fixed sign Taurus or Leo.

Fertilize and Compost

Fertilize when the Moon is in a fruitful sign (Cancer, Scorpio, Pisces). Organic fertilizers are best when the Moon is waning. Use chemical fertilizers when the Moon is waxing. Start compost when the Moon is in the fourth quarter in a water sign.

Find Hidden Treasure

Let the Moon be in good aspect to Jupiter or Venus. If you erect a horoscope for this election, place the Moon in the Fourth House.

Find Lost Articles

Search for lost articles during the first quarter and when your Sun sign is marked favorable. Also check to see that the planet ruling the lost item is trine, sextile, or conjunct the Moon. The Moon rules household utensils; Mercury rules letters and books; and Venus rules clothing, jewelry, and money.

Fishing

During the summer months, the best time of the day to fish is from sunrise to three hours after, and from two hours before sunset until one hour after. Fish do not bite in cooler months until the air is warm, from noon to 3 pm. Warm, cloudy days are good. The most favorable winds are from the south and southwest. Easterly winds are unfavorable. The best days of the month for fishing are when the Moon changes quarters, especially if the change occurs on a day when the Moon is in a water sign (Cancer, Scorpio, Pisces). The best period in any month is the day after the Full Moon.

Friendship

The need for friendship is greater when the Moon is in Aquarius, or when Uranus aspects the Moon. Friendship prospers when Venus or Uranus is trine, sextile, or conjunct the Moon. The Moon in Gemini facilitates the chance meeting of acquaintances and friends.

Grafting or Budding

Grafting is the process of introducing new varieties of fruit on less desirable trees. For this process you should use the increasing phase of the Moon in fruitful signs such as Cancer, Scorpio, or Pisces. Capricorn may be used, too. Cut your grafts while trees are dormant, from December to March. Keep them in a cool, dark, not too dry or too damp place. Do the grafting before the sap starts to flow and while the Moon is waxing, and preferably while it is in Cancer, Scorpio, or Pisces. The type of plant should determine both cutting and planting times.

Habit (Breaking)

To end an undesirable habit, and this applies to ending everything from a bad relationship to smoking, start on a day when the Moon is in the fourth quarter and in the barren sign of Gemini, Leo, or Aquarius. Aries, Virgo, and Capricorn may be suitable as well, depending on the habit you want to be rid of. Make sure that your lunar cycle is favorable. Avoid lunar aspects to Mars or Jupiter. However, favorable aspects to Pluto are helpful.

Haircuts

Cut hair when the Moon is in Gemini, Sagittarius, Pisces, Taurus, or Capricorn, but not in Virgo. Look for favorable aspects to Venus. For faster growth, cut hair when the Moon is increasing in Cancer or Pisces. To make hair grow thicker, cut when the Moon is full in the signs of Taurus, Cancer, or Leo. If you want your hair to grow more slowly, have the Moon be decreasing in Aries, Gemini, or Virgo, and have the Moon square or opposing Saturn.

Permanents, straightening, and hair coloring will take well if the Moon is in Taurus or Leo and trine or sextile Venus. Avoid hair treatments if Mars is marked as square or in opposition, especially if heat is to be used. For permanents, a trine to Jupiter is helpful. The Moon also should be in the first quarter. Check the lunar cycle for a favorable day in relation to your Sun sign.

Harvest Crops

Harvest root crops when the Moon is in a dry sign (Aries, Leo, Sagittarius, Gemini, Aquarius) and waning. Harvest grain for storage just after the Full Moon, avoiding Cancer, Scorpio, or Pisces. Harvest in the third and fourth quarters in dry signs. Dry crops in the third quarter in fire signs.

Health

A diagnosis is more likely to be successful when the Moon is in Aries, Cancer, Libra, or Capricorn; and less so when in Gemini, Sagittarius, Pisces, or Virgo. Begin a recuperation program when the Moon is in a cardinal or fixed sign and the day is favorable to your Sun sign. Enter hospitals at these times, too. For surgery, see "Surgical Procedures." Buy medicines when the Moon is in Virgo or Scorpio.

Home (Buy new)

If you desire a permanent home, buy when the New Moon is in a fixed sign—Taurus or Leo—for example. Each sign will affect your decision in a different way. A house bought when the Moon is in Taurus is likely to be more practical and have a country look—right down to the split-rail fence. A house purchased when the Moon is in Leo will more likely be a real showplace.

If you're buying for speculation and a quick turnover, be certain that the Moon is in a cardinal sign (Aries, Cancer, Libra, Capricorn). Avoid buying when the Moon is in a fixed sign (Leo, Scorpio, Aquarius, Taurus).

Home (Make repairs)

In all repairs, avoid squares, oppositions, or conjunctions to the planet ruling the place or thing to be repaired. For example, bathrooms are ruled by Scorpio and Cancer. You would not want to start a project in those rooms when the Moon or Pluto is receiving hard aspects. The front entrance, hall, dining room, and porch are ruled by the Sun. So you would want to avoid times when Saturn or Mars are square, opposing, or conjunct the Sun. Also, let the Moon be waxing.

Home (Sell)

Make a strong effort to list your property for sale when the Sun is marked favorable in your sign and in good aspect to Jupiter. Avoid adverse aspects to as many planets as possible.

Home Furnishings (Buy new)

Saturn days (Saturday) are good for buying, and Jupiter days (Thursday) are good for selling. Items bought on days when Saturn is well aspected tend to wear longer and purchases tend to be more conservative.

Job (Start new)

Jupiter and Venus should be sextile, trine, or conjunct the Moon. A day when your Sun is receiving favorable aspects is preferred.

Legal Matters

Good Moon-Jupiter aspects improve the outcome in legal decisions. To gain damages through a lawsuit, begin the process during the increasing Moon. To avoid paying damages, a court date during the decreasing Moon is desirable. Good Moon-Sun aspects strengthen your chance of success. A well-aspected Moon in Cancer or Leo, making good aspects to the Sun, brings the best results in custody cases. In divorce cases, a favorable Moon-Venus aspect is best.

Loan (Ask for)

A first and second quarter phase favors the lender, the third and fourth quarters favor the borrower. Good aspects of Jupiter and

Venus to the Moon are favorable to both, as is having the Moon in Leo or Taurus.

Machinery, Appliances, or Tools (Buy)

Tools, machinery, and other implements should be bought on days when your lunar cycle is favorable and when Mars and Uranus are trine, sextile, or conjunct the Moon. Any quarter of the Moon is suitable. When buying gas or electrical appliances, the Moon should be in Aquarius.

Make a Will

Let the Moon be in a fixed sign (Taurus, Leo, Scorpio, or Aquarius) to ensure permanence. If the Moon is in a cardinal sign (Aries, Cancer, Libra, or Capricorn), the will could be altered. Let the Moon be waxing—increasing in light—and in good aspect to Saturn, Venus, or Mercury. In the case the will is made in an emergency during illness, and the Moon is slow in motion, void-of-course, combust, or under the Sun's beams, the testator will die and the will remain unaltered. There is some danger that it will be lost or stolen, however.

Marriage

The best time for marriage to take place is when the Moon is increasing, but not yet full. Good signs for the Moon to be in are Taurus, Cancer, Leo, or Libra.

The Moon in Taurus produces the most steadfast marriages, but if the partners later want to separate, they may have a difficult time. Make sure that the Moon is well aspected, especially to Venus or Jupiter. Avoid aspects to Mars, Uranus, or Pluto, and the signs Aries, Gemini, Virgo, Scorpio, or Aquarius.

The values of the signs are as follows:

- Aries is not favored for marriage
- Taurus from 0 to 19 degrees is good, the remaining degrees are less favorable

- Cancer is unfavorable unless you are marrying a widow
- Leo is favored, but it may cause one party to deceive the other as to his or her money or possessions
- Virgo is not favored except when marrying a widow
- Libra is good for engagements but not for marriage
- Scorpio from 0 to 15 degrees is good, but the last fifteen degrees are entirely unfortunate. The woman may be fickle, envious, and quarrelsome
- Sagittarius is neutral
- Capricorn, from 0 to 10 degrees, is difficult for marriage; however, the remaining degrees are favorable, especially when marrying a widow
- Aquarius is not favored
- Pisces is favored, although marriage under this sign can incline a woman to chatter a lot

These effects are strongest when the Moon is in the sign. If the Moon and Venus are in a cardinal sign, happiness between the couple may not continue long.

On no account should the Moon apply to Saturn or Mars, even by good aspect.

Medical Treatment for the Eyes

Let the Moon be increasing in light and motion and making favorable aspects to Venus or Jupiter, and be unaspected by Mars. Keep the Moon out of Taurus, Capricorn, or Virgo. If an aspect between the Moon and Mars is unavoidable, let it be separating.

Medical Treatment for the Head

If possible, have Mars and Saturn free of hard aspects. Let the Moon be in Aries or Taurus, decreasing in light, in conjunction or aspect with Venus or Jupiter, and free of hard aspects. The Sun should not be in any aspect to the Moon.

Medical Treatment for the Nose

Let the Moon be in Cancer, Leo, or Virgo, and not aspecting Mars or Saturn, and not in conjunction with a weak or retrograde planet.

Mining

Saturn rules mining. Begin work when Saturn is marked conjunct, trine, or sextile. Mine for gold when the Sun is marked conjunct, trine, or sextile. Mercury rules quicksilver, Venus rules copper, Jupiter rules tin, Saturn rules lead and coal, Uranus rules radioactive elements, Neptune rules oil, the Moon rules water. Mine for these items when the ruling planet is marked conjunct, trine, or sextile.

Move to New Home

If you have a choice, and sometimes we don't, make sure that Mars is not aspecting the Moon. Move on a day favorable to your Sun sign, or when the Moon is conjunct, sextile, or trine the Sun.

Mow Lawn

Mow in the first and second quarters (waxing phase) to increase growth and lushness, and in the third and fourth quarters (waning phase) to decrease growth.

Negotiate

When you are choosing a time to negotiate, consider what the meeting is about and what you want to have happen. If it is agreement or compromise between two parties that you desire, have the Moon be in the sign of Libra. When you are making contracts, it is best to have the Moon in the same element. For example, if your concern is communication, then elect a time when the Moon is in an air sign. If, on the other hand, your concern is about possessions, an earth sign would be more appropriate. Fixed signs are unfavorable, with the exception of Leo; so are cardinal signs, except for Capricorn. If you are negotiating the end of something, use the rules that apply to ending habits.

Occupational Training

When you begin training, see that your lunar cycle is favorable that day, and that the planet ruling your occupation is marked conjunct or trine.

Paint

Paint buildings during the waning Libra or Aquarius Moon. If the weather is hot, paint when the Moon is in Taurus. If the weather is cold, paint when the Moon is in Leo. Schedule the painting to start in the fourth quarter as the wood is drier and paint will penetrate wood better. Avoid painting around the New Moon, though, as the wood is likely to be damp, making the paint subject to scalding when hot weather hits it. If the temperature is below 70 degrees Fahrenheit, it is not advisable to paint while the Moon is in Cancer, Scorpio, or Pisces as the paint is apt to creep, check, or run.

Party (Host or attend)

A party timed so the Moon is in Gemini, Leo, Libra, or Sagittarius, with good aspects to Venus and Jupiter, will be fun and well attended. There should be no aspects between the Moon and Mars or Saturn.

Pawn

Do not pawn any article when Jupiter is receiving a square or opposition from Saturn or Mars, or when Jupiter is within 17 degrees of the Sun, for you will have little chance to redeem the items.

Pick Mushrooms

Mushrooms, one of the most promising traditional medicines in the world, should be gathered at the Full Moon.

Plant

Root crops, like carrots and potatoes, are best if planted in the sign Taurus or Capricorn. Beans, peas, tomatoes, peppers, and other fruit-bearing plants are best if planted in a sign that supports seed growth. Leaf plants, like lettuce, broccoli, or cauliflower, are best planted when the Moon is in a water sign.

It is recommended that you transplant during a decreasing Moon, when forces are streaming into the lower part of the plant. This helps root growth.

Promotion (Ask for)

Choose a day favorable to your Sun sign. Mercury should be marked conjunct, trine, or sextile. Avoid days when Mars or Saturn is aspected.

Prune

Prune during the third and fourth quarter of a Scorpio Moon to retard growth and to promote better fruit. Prune when the Moon is in cardinal Capricorn to promote healing.

Reconcile with People

If the reconciliation be with a woman, let Venus be strong and well aspected. If elders or superiors are involved, see that Saturn is receiving good aspects; if the reconciliation is between young people or between an older and younger person, see that Mercury is well aspected.

Romance

There is less control of when a romance starts, but romances begun under an increasing Moon are more likely to be permanent or satisfying, while those begun during the decreasing Moon tend to transform the participants. The tone of the relationship can be guessed from the sign the Moon is in. Romances begun with the Moon in Aries may be impulsive. Those begun in Capricorn will take greater effort to bring to a desirable conclusion, but they may be very rewarding. Good aspects between the Moon and Venus will have a positive influence on the relationship. Avoid unfavorable aspects to Mars, Uranus, and Pluto. A decreasing Moon, particularly the fourth quarter, facilitates ending a relationship, and causes the least pain.

Roof a Building
Begin roofing a building during the third or fourth quarter, when the Moon is in Aries or Aquarius. Shingles laid during the New Moon have a tendency to curl at the edges.

Sauerkraut
The best-tasting sauerkraut is made just after the Full Moon in the fruitful signs of Cancer, Scorpio, or Pisces.

Select a Child's Sex
Count from the last day of menstruation to the first day of the next cycle and divide the interval between the two dates in half. Pregnancy in the first half produces females, but copulation should take place with the Moon in a feminine sign. Pregnancy in the latter half, up to three days before the beginning of menstruation, produces males, but copulation should take place with the Moon in a masculine sign. The three-day period before the next period again produces females.

Sell or Canvas
Begin these activities during a day favorable to your Sun sign. Otherwise, sell on days when Jupiter, Mercury, or Mars is trine, sextile, or conjunct the Moon. Avoid days when Saturn is square or opposing the Moon, for that always hinders business and causes discord. If the Moon is passing from the first quarter to full, it is best to have the Moon swift in motion and in good aspect with Venus and/or Jupiter.

Sign Papers

Sign contracts or agreements when the Moon is increasing in a fruitful sign and on a day when the Moon is making favorable aspects to Mercury. Avoid days when Mars, Saturn, or Neptune are square or opposite the Moon.

Spray and Weed

Spray pests and weeds during the fourth quarter when the Moon is in the barren sign Leo or Aquarius, and making favorable aspects to Pluto. Weed during a waning Moon in a barren sign. For the best days to kill weeds and pests, see pages 70 and 71.

Staff (Fire)

Have the Moon in the third or fourth quarter, but not full. The Moon should not be square any planets.

Staff (Hire)

The Moon should be in the first or second quarter, and preferably in the sign of Gemini or Virgo. The Moon should be conjunct, trine, or sextile Mercury or Jupiter.

Stocks (Buy)

The Moon should be in Taurus or Capricorn, and there should be a sextile or trine to Jupiter or Saturn.

Surgical Procedures

Blood flow, like ocean tides, appears to be related to Moon phases. To reduce hemorrhage after a surgery, schedule it within one week before or after a New Moon. Schedule surgery to occur during the increase of the Moon if possible, as wounds heal better and vitality is greater than during the decrease of the Moon. Avoid surgery within one week before or after the Full Moon. Select a date when the Moon is past the sign governing the part of the body involved in the operation. For example, abdominal operations should be done when the Moon is in Sagittarius,

Capricorn, or Aquarius. To find the signs and the body parts they rule, refer to the illustration on page 91. The further removed the Moon sign is from the sign ruling the afflicted part of the body, the better.

For successful operations, avoid times when the Moon is applying to any aspect of Mars. (This tends to promote inflammation and complications.) See the Lunar Aspectarian on odd pages 135–157 to find days with negative Mars aspects and positive Venus and Jupiter aspects. Never operate with the Moon in the same sign as a person's Sun sign or Ascendant. Let the Moon be in a fixed sign and avoid square or opposing aspects. The Moon should not be void-of-course. Cosmetic surgery should be done in the increase of the Moon, when the Moon is not square or in opposition to Mars. Avoid days when the Moon is square or opposing Saturn or the Sun.

Travel (Air)

Start long trips when the Moon is making favorable aspects to the Sun. For enjoyment, aspects to Jupiter are preferable; for visiting, look for favorable aspects to Mercury. To prevent accidents, avoid squares or oppositions to Mars, Saturn, Uranus, or Pluto. Choose a day when the Moon is in Sagittarius or Gemini and well aspected to Mercury, Jupiter, or Uranus. Avoid adverse aspects of Mars, Saturn, or Uranus.

Visit

On setting out to visit a person, let the Moon be in aspect with any retrograde planet, for this ensures that the person you're visiting will be at home. If you desire to stay a long time in a place, let the Moon be in good aspect to Saturn. If you desire to leave the place quickly, let the Moon be in a cardinal sign.

Wean Children

To wean a child successfully, do so when the Moon is in Sagittarius, Capricorn, Aquarius, or Pisces—signs that do not rule vital human organs. By observing this astrological rule, much trouble for parents and child may be avoided.

Weight (Reduce)

If you want to lose weight, the best time to get started is when the Moon is in the third or fourth quarter, and in the barren sign of Virgo. Review the section on How to Use the Moon Tables and Lunar Aspectarian beginning on page 134 to help you select a date that is favorable to begin your weight-loss program.

Wine and Drink Other Than Beer

Start brewing when the Moon is in Pisces or Taurus. Sextiles or trines to Venus are favorable, but avoid aspects to Mars or Saturn.

Write

Write for pleasure or publication when the Moon is in Gemini. Mercury should be making favorable aspects to Uranus and Neptune.

How to Use the Moon Tables and Lunar Aspectarian

Timing activities is one of the most important things you can do to ensure success. In many eastern countries, timing by the planets is so important that practically no event takes place without first setting up a chart for it. Weddings have occurred in the middle of the night because the influences were best then. You may not want to take it that far, but you can still make use of the influences of the Moon whenever possible. It's easy and it works!

In the *Moon Sign Book* is information to help you plan just about any activity: weddings, fishing, making purchases, cutting your hair, traveling, and more. We provide the guidelines you need to pick the best day out of the several from which you have to choose. The Moon Tables are the *Moon Sign Book's* primary method for choosing dates. Following are instructions, examples, and directions on how to read the Moon Tables. More advanced information on using the tables containing the Lunar Aspectarian and favorable and unfavorable days (found on odd-numbered pages opposite the Moon Tables), Moon void-of-course and retrograde information to choose the dates best for you is also included.

The Five Basic Steps

Step 1: Directions for Choosing Dates
Look up the directions for choosing dates for the activity that you wish to begin, then go to step 2.

Step 2: Check the Moon Tables
You'll find two tables for each month of the year beginning on page 134. The Moon Tables (on the left-hand pages) include the day, date, and sign the Moon is in; the element and nature of the sign; the Moon's phase; and when it changes sign or phase. If there is a time listed after a date, that time is the time when the Moon moves into that zodiac sign. Until then, the Moon is considered to be in the sign for the previous day.

The abbreviation Full signifies Full Moon and New signifies New Moon. The times listed with dates indicate when the Moon changes sign. The times listed after the phase indicate when the Moon changes phase.

Turn to the month you would like to begin your activity. You will be using the Moon's sign and phase information most often when you begin choosing your own dates. Use the Time Zone Map on page 162 and the Time Zone Conversions table on page 163 to convert time to your own time zone.

When you find dates that meet the criteria for the correct Moon phase and sign for your activity, you may have completed the process. For certain simple activities, such as getting a haircut, the phase and sign information is all that is needed. If the directions for your activity include information on certain lunar aspects, however, you should consult the Lunar Aspectarian. An example of this would be if the directions told you not to perform a certain activity when the Moon is square (Q) Jupiter.

Step 3: Check the Lunar Aspectarian

On the pages opposite the Moon Tables you will find tables containing the Lunar Aspectarian and Favorable and Unfavorable Days. The Lunar Aspectarian gives the aspects (or angles) of the Moon to other planets. Some aspects are favorable, while others are not. To use the Lunar Aspectarian, find the planet that the directions list as favorable for your activity, and run down the column to the date desired. For example, you should avoid aspects to Mars if you are planning surgery. So you would look for Mars across the top and then run down that column looking for days where there are no aspects to Mars (as signified by empty boxes). If you want to find a favorable aspect (sextile (X) or trine (T)) to Mercury, run your finger down the column under Mercury until you find an X or T. Adverse aspects to planets are squares (Q) or oppositions (O). A conjunction (C) is sometimes beneficial, sometimes not, depending on the activity or planets involved.

Step 4: Favorable and Unfavorable Days

The tables listing favorable and unfavorable days are helpful when you want to choose your personal best dates because your Sun sign is taken into consideration. The twelve Sun signs are listed on the right side of the tables. Once you have determined which days meet your criteria for phase, sign, and aspects, you can determine whether or not those days are positive for you by checking the favorable and unfavorable days for your Sun sign.

To find out if a day is positive for you, find your Sun sign and then look down the column. If it is marked F, it is very favorable. The Moon is in the same sign as your Sun on a favorable day. If it is marked f, it is slightly favorable; U is very unfavorable; and u means slightly unfavorable. A day marked very unfavorable (U) indicates that the Moon is in the sign opposing your Sun.

Once you have selected good dates for the activity you are about to begin, you can go straight to "Using What You've

Learned," beginning on the next page. To learn how to fine-tune your selections even further, read on.

Step 5: Void-of-Course Moon and Retrogrades

This last step is perhaps the most advanced portion of the procedure. It is generally considered poor timing to make decisions, sign important papers, or start special activities during a Moon void-of-course period or during a Mercury retrograde. Once you have chosen the best date for your activity based on steps one through four, you can check the Void-of-Course tables, beginning on page 73, to find out if any of the dates you have chosen have void periods.

The Moon is said to be void-of-course after it has made its last aspect to a planet within a particular sign, but before it has moved into the next sign. Put simply, the Moon is "resting" during the void-of-course period, so activities initiated at this time generally don't come to fruition. You will notice that there are many void periods during the year, and it is nearly impossible to avoid all of them. Some people choose to ignore these altogether and do not take them into consideration when planning activities.

Next, you can check the Retrograde Planets tables on page 158 to see what planets are retrograde during your chosen date(s).

A planet is said to be retrograde when it appears to move backward in the sky as viewed from the Earth. Generally, the farther a planet is away from the Sun, the longer it can stay retrograde. Some planets will retrograde for several months at a time. Avoiding retrogrades is not as important in lunar planning as avoiding the Moon void-of-course, with the exception of the planet Mercury.

Mercury rules thought and communication, so it is advisable not to sign important papers, initiate important business or legal work, or make crucial decisions during these times. As with the Moon void-of-course, it is difficult to avoid all planetary retrogrades when beginning events, and you may choose to ignore this step of the process. Following are some examples using some or all of the steps outlined above.

Using What You've Learned

Let's say it's a new year and you want to have your hair cut. It's thin and you would like it to look fuller, so you find the directions for hair care and you see that for thicker hair you should cut hair while the Moon is Full and in the sign of Taurus, Cancer, or Leo. You should avoid the Moon in Aries, Gemini, or Virgo. Look at the January Moon Table on page 134. You see that the Full Moon is on January 3 at 8:57 am. The Moon moves into the sign of Leo the next day, and remains in Leo until January 7 at 1:18 am, so January 4–6 meets both the phase and sign criteria.

Let's move on to a more difficult example using the sign and phase of the Moon. You want to buy a permanent home. After checking the instructions for purchasing a house: "Home (Buy new)" on page 116, you see that you should buy a home when the Moon is in Taurus, Cancer, or Leo. You need to get a loan, so you should also look under "Loan (Ask for)" on page 117. Here it says that the third and fourth quarters favor the borrower (you). You are going to buy the house in October so go to page 152. The Moon is in the third quarter October 27–31. The Moon is in Cancer from 8:49 pm on October 29 through October 31. The best days for obtaining a loan would be October 29–31, while the Moon is in Cancer.

Just match up the best sign and phase (quarter) to come up with the best date. With all activities, be sure to check the favorable and unfavorable days for your Sun sign in the table adjoining the Lunar Aspectarian. If there is a choice between several dates, pick the one most favorable for you. Because buying a home is an important business decision, you may also wish to see if the Moon is void or if Mercury is retrograde during these dates.

Now let's look at an example that uses signs, phases, and aspects. Our example is starting new home construction. We will

131

use the month of April. Look under "Build (Start foundation)" on page 109 and you'll see that the Moon should be in the first quarter of Taurus or Leo. You should select a time when the Moon is not making unfavorable aspects to Saturn. (Conjunctions are usually considered good if they are not to Mars, Saturn, or Neptune.) Look in the April Moon Table. You will see that the Moon is in the first quarter April 18–23. The Moon is in Leo from 7:38 pm on April 23 until April 24 at 2:35 am. Now, look to the Lunar Aspectarian for April. We see that there are no squares or oppositions to Saturn on any of these dates, but there is a square to Mercury on April 23. These are not good dates to start a foundation. You'll have to build in a different month.

A Note About Time and Time Zones

All tables in the *Moon Sign Book* use Eastern Time. You must calculate the difference between your time zone and the Eastern Time Zone. Please refer to the Time Zone Conversions chart on 163 for help with time conversions. The sign the Moon is in at midnight is the sign shown in the Aspectarian and Favorable and Unfavorable Days tables.

How Does the Time Matter?

Due to the three-hour time difference between the east and west coasts of the United States, those of you living on the East Coast may be, for example, under the influence of a Virgo Moon, while those of you living on the West Coast will still have a Leo Moon influence.

We follow a commonly held belief among astrologers: whatever sign the Moon is in at the start of a day—12:00 am Eastern Time—is considered the dominant influence of the day. That sign is indicated in the Moon Tables. If the date you select for an activity shows the Moon changing signs, you can decide how important the sign change may be for your specific election and adjust your election date and time accordingly.

Use Common Sense

Some activities depend on outside factors. Obviously, you can't go out and plant when there is a foot of snow on the ground. You should adjust to the conditions at hand. If the weather was bad during the first quarter, when it was best to plant crops, do it during the second quarter while the Moon is in a fruitful sign. If the Moon is not in a fruitful sign during the first or second quarter, choose a day when it is in a semi-fruitful sign. The best advice is to choose either the sign or phase that is most favorable, when the two don't coincide.

To Summarize

First, look up the activity under the proper heading, then look for the information given in the tables. Choose the best date considering the number of positive factors in effect. If most of the dates are favorable, there is no problem choosing the one that will fit your schedule. However, if there aren't any really good dates, pick the ones with the least number of negative influences. Please keep in mind that the information found here applies in the broadest sense to the events you want to plan or are considering. To be the most effective, when you use electional astrology, you should also consider your own birth chart in relation to a chart drawn for the time or times you have under consideration. The best advice we can offer you is: read the entire introduction to each section.

January Moon Table

Date	Sign	Element	Nature	Phase
1 Mon	Gemini	Air	Barren	2nd
2 Tue 10:14 am	Cancer	Water	Fruitful	2nd
3 Wed	Cancer	Water	Fruitful	Full 8:57 am
4 Thu 4:14 pm	Leo	Fire	Barren	3rd
5 Fri	Leo	Fire	Barren	3rd
6 Sat	Leo	Fire	Barren	3rd
7 Sun 1:18 am	Virgo	Earth	Barren	3rd
8 Mon	Virgo	Earth	Barren	3rd
9 Tue 1:15 pm	Libra	Air	Semi-fruitful	3rd
10 Wed	Libra	Air	Semi-fruitful	3rd
11 Thu	Libra	Air	Semi-fruitful	4th 7:44 am
12 Fri 2:08 am	Scorpio	Water	Fruitful	4th
13 Sat	Scorpio	Water	Fruitful	4th
14 Sun 1:11 pm	Sagittarius	Fire	Barren	4th
15 Mon	Sagittarius	Fire	Barren	4th
16 Tue 8:49 pm	Capricorn	Earth	Semi-fruitful	4th
17 Wed	Capricorn	Earth	Semi-fruitful	4th
18 Thu	Capricorn	Earth	Semi-fruitful	New 11:01 pm
19 Fri 1:15 am	Aquarius	Air	Barren	1st
20 Sat	Aquarius	Air	Barren	1st
21 Sun 3:48 am	Pisces	Water	Fruitful	1st
22 Mon	Pisces	Water	Fruitful	1st
23 Tue 5:52 am	Aries	Fire	Barren	1st
24 Wed	Aries	Fire	Barren	1st
25 Thu 8:28 am	Taurus	Earth	Semi-fruitful	2nd 6:01 pm
26 Fri	Taurus	Earth	Semi-fruitful	2nd
27 Sat 12:10 pm	Gemini	Air	Barren	2nd
28 Sun	Gemini	Air	Barren	2nd
29 Mon 5:16 pm	Cancer	Water	Fruitful	2nd
30 Tue	Cancer	Water	Fruitful	2nd
31 Wed	Cancer	Water	Fruitful	2nd

Aspectarian/Favorable & Unfavorable Days

Date	Sun	Mercury	Venus	Mars	Jupiter	Saturn	Uranus	Neptune	Pluto	Aries	Taurus	Gemini	Cancer	Leo	Virgo	Libra	Scorpio	Sagittarius	Capricorn	Aquarius	Pisces
1				T		Q		T		f		F		f	u	f		U		f	u
2				X					O	u	f		F		f	u	f		U		f
3	O	O						T		u	f		F		f	u	f		U		f
4			O							f	u	f		F		f	u	f		U	
5						T				f	u	f		F		f	u	f		U	
6			T		C			O	T	f	u	f		F		f	u	f		U	
7				Q							f	u	f		F		f	u	f		U
8	T	T						O			f	u	f		F		f	u	f		U
9			Q						Q		f	u	f		F		f	u	f		U
10			T	X						U		f	u	f		F		f	u	f	
11	Q	Q		X	X			T	X	U		f	u	f		F		f	u	f	
12										U		f	u	f		F		f	u	f	
13		Q						T	Q		U		f	u	f		F		f	u	f
14	X	X				Q					U		f	u	f		F		f	u	f
15		X			C	Q				f		U		f	u	f		F		f	u
16			C		T			X	C	f		U		f	u	f		F		f	u
17						X				u	f		U		f	u	f		F		f
18	C									u	f		U		f	u	f		F		f
19		C		X						u	f		U		f	u	f		F		f
20			C			O		C		f	u	f		U		f	u	f		F	
21				X					X	f	u	f		U		f	u	f		F	
22				Q		C					f	u	f		U		f	u	f		F
23	X			Q					Q		f	u	f		U		f	u	f		F
24		X			T	T		X		F		f	u	f		U		f	u	f	
25	Q		X	T					T	F		f	u	f		U		f	u	f	
26		Q				Q	X	Q			F		f	u	f		U		f	u	f
27		Q									F		f	u	f		U		f	u	f
28	T						O	Q	T	f		F		f	u	f		U		f	u
29		T	T			X			O	f		F		f	u	f		U		f	u
30			O			T				u	f		F		f	u	f		U		f
31										u	f		F		f	u	f		U		f

February Moon Table

Date	Sign	Element	Nature	Phase
1 Thu 12:14 am	Leo	Fire	Barren	2nd
2 Fri	Leo	Fire	Barren	Full 12:45 am
3 Sat 9:34 am	Virgo	Earth	Barren	3rd
4 Sun	Virgo	Earth	Barren	3rd
5 Mon 9:15 pm	Libra	Air	Semi-fruitful	3rd
6 Tue	Libra	Air	Semi-fruitful	3rd
7 Wed	Libra	Air	Semi-fruitful	3rd
8 Thu 10:09 am	Scorpio	Water	Fruitful	3rd
9 Fri	Scorpio	Water	Fruitful	3rd
10 Sat 10:01 pm	Sagittarius	Fire	Barren	4th 4:51 am
11 Sun	Sagittarius	Fire	Barren	4th
12 Mon	Sagittarius	Fire	Barren	4th
13 Tue 6:42 am	Capricorn	Earth	Semi-fruitful	4th
14 Wed	Capricorn	Earth	Semi-fruitful	4th
15 Thu 11:34 am	Aquarius	Air	Barren	4th
16 Fri	Aquarius	Air	Barren	4th
17 Sat 1:30 pm	Pisces	Water	Fruitful	New 11:14 am
18 Sun	Pisces	Water	Fruitful	1st
19 Mon 2:06 pm	Aries	Fire	Barren	1st
20 Tue	Aries	Fire	Barren	1st
21 Wed 3:03 pm	Taurus	Earth	Semi-fruitful	1st
22 Thu	Taurus	Earth	Semi-fruitful	1st
23 Fri 5:42 pm	Gemini	Air	Barren	1st
24 Sat	Gemini	Air	Barren	2nd 2:56 am
25 Sun 10:47 pm	Cancer	Water	Fruitful	2nd
26 Mon	Cancer	Water	Fruitful	2nd
27 Tue	Cancer	Water	Fruitful	2nd
28 Wed 6:29 am	Leo	Fire	Barren	2nd

Aspectarian/Favorable & Unfavorable Days

Date	Sun	Mercury	Venus	Mars	Jupiter	Saturn	Uranus	Neptune	Pluto	Aries	Taurus	Gemini	Cancer	Leo	Virgo	Libra	Scorpio	Sagittarius	Capricorn	Aquarius	Pisces
1										u	f		F		f	u	f		U		
2	O				T	C		O		f	u	f		F		f	u	f		U	
3		O							T	f	u	f		F		f	u	f		U	
4			O	T	Q			O			f	u	f		F		f	u	f		U
5									Q		f	u	f		F		f	u	f		U
6										U		f	u	f		F		f	u	f	
7	T			Q	X	X		T		U		f	u	f		F		f	u	f	
8									X	U		f	u	f		F		f	u	f	
9		T	T	X		T					U		f	u	f		F		f	u	f
10	Q				Q			Q			U		f	u	f		F		f	u	f
11		Q					Q			f		U		f	u	f		F		f	u
12	X		Q		C	T	X			f		U		f	u	f		F		f	u
13									C	f		U		f	u	f		F		f	u
14		X	X	C			X			u	f		U		f	u	f		F		f
15										u	f		U		f	u	f		F		f
16					X	O			C	f	u	f		U		f	u	f		F	
17	C								X	f	u	f		U		f	u	f		F	
18		C			Q		C				f	u	f		U		f	u	f		F
19			C	X					Q		f	u	f		U		f	u	f		F
20					T	T		X		F		f	u	f		U		f	u	f	
21	X	X		Q					T	F		f	u	f		U		f	u	f	
22							X				F		f	u	f		U		f	u	f
23		Q	X	T		Q			Q		F		f	u	f		U		f	u	f
24	Q							Q		f		F		f	u	f		U		f	u
25					O	X		T	O	f		F		f	u	f		U		f	u
26	T	T	Q							u	f		F		f	u	f		U		f
27							T			u	f		F		f	u	f		U		f
28			O							u	f		F		f	u	f		U		f

March Moon Table

Date	Sign	Element	Nature	Phase
1 Thu	Leo	Fire	Barren	2nd
2 Fri 4:32 pm	Virgo	Earth	Barren	2nd
3 Sat	Virgo	Earth	Barren	Full 6:17 pm
4 Sun	Virgo	Earth	Barren	3rd
5 Mon 4:25 am	Libra	Air	Semi-fruitful	3rd
6 Tue	Libra	Air	Semi-fruitful	3rd
7 Wed 5:16 pm	Scorpio	Water	Fruitful	3rd
8 Thu	Scorpio	Water	Fruitful	3rd
9 Fri	Scorpio	Water	Fruitful	3rd
10 Sat 5:37 am	Sagittarius	Fire	Barren	3rd
11 Sun	Sagittarius	Fire	Barren	4th 11:54 pm
12 Mon 4:34 pm	Capricorn	Earth	Semi-fruitful	4th
13 Tue	Capricorn	Earth	Semi-fruitful	4th
14 Wed 10:52 pm	Aquarius	Air	Barren	4th
15 Thu	Aquarius	Air	Barren	4th
16 Fri	Aquarius	Air	Barren	4th
17 Sat 1:30 am	Pisces	Water	Fruitful	4th
18 Sun	Pisces	Water	Fruitful	New 10:42 pm
19 Mon 1:41 am	Aries	Fire	Barren	1st
20 Tue	Aries	Fire	Barren	1st
21 Wed 1:15 am	Taurus	Earth	Semi-fruitful	1st
22 Thu	Taurus	Earth	Semi-fruitful	1st
23 Fri 2:06 am	Gemini	Air	Barren	1st
24 Sat	Gemini	Air	Barren	1st
25 Sun 5:49 am	Cancer	Water	Fruitful	2nd 2:16 pm
26 Mon	Cancer	Water	Fruitful	2nd
27 Tue 1:04 pm	Leo	Fire	Barren	2nd
28 Wed	Leo	Fire	Barren	2nd
29 Thu 11:27 pm	Virgo	Earth	Barren	2nd
30 Fri	Virgo	Earth	Barren	2nd
31 Sat	Virgo	Earth	Barren	2nd

Aspectarian/Favorable & Unfavorable Days

Date	Sun	Mercury	Venus	Mars	Jupiter	Saturn	Uranus	Neptune	Pluto	Aries	Taurus	Gemini	Cancer	Leo	Virgo	Libra	Scorpio	Sagittarius	Capricorn	Aquarius	Pisces
1		T		T	C		O			f	u	f		F		f	u	f		U	
2		O							T	f	u	f		F		f	u	f		U	
3	O					O					f	u	f		F		f	u	f		U
4			Q								f	u	f		F		f	u	f		U
5				T					Q		f	u	f		F		f	u	f		U
6			O		X	X		T		U		f	u	f		F		f	u	f	
7		T							X	U		f	u	f		F		f	u	f	
8			Q				T				U		f	u	f		F		f	u	f
9	T	Q				Q		Q			U		f	u	f		F		f	u	f
10			X								U		f	u	f		F		f	u	f
11	Q			X	C	T	Q	X		f		U		f	u	f		F		f	u
12		X	T						C	f		U		f	u	f		F		f	u
13							X			u	f		U		f	u	f		F		f
14	X		Q							u	f		U		f	u	f		F		f
15				C						f	u	f		U		f	u	f		F	
16		C			X	O		C	X	f	u	f		U		f	u	f		F	
17										f	u	f		U		f	u	f		F	
18	C				Q		C		Q		f	u	f		U		f	u	f		F
19											f	u	f		U		f	u	f		F
20				X	T	T		X	T	F		f	u	f		U		f	u	f	
21		X	C							F		f	u	f		U		f	u	f	
22			Q			Q	X	Q			F		f	u	f		U		f	u	f
23	X	Q									F		f	u	f		U		f	u	f
24				T	O	X	Q	T		f		F		f	u	f		U		f	u
25	Q	T	X						O	f		F		f	u	f		U		f	u
26							T			u	f		F		f	u	f		U		f
27										u	f		F		f	u	f		U		f
28	T		Q				C			f	u	f		F		f	u	f		U	
29			O	T	C			O	T	f	u	f		F		f	u	f		U	
30											f	u	f		F		f	u	f		U
31		O	T		Q		O				f	u	f		F		f	u	f		U

April Moon Table

Date	Sign	Element	Nature	Phase
1 Sun 11:43 am	Libra	Air	Semi-fruitful	2nd
2 Mon	Libra	Air	Semi-fruitful	Full 1:15 pm
3 Tue	Libra	Air	Semi-fruitful	3rd
4 Wed 12:35 am	Scorpio	Water	Fruitful	3rd
5 Thu	Scorpio	Water	Fruitful	3rd
6 Fri 12:56 pm	Sagittarius	Fire	Barren	3rd
7 Sat	Sagittarius	Fire	Barren	3rd
8 Sun 11:36 pm	Capricorn	Earth	Semi-fruitful	3rd
9 Mon	Capricorn	Earth	Semi-fruitful	3rd
10 Tue	Capricorn	Earth	Semi-fruitful	4th 2:04 pm
11 Wed 7:23 am	Aquarius	Air	Barren	4th
12 Thu	Aquarius	Air	Barren	4th
13 Fri 11:38 am	Pisces	Water	Fruitful	4th
14 Sat	Pisces	Water	Fruitful	4th
15 Sun 12:46 pm	Aries	Fire	Barren	4th
16 Mon	Aries	Fire	Barren	4th
17 Tue 12:11 pm	Taurus	Earth	Semi-fruitful	New 7:36 am
18 Wed	Taurus	Earth	Semi-fruitful	1st
19 Thu 11:51 am	Gemini	Air	Barren	1st
20 Fri	Gemini	Air	Barren	1st
21 Sat 1:50 pm	Cancer	Water	Fruitful	1st
22 Sun	Cancer	Water	Fruitful	1st
23 Mon 7:38 pm	Leo	Fire	Barren	1st
24 Tue	Leo	Fire	Barren	2nd 2:35 am
25 Wed	Leo	Fire	Barren	2nd
26 Thu 5:24 am	Virgo	Earth	Barren	2nd
27 Fri	Virgo	Earth	Barren	2nd
28 Sat 5:44 pm	Libra	Air	Semi-fruitful	2nd
29 Sun	Libra	Air	Semi-fruitful	2nd
30 Mon	Libra	Air	Semi-fruitful	2nd

Aspectarian/Favorable & Unfavorable Days

Date	Sun	Mercury	Venus	Mars	Jupiter	Saturn	Uranus	Neptune	Pluto	Aries	Taurus	Gemini	Cancer	Leo	Virgo	Libra	Scorpio	Sagittarius	Capricorn	Aquarius	Pisces
1								Q			f	u	f		F			f	u	f	U
2	O									U		f	u	f		F		f	u	f	
3				T	X	X		T	X	U		f	u	f		F		f	u	f	
4										U		f	u	f		F		f	u	f	
5		T	O			Q	T	Q			U		f	u	f		F		f	u	f
6			Q								U		f	u	f		F		f	u	f
7							Q			f		U		f	u	f		F		f	u
8	T	Q				C	T		X	C	f		U		f	u	f		F		f	u
9			X								u	f		U		f	u	f		F		f
10	Q						X			u	f		U		f	u	f		F		f
11		X	T							u	f		U		f	u	f		F		f
12	X			X	O			C		f	u	f		U		f	u	f		F	
13		Q	C					X		f	u	f		U		f	u	f		F	
14				Q		C					f	u	f		U		f	u	f		F
15			X					Q			f	u	f		U		f	u	f		F
16		C			T	T		X		F		f	u	f		U		f	u	f	
17	C							T		F		f	u	f		U		f	u	f	
18			X		Q	X	Q				F		f	u	f		U		f	u	f
19											F		f	u	f		U		f	u	f
20		X	C	Q	O	X	Q	T		f		F		f	u	f		U		f	u
21	X							O		f		F		f	u	f		U		f	u
22				T			T			u	f		F		f	u	f		U		f
23		Q								u	f		F		f	u	f		U		f
24	Q									f	u	f		F		f	u	f		U	
25			X		T	C		O		f	u	f		F		f	u	f		U	
26	T	T						T		f	u	f		F		f	u	f		U	
27			Q	O	Q		O					f	u	f		F		f	u	f	U
28								Q				f	u	f		F		f	u	f	U
29										U		f	u	f		F		f	u	f	
30			T		X	X		T		U		f	u	f		F		f	u	f	

141

May Moon Table

Date	Sign	Element	Nature	Phase
1 Tue 6:41 am	Scorpio	Water	Fruitful	2nd
2 Wed	Scorpio	Water	Fruitful	Full 6:09 am
3 Thu 6:47 pm	Sagittarius	Fire	Barren	3rd
4 Fri	Sagittarius	Fire	Barren	3rd
5 Sat	Sagittarius	Fire	Barren	3rd
6 Sun 5:21 am	Capricorn	Earth	Semi-fruitful	3rd
7 Mon	Capricorn	Earth	Semi-fruitful	3rd
8 Tue 1:48 pm	Aquarius	Air	Barren	3rd
9 Wed	Aquarius	Air	Barren	3rd
10 Thu 7:31 pm	Pisces	Water	Fruitful	4th 12:27 am
11 Fri	Pisces	Water	Fruitful	4th
12 Sat 10:19 pm	Aries	Fire	Barren	4th
13 Sun	Aries	Fire	Barren	4th
14 Mon 10:48 pm	Taurus	Earth	Semi-fruitful	4th
15 Tue	Taurus	Earth	Semi-fruitful	4th
16 Wed 10:34 pm	Gemini	Air	Barren	New 3:27 pm
17 Thu	Gemini	Air	Barren	1st
18 Fri 11:38 pm	Cancer	Water	Fruitful	1st
19 Sat	Cancer	Water	Fruitful	1st
20 Sun	Cancer	Water	Fruitful	1st
21 Mon 3:56 am	Leo	Fire	Barren	1st
22 Tue	Leo	Fire	Barren	1st
23 Wed 12:26 pm	Virgo	Earth	Barren	2nd 5:02 pm
24 Thu	Virgo	Earth	Barren	2nd
25 Fri	Virgo	Earth	Barren	2nd
26 Sat 12:16 am	Libra	Air	Semi-fruitful	2nd
27 Sun	Libra	Air	Semi-fruitful	2nd
28 Mon 1:11 pm	Scorpio	Water	Fruitful	2nd
29 Tue	Scorpio	Water	Fruitful	2nd
30 Wed	Scorpio	Water	Fruitful	2nd
31 Thu 1:06 am	Sagittarius	Fire	Barren	Full 9:04 pm

Date	Sun	Mercury	Venus	Mars	Jupiter	Saturn	Uranus	Neptune	Pluto	Aries	Taurus	Gemini	Cancer	Leo	Virgo	Libra	Scorpio	Sagittarius	Capricorn	Aquarius	Pisces
1								X		U		f	u	f			F	f	u	f	
2	O	O		T		Q	T				U		f	u	f			F	f	u	f
3								Q			U		f	u	f			F	f	u	f
4										f		U		f	u	f			F	f	u
5				Q	C	T	Q	X		f		U		f	u	f			F	f	u
6			O						C	f		U		f	u	f			F	f	u
7	T	T					X			u	f		U		f	u	f			F	f
8		T		X						u	f		U		f	u	f			F	f
9	Q			X	O					f	u	f		U		f	u	f			F
10	Q	Q						C	X	f	u	f		U		f	u	f			F
11			T							F	f	u	f		U		f	u	f		
12	X			C	Q		C		Q	F	f	u	f		U		f	u	f		
13		X	Q								F	f	u	f		U		f	u	f	
14						T	T	X	T		F	f	u	f		U		f	u	f	
15			X									F	f	u	f		U		f	u	f
16	C					Q	X	Q				F	f	u	f		U		f	u	f
17		C		X						f			F	f	u	f		U		f	u
18				O	X	Q	T		O	f			F	f	u	f		U		f	u
19				Q						u	f			F	f	u	f		U		f
20							T			u	f			F	f	u	f		U		f
21	X			T						u	f			F	f	u	f		U		f
22		X			T	C		O		f	u	f			F	f	u	f		U	
23	Q							T		f	u	f			F	f	u	f		U	
24				Q							f	u	f			F	f	u	f		U
25		Q	X			O			Q		f	u	f			F	f	u	f		U
26	T		O								f	u	f			F	f	u	f		U
27			Q		X	X		T		U		f	u	f			F	f	u	f	
28		T						X		U		f	u	f			F	f	u	f	
29						T					U		f	u	f			F	f	u	f
30			T			Q	T	Q			U		f	u	f			F	f	u	f
31	O										U		f	u	f			F	f	u	f

June Moon Table

Date	Sign	Element	Nature	Phase
1 Fri	Sagittarius	Fire	Barren	3rd
2 Sat 11:09 am	Capricorn	Earth	Semi-fruitful	3rd
3 Sun	Capricorn	Earth	Semi-fruitful	3rd
4 Mon 7:15 pm	Aquarius	Air	Barren	3rd
5 Tue	Aquarius	Air	Barren	3rd
6 Wed	Aquarius	Air	Barren	3rd
7 Thu 1:24 am	Pisces	Water	Fruitful	3rd
8 Fri	Pisces	Water	Fruitful	4th 7:43 am
9 Sat 5:26 am	Aries	Fire	Barren	4th
10 Sun	Aries	Fire	Barren	4th
11 Mon 7:29 am	Taurus	Earth	Semi-fruitful	4th
12 Tue	Taurus	Earth	Semi-fruitful	4th
13 Wed 8:24 am	Gemini	Air	Barren	4th
14 Thu	Gemini	Air	Barren	New 11:13 pm
15 Fri 9:45 am	Cancer	Water	Fruitful	1st
16 Sat	Cancer	Water	Fruitful	1st
17 Sun 1:25 pm	Leo	Fire	Barren	1st
18 Mon	Leo	Fire	Barren	1st
19 Tue 8:45 pm	Virgo	Earth	Barren	1st
20 Wed	Virgo	Earth	Barren	1st
21 Thu	Virgo	Earth	Barren	1st
22 Fri 7:43 am	Libra	Air	Semi-fruitful	2nd 9:15 am
23 Sat	Libra	Air	Semi-fruitful	2nd
24 Sun 8:26 pm	Scorpio	Water	Fruitful	2nd
25 Mon	Scorpio	Water	Fruitful	2nd
26 Tue	Scorpio	Water	Fruitful	2nd
27 Wed 8:23 am	Sagittarius	Fire	Barren	2nd
28 Thu	Sagittarius	Fire	Barren	2nd
29 Fri 6:05 pm	Capricorn	Earth	Semi-fruitful	2nd
30 Sat	Capricorn	Earth	Semi-fruitful	Full 9:49 am

Aspectarian/Favorable & Unfavorable Days

Date	Sun	Mercury	Venus	Mars	Jupiter	Saturn	Uranus	Neptune	Pluto	Aries	Taurus	Gemini	Cancer	Leo	Virgo	Libra	Scorpio	Sagittarius	Capricorn	Aquarius	Pisces
1				T	C	T	Q	X		f		U		f	u	f		F		f	u
2		O							C	f		U		f	u	f		F		f	u
3			Q				X			u	f		U		f	u	f		F		f
4			O							u	f		U		f	u	f		F		f
5	T				X					f	u	f		U		f	u	f		F	
6				X		O		C	X	f	u	f		U		f	u	f		F	
7		T								f	u	f		U		f	u	f		F	
8	Q				Q		C				f	u	f		U		f	u	f		F
9		Q	T						Q		f	u	f		U		f	u	f		F
10	X			C	T	T		X		F		f	u	f		U		f	u	f	
11			Q						T	F		f	u	f		U		f	u	f	
12		X				Q	X	Q			F		f	u	f		U		f	u	f
13		X									F		f	u	f		U		f	u	f
14	C			X	O	X	Q	T		f		F		f	u	f		U		f	u
15									O	f		F		f	u	f		U		f	u
16		C				T				u	f		F		f	u	f		U		f
17			Q							u	f		F		f	u	f		U		f
18			C	T						f	u	f		F		f	u	f		U	
19	X			T		C		O	T	f	u	f		F		f	u	f		U	
20		X		Q							f	u	f		F		f	u	f		U
21						O					f	u	f		F		f	u	f		U
22	Q								Q		f	u	f		F		f	u	f		U
23		Q	X	X						U		f	u	f		F		f	u	f	
24			O		X			T	X	U		f	u	f		F		f	u	f	
25	T	T									U		f	u	f		F		f	u	f
26			Q		Q	T	Q				U		f	u	f		F		f	u	f
27											U		f	u	f		F		f	u	f
28				C		Q				f		U		f	u	f		F		f	u
29			T		T			X	C	f		U		f	u	f		F		f	u
30	O	O		T						u	f		U		f	u	f		F		f

July Moon Table

Date	Sign	Element	Nature	Phase
1 Sun	Capricorn	Earth	Semi-fruitful	3rd
2 Mon 1:24 am	Aquarius	Air	Barren	3rd
3 Tue	Aquarius	Air	Barren	3rd
4 Wed 6:52 am	Pisces	Water	Fruitful	3rd
5 Thu	Pisces	Water	Fruitful	3rd
6 Fri 10:56 am	Aries	Fire	Barren	3rd
7 Sat	Aries	Fire	Barren	4th 12:53 pm
8 Sun 1:54 pm	Taurus	Earth	Semi-fruitful	4th
9 Mon	Taurus	Earth	Semi-fruitful	4th
10 Tue 4:10 pm	Gemini	Air	Barren	4th
11 Wed	Gemini	Air	Barren	4th
12 Thu 6:39 pm	Cancer	Water	Fruitful	4th
13 Fri	Cancer	Water	Fruitful	4th
14 Sat 10:43 pm	Leo	Fire	Barren	New 8:04 am
15 Sun	Leo	Fire	Barren	1st
16 Mon	Leo	Fire	Barren	1st
17 Tue 5:39 am	Virgo	Earth	Barren	1st
18 Wed	Virgo	Earth	Barren	1st
19 Thu 3:53 pm	Libra	Air	Semi-fruitful	1st
20 Fri	Libra	Air	Semi-fruitful	1st
21 Sat	Libra	Air	Semi-fruitful	1st
22 Sun 4:18 am	Scorpio	Water	Fruitful	2nd 2:29 am
23 Mon	Scorpio	Water	Fruitful	2nd
24 Tue 4:29 pm	Sagittarius	Fire	Barren	2nd
25 Wed	Sagittarius	Fire	Barren	2nd
26 Thu	Sagittarius	Fire	Barren	2nd
27 Fri 2:21 am	Capricorn	Earth	Semi-fruitful	2nd
28 Sat	Capricorn	Earth	Semi-fruitful	2nd
29 Sun 9:13 am	Aquarius	Air	Barren	Full 8:48 pm
30 Mon	Aquarius	Air	Barren	3rd
31 Tue 1:40 pm	Pisces	Water	Fruitful	3rd

Aspectarian/Favorable & Unfavorable Days

Date	Sun	Mercury	Venus	Mars	Jupiter	Saturn	Uranus	Neptune	Pluto	Aries	Taurus	Gemini	Cancer	Leo	Virgo	Libra	Scorpio	Sagittarius	Capricorn	Aquarius	Pisces
1						X			u	u	f		U		f	u	f		F		f
2				Q	X					f	u	f		U		f	u	f		F	
3			O		O			C		f	u	f		U		f	u	f		F	
4		T		X					X	f	u	f		U		f	u	f		F	
5	T				Q	C					f	u	f		U		f	u	f		F
6		Q							Q		f	u	f		U		f	u	f		F
7	Q				T			X		F		f	u	f		U		f	u	f	
8		X	T		T			T		F		f	u	f		U		f	u	f	
9	X			C			X				F		f	u	f		U		f	u	f
10		Q			Q		Q				F		f	u	f		U		f	u	f
11				O		Q				f		F		f	u	f		U		f	u
12		C	X		X			T	O	f		F		f	u	f		U		f	u
13				X						u	f		F		f	u	f		U		f
14	C					T				u	f		F		f	u	f		U		f
15					T					f	u	f		F		f	u	f		U	
16			Q		C			O	T	f	u	f		F		f	u	f		U	
17		X	C							f	u	f		F		f	u	f		U	
18			T	Q		O					f	u	f		F		f	u	f		U
19	X							Q			f	u	f		F		f	u	f		U
20		Q		X						U		f	u	f		F		f	u	f	
21					X			T	X	U		f	u	f		F		f	u	f	
22	Q		X							U		f	u	f		F		f	u	f	
23		T		O		T	Q				U		f	u	f		F		f	u	f
24	T		Q		Q						U		f	u	f		F		f	u	f
25					C					f		U		f	u	f		F		f	u
26						T	Q	X	C	f		U		f	u	f		F		f	u
27			T							f		U		f	u	f		F		f	u
28		O		T				X		u	f		U		f	u	f		F		f
29	O									u	f		U		f	u	f		F		f
30					X			C		f	u	f		U		f	u	f		F	
31			O	Q		O			X	f	u	f		U		f	u	f		F	

August Moon Table

Date	Sign	Element	Nature	Phase
1 Wed	Pisces	Water	Fruitful	3rd
2 Thu 4:43 pm	Aries	Fire	Barren	3rd
3 Fri	Aries	Fire	Barren	3rd
4 Sat 7:16 pm	Taurus	Earth	Semi-fruitful	3rd
5 Sun	Taurus	Earth	Semi-fruitful	4th 5:19 pm
6 Mon 10:01 pm	Gemini	Air	Barren	4th
7 Tue	Gemini	Air	Barren	4th
8 Wed	Gemini	Air	Barren	4th
9 Thu 1:36 am	Cancer	Water	Fruitful	4th
10 Fri	Cancer	Water	Fruitful	4th
11 Sat 6:42 am	Leo	Fire	Barren	4th
12 Sun	Leo	Fire	Barren	New 7:02 pm
13 Mon 2:03 pm	Virgo	Earth	Barren	1st
14 Tue	Virgo	Earth	Barren	1st
15 Wed	Virgo	Earth	Barren	1st
16 Thu 12:04 am	Libra	Air	Semi-fruitful	1st
17 Fri	Libra	Air	Semi-fruitful	1st
18 Sat 12:13 pm	Scorpio	Water	Fruitful	1st
19 Sun	Scorpio	Water	Fruitful	1st
20 Mon	Scorpio	Water	Fruitful	2nd 7:54 pm
21 Tue 12:44 am	Sagittarius	Fire	Barren	2nd
22 Wed	Sagittarius	Fire	Barren	2nd
23 Thu 11:20 am	Capricorn	Earth	Semi-fruitful	2nd
24 Fri	Capricorn	Earth	Semi-fruitful	2nd
25 Sat 6:35 pm	Aquarius	Air	Barren	2nd
26 Sun	Aquarius	Air	Barren	2nd
27 Mon 10:34 pm	Pisces	Water	Fruitful	2nd
28 Tue	Pisces	Water	Fruitful	Full 6:35 am
29 Wed	Pisces	Water	Fruitful	3rd
30 Thu 12:24 am	Aries	Fire	Barren	3rd
31 Fri	Aries	Fire	Barren	3rd

Aspectarian/Favorable & Unfavorable Days

Date	Sun	Mercury	Venus	Mars	Jupiter	Saturn	Uranus	Neptune	Pluto	Aries	Taurus	Gemini	Cancer	Leo	Virgo	Libra	Scorpio	Sagittarius	Capricorn	Aquarius	Pisces
1					Q		C				f	u	f		U		f	u	f		F
2		T		X					Q		f	u	f		U		f	u	f		F
3	T				T					F		f	u	f		U	f	u	f		
4		Q	T			T		X	T	F		f	u	f		U	f	u	f		
5	Q										F		f	u	f		U		f	u	f
6			Q	C		Q	X	Q			F		f	u	f		U		f	u	f
7		X			O					f		F	f	u	f		U			f	u
8	X					X	Q	T	O	f		F	f	u	f		U			f	u
9			X							f		F	f	u	f		U			f	u
10						T				u	f		F	f	u	f		U			f
11			X							u	f		F	f	u	f		U			f
12	C	C			T			O		f	u	f		F		f	u	f		U	
13		C	Q		C				T	f	u	f		F		f	u	f		U	
14				Q		O				f	u	f		F		f	u	f			U
15									Q	f	u	f		F		f	u	f			U
16			T	X						f	u	f		F		f	u	f			U
17								T		U		f	u	f	F		f	u	f		
18	X	X	X			X			X	U		f	u	f	F		f	u	f		
19						T					U		f	u	f		F		f	u	f
20	Q		Q		Q		Q				U		f	u	f		F		f	u	f
21		Q		O	C						U		f	u	f		F		f	u	f
22			T			Q	X			f		U		f	u	f		F		f	u
23	T				T				C	f		U		f	u	f		F		f	u
24		T					X			u	f		U	f	u	f		F			f
25										u	f		U	f	u	f		F			f
26			T	X						f	u	f		U		f	u	f		F	
27		O			O		C	X		f	u	f		U		f	u	f		F	
28	O			Q	Q					f	u	f			U		f	u	f		F
29		O					C		Q	f	u	f			U		f	u	f		F
30					T					f	u	f			U		f	u	f		F
31			T	X				X	T	F		f	u	f		U	f	u	f		

149

September Moon Table

Date	Sign	Element	Nature	Phase
1 Sat 1:35 am	Taurus	Earth	Semi-fruitful	3rd
2 Sun	Taurus	Earth	Semi-fruitful	3rd
3 Mon 3:30 am	Gemini	Air	Barren	4th 10:32 pm
4 Tue	Gemini	Air	Barren	4th
5 Wed 7:08 am	Cancer	Water	Fruitful	4th
6 Thu	Cancer	Water	Fruitful	4th
7 Fri 12:59 pm	Leo	Fire	Barren	4th
8 Sat	Leo	Fire	Barren	4th
9 Sun 9:10 pm	Virgo	Earth	Barren	4th
10 Mon	Virgo	Earth	Barren	4th
11 Tue	Virgo	Earth	Barren	New 8:44 am
12 Wed 7:31 am	Libra	Air	Semi-fruitful	1st
13 Thu	Libra	Air	Semi-fruitful	1st
14 Fri 7:37 pm	Scorpio	Water	Fruitful	1st
15 Sat	Scorpio	Water	Fruitful	1st
16 Sun	Scorpio	Water	Fruitful	1st
17 Mon 8:21 am	Sagittarius	Fire	Barren	1st
18 Tue	Sagittarius	Fire	Barren	1st
19 Wed 7:51 pm	Capricorn	Earth	Semi-fruitful	2nd 12:48 pm
20 Thu	Capricorn	Earth	Semi-fruitful	2nd
21 Fri	Capricorn	Earth	Semi-fruitful	2nd
22 Sat 4:18 am	Aquarius	Air	Barren	2nd
23 Sun	Aquarius	Air	Barren	2nd
24 Mon 8:55 am	Pisces	Water	Fruitful	2nd
25 Tue	Pisces	Water	Fruitful	2nd
26 Wed 10:22 am	Aries	Fire	Barren	Full 3:45 pm
27 Thu	Aries	Fire	Barren	3rd
28 Fri 10:17 am	Taurus	Earth	Semi-fruitful	3rd
29 Sat	Taurus	Earth	Semi-fruitful	3rd
30 Sun 10:34 am	Gemini	Air	Barren	3rd

Aspectarian/Favorable & Unfavorable Days

Date	Sun	Mercury	Venus	Mars	Jupiter	Saturn	Uranus	Neptune	Pluto	Aries	Taurus	Gemini	Cancer	Leo	Virgo	Libra	Scorpio	Sagittarius	Capricorn	Aquarius	Pisces
1	T					T				F		f	u	f			U	f	u	f	
2		T	Q					X	Q		F		f	u	f			U	f	u	f
3	Q				O	Q					F		f	u	f			U	f	u	f
4			X	C			Q	T		f		F		f	u	f			U	f	u
5		Q				X			O	f		F		f	u	f			U	f	u
6	X						T			u	f		F		f	u	f			U	f
7		X								u	f		F		f	u	f			U	f
8			C		T					f	u	f		F		f	u	f			U
9			X			C		O	T	f	u	f		F		f	u	f			U
10				Q						U	f	u	f		F		f	u	f		
11	C			Q		O			Q	U	f	u	f		F		f	u	f		
12									Q	U	f	u	f		F		f	u	f		
13		C	X	X				T			U	f	u	f		F		f	u	f	
14			T		X				X		U	f	u	f		F		f	u	f	
15												U	f	u	f		F		f	u	f
16	X		Q					T	Q			U	f	u	f		F		f	u	f
17					Q							U	f	u	f		F		f	u	f
18		X	T		C			Q	X	f			U	f	u	f		F		f	u
19	Q			O					C	f			U	f	u	f		F		f	u
20					T					u	f			U	f	u	f		F		f
21		Q				X				u	f			U	f	u	f		F		f
22	T									u	f			U	f	u	f		F		f
23			O	X		C				f	u	f			U	f	u	f		F	
24		T		T	O				X	f	u	f			U	f	u	f		F	
25				Q	C						f	u	f			U	f	u	f		F
26	O			Q					Q		f	u	f			U	f	u	f		F
27			T		T			X		F		f	u	f			U	f	u	f	
28		O	X		T				T	F		f	u	f			U	f	u	f	
29			Q					X	Q		F		f	u	f			U	f	u	f
30	T		Q		Q						F		f	u	f			U	f	u	f

October Moon Table

Date	Sign	Element	Nature	Phase
1 Mon	Gemini	Air	Barren	3rd
2 Tue 12:57 pm	Cancer	Water	Fruitful	3rd
3 Wed	Cancer	Water	Fruitful	4th 6:06 am
4 Thu 6:27 pm	Leo	Fire	Barren	4th
5 Fri	Leo	Fire	Barren	4th
6 Sat	Leo	Fire	Barren	4th
7 Sun 3:03 am	Virgo	Earth	Barren	4th
8 Mon	Virgo	Earth	Barren	4th
9 Tue 1:57 pm	Libra	Air	Semi-fruitful	4th
10 Wed	Libra	Air	Semi-fruitful	4th
11 Thu	Libra	Air	Semi-fruitful	New 1:01 am
12.Fri 2:13 am	Scorpio	Water	Fruitful	1st
13 Sat	Scorpio	Water	Fruitful	1st
14 Sun 2:58 pm	Sagittarius	Fire	Barren	1st
15 Mon	Sagittarius	Fire	Barren	1st
16 Tue	Sagittarius	Fire	Barren	1st
17 Wed 3:03 am	Capricorn	Earth	Semi-fruitful	1st
18 Thu	Capricorn	Earth	Semi-fruitful	1st
19 Fri 12:52 pm	Aquarius	Air	Barren	2nd 4:33 am
20 Sat	Aquarius	Air	Barren	2nd
21 Sun 7:02 pm	Pisces	Water	Fruitful	2nd
22 Mon	Pisces	Water	Fruitful	2nd
23 Tue 9:24 pm	Aries	Fire	Barren	2nd
24 Wed	Aries	Fire	Barren	2nd
25 Thu 9:07 pm	Taurus	Earth	Semi-fruitful	2nd
26 Fri	Taurus	Earth	Semi-fruitful	Full 12:51 am
27 Sat 8:11 pm	Gemini	Air	Barren	3rd
28 Sun	Gemini	Air	Barren	3rd
29 Mon 8:49 pm	Cancer	Water	Fruitful	3rd
30 Tue	Cancer	Water	Fruitful	3rd
31 Wed	Cancer	Water	Fruitful	3rd

Aspectarian/Favorable & Unfavorable Days

Date	Sun	Mercury	Venus	Mars	Jupiter	Saturn	Uranus	Neptune	Pluto	Aries	Taurus	Gemini	Cancer	Leo	Virgo	Libra	Scorpio	Sagittarius	Capricorn	Aquarius	Pisces
1				O		Q	T		f		F		f	u	f		U		f	u	f
2		T	X	C		X			O	f		F		f	u	f		U		f	u
3	Q						T			u	f		F		f	u	f		U		f
4										u	f		F		f	u	f		U		f
5	X	Q			T					f	u	f		F		f	u	f		U	
6							O	T		f	u	f		F		f	u	f		U	
7		X	C	X		C				f	u	f		F		f	u	f		U	
8					Q		O				f	u	f		F		f	u	f		U
9			Q						Q		f	u	f		F		f	u	f		U
10				X						U		f	u	f		F		f	u	f	
11	C					T	X			U		f	u	f		F		f	u	f	
12		C	X	T		X				U		f	u	f		F		f	u	f	
13						T	Q				U		f	u	f		F		f	u	f
14											U		f	u	f		F		f	u	f
15			Q			Q	Q			f		U		f	u	f		F		f	u
16	X			C			X	C		f		U		f	u	f		F		f	u
17		X	T	O		T				f		U		f	u	f		F		f	u
18						X				u	f		U		f	u	f		F		f
19	Q	Q								u	f		U		f	u	f		F		f
20				X						f	u	f		U		f	u	f		F	
21	T	T						C	X	f	u	f		U		f	u	f		F	
22			O	T		O	C				f	u	f		U		f	u	f		F
23				Q					Q		f	u	f		U		f	u	f		F
24			Q							F		f	u	f		U		f	u	f	
25		O			T			X	T	F		f	u	f		U		f	u	f	
26	O		T	X		T	X				F		f	u	f		U		f	u	f
27							Q				F		f	u	f		U		f	u	f
28					Q	Q				f		F		f	u	f		U		f	u
29		T	Q		O			T	O	f		F		f	u	f		U		f	u
30	T			C		X	T			u	f		F		f	u	f		U		f
31		Q	X							u	f		F		f	u	f		U		f

November Moon Table

Date	Sign	Element	Nature	Phase
1 Thu 12:48 am	Leo	Fire	Barren	4th 5:18 pm
2 Fri	Leo	Fire	Barren	4th
3 Sat 8:44 am	Virgo	Earth	Barren	4th
4 Sun	Virgo	Earth	Barren	4th
5 Mon 6:47 pm	Libra	Air	Semi-fruitful	4th
6 Tue	Libra	Air	Semi-fruitful	4th
7 Wed	Libra	Air	Semi-fruitful	4th
8 Thu 7:18 am	Scorpio	Water	Fruitful	4th
9 Fri	Scorpio	Water	Fruitful	New 6:03 pm
10 Sat 7:59 pm	Sagittarius	Fire	Barren	1st
11 Sun	Sagittarius	Fire	Barren	1st
12 Mon	Sagittarius	Fire	Barren	1st
13 Tue 8:00 am	Capricorn	Earth	Semi-fruitful	1st
14 Wed	Capricorn	Earth	Semi-fruitful	1st
15 Thu 6:30 pm	Aquarius	Air	Barren	1st
16 Fri	Aquarius	Air	Barren	1st
17 Sat	Aquarius	Air	Barren	2nd 5:32 pm
18 Sun 2:14 am	Pisces	Water	Fruitful	2nd
19 Mon	Pisces	Water	Fruitful	2nd
20 Tue 6:24 am	Aries	Fire	Barren	2nd
21 Wed	Aries	Fire	Barren	2nd
22 Thu 7:18 am	Taurus	Earth	Semi-fruitful	2nd
23 Fri	Taurus	Earth	Semi-fruitful	2nd
24 Sat 6:29 am	Gemini	Air	Barren	Full 9:30 am
25 Sun	Gemini	Air	Barren	3rd
26 Mon 6:07 am	Cancer	Water	Fruitful	3rd
27 Tue	Cancer	Water	Fruitful	3rd
28 Wed 8:23 am	Leo	Fire	Barren	3rd
29 Thu	Leo	Fire	Barren	3rd
30 Fri 2:44 pm	Virgo	Earth	Barren	3rd

Aspectarian/Favorable & Unfavorable Days

Date	Sun	Mercury	Venus	Mars	Jupiter	Saturn	Uranus	Neptune	Pluto	Aries	Taurus	Gemini	Cancer	Leo	Virgo	Libra	Scorpio	Sagittarius	Capricorn	Aquarius	Pisces
1	Q									u	f		F		f	u	f		U		
2		X		T				O		f	u	f		F		f	u	f		U	
3						C			T	f	u	f		F		f	u	f		U	
4	X			X	Q		O				f	u	f		F		f	u	f		U
5			C						Q		f	u	f		F		f	u	f		U
6			Q							U		f	u	f		F		f	u	f	
7				X				T		U		f	u	f		F		f	u	f	
8		C			X				X	U		f	u	f		F		f	u	f	
9	C			T			T	Q			U		f	u	f		F		f	u	f
10											U		f	u	f		F		f	u	f
11			X			Q				f		U		f	u	f		F		f	u
12				C			Q	X		f		U		f	u	f		F		f	u
13		X	Q			T			C	f		U		f	u	f		F		f	u
14				O			X			u	f		U		f	u	f		F		f
15	X									u	f		U		f	u	f		F		f
16		Q	T							f	u	f		U		f	u	f		F	
17	Q			X				C	X	f	u	f		U		f	u	f		F	
18		T			O					f	u	f		U		f	u	f		F	
19				T	Q		C				f	u	f		U		f	u	f		F
20	T								Q		f	u	f		U		f	u	f		F
21			O	Q	T			X		F		f	u	f		U		f	u	f	
22						T			T	F		f	u	f		U		f	u	f	
23		O		X		X	Q				F		f	u	f		U		f	u	f
24	O				Q						F		f	u	f		U		f	u	f
25			T		O		Q	T		f		F		f	u	f		U		f	u
26						X			O	f		F		f	u	f		U		f	u
27		T	Q	C			T			u	f		F		f	u	f		U		f
28	T									u	f		F		f	u	f		U		f
29								O		f	u	f		F		f	u	f		U	
30		Q	X		T				T	f	u	f		F		f	u	f		U	

155

December Moon Table

Date	Sign	Element	Nature	Phase
1 Sat	Virgo	Earth	Barren	4th 7:44 am
2 Sun	Virgo	Earth	Barren	4th
3 Mon 1:01 am	Libra	Air	Semi-fruitful	4th
4 Tue	Libra	Air	Semi-fruitful	4th
5 Wed 1:31 pm	Scorpio	Water	Fruitful	4th
6 Thu	Scorpio	Water	Fruitful	4th
7 Fri	Scorpio	Water	Fruitful	4th
8 Sat 2:11 am	Sagittarius	Fire	Barren	4th
9 Sun	Sagittarius	Fire	Barren	New 12:40 pm
10 Mon 1:50 pm	Capricorn	Earth	Semi-fruitful	1st
11 Tue	Capricorn	Earth	Semi-fruitful	1st
12 Wed	Capricorn	Earth	Semi-fruitful	1st
13 Thu 12:01 am	Aquarius	Air	Barren	1st
14 Fri	Aquarius	Air	Barren	1st
15 Sat 8:15 am	Pisces	Water	Fruitful	1st
16 Sun	Pisces	Water	Fruitful	1st
17 Mon 1:52 pm	Aries	Fire	Barren	2nd 5:17 am
18 Tue	Aries	Fire	Barren	2nd
19 Wed 4:38 pm	Taurus	Earth	Semi-fruitful	2nd
20 Thu	Taurus	Earth	Semi-fruitful	2nd
21 Fri 5:14 pm	Gemini	Air	Barren	2nd
22 Sat	Gemini	Air	Barren	2nd
23 Sun 5:18 pm	Cancer	Water	Fruitful	Full 8:15 pm
24 Mon	Cancer	Water	Fruitful	3rd
25 Tue 6:52 pm	Leo	Fire	Barren	3rd
26 Wed	Leo	Fire	Barren	3rd
27 Thu 11:44 pm	Virgo	Earth	Barren	3rd
28 Fri	Virgo	Earth	Barren	3rd
29 Sat	Virgo	Earth	Barren	3rd
30 Sun 8:37 am	Libra	Air	Semi-fruitful	3rd
31 Mon	Libra	Air	Semi-fruitful	4th 2:51 am

Aspectarian/Favorable & Unfavorable Days

Date	Sun	Mercury	Venus	Mars	Jupiter	Saturn	Uranus	Neptune	Pluto	Aries	Taurus	Gemini	Cancer	Leo	Virgo	Libra	Scorpio	Sagittarius	Capricorn	Aquarius	Pisces
1	Q			X		C	O				f	u	f		F		f	u	f		U
2					Q				Q		f	u	f		F		f	u	f		U
3		X		Q							f	u	f		F		f	u	f		U
4	X							T		U		f	u	f		F		f	u	f	
5			C		X				X	U		f	u	f		F		f	u	f	
6			T		X	T					U		f	u	f		F		f	u	f
7			T					Q			U		f	u	f		F		f	u	f
8					Q						U		f	u	f		F		f	u	f
9	C	C						Q	X	f		U		f	u	f		F		f	u
10						C			C	f		U		f	u	f		F		f	u
11			X	O	T	X				u	f		U		f	u	f		F		f
12										u	f		U		f	u	f		F		f
13			Q							u	f		U		f	u	f		F		f
14	X	X						C		f	u	f		U		f	u	f		F	
15					T	X	O		X	f	u	f		U		f	u	f		F	
16			T					C			f	u	f		U		f	u	f		F
17	Q	Q		Q	Q				Q		f	u	f		U		f	u	f		F
18							X			F		f	u	f		U		f	u	f	
19	T	T		X	T				T	F		f	u	f		U		f	u	f	
20			O		T	X					F		f	u	f		U		f	u	f
21						Q					F		f	u	f		U		f	u	f
22					Q	Q				f		F		f	u	f		U		f	u
23	O		C	O				T	O	f		F		f	u	f		U		f	u
24		O			X	T				u	f		F		f	u	f		U		f
25			T							u	f		F		f	u	f		U		f
26										f	u	f		F		f	u	f		U	
27			Q					O	T	f	u	f		F		f	u	f		U	
28	T			X	T	C					f	u	f		F		f	u	f		U
29		T					O				f	u	f		F		f	u	f		U
30			X	Q	Q				Q		f	u	f		F		f	u	f		U
31	Q	Q								U		f	u	f		F		f	u	f	

2007 Retrograde Planets

Planet	Begin	EST	**PST**	End	EST	**PST**
Saturn	12/05/06	11:06 pm	**8:06 pm**	04/19/07	5:24 pm	**2:24 pm**
Mercury	02/13/07	11:38 pm	**8:38 pm**	03/07/07	11:44 pm	**8:44 pm**
Pluto	03/31/07	6:45 pm	**3:45 pm**	09/07/07	10:54 am	**7:54 am**
Jupiter	04/05/07	9:22 pm	**6:22 pm**	08/06/07	10:04 pm	**7:04 pm**
Neptune	05/24/07	9:08 pm	**6:08 pm**	10/31/07	4:07 pm	**1:07 pm**
Mercury	06/15/07	7:40 pm	**4:40 pm**	07/09/07	10:15 pm	**7:15 pm**
Uranus	06/23/07	10:42 am	**7:42 am**	11/24/07	5:15 am	**2:15 am**
Venus	07/27/07	1:28 pm	**10:28 am**	09/08/07	12:14 pm	**9:14 am**
Mercury	10/11/07		**9:00 pm**			
Mercury	10/12/07	12:00 am		11/01/07	6:58 pm	**3:58 pm**
Mars	11/15/07	3:24 am	**12:24 am**	01/30/08	5:33 pm	**2:33 pm**
Saturn	12/19/07	9:09 am	**6:09 am**	05/02/08	11:07 pm	**8:07 pm**

Eastern Time in plain type, **Pacific Time in bold type**

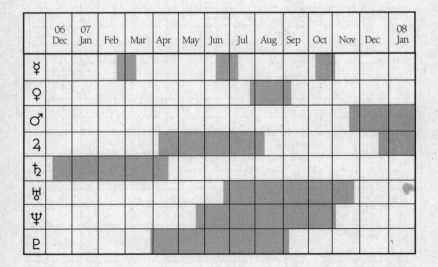

158

Notes:

Hunting and Fishing Dates

Date	Qtr.	Sign
Jan 2, 10:14 am–Jan 4, 4:14 pm	2nd	Cancer
Jan 12, 2:08 am–Jan 14, 1:11 pm	4th	Scorpio
Jan 21, 3:48 am–Jan 23, 5:52 am	1st	Pisces
Jan 29, 5:16 pm–Jan 31, 9:14 pm	2nd	Cancer
Feb 8, 10:09 am–Feb 10, 10:01 pm	2nd	Scorpio
Feb 17, 1:30 pm–Feb 19, 2:06 pm	1st	Pisces
Feb 25, 10:47 pm–Feb 28, 6:29 am	1st	Cancer
Mar 7, 5:16 pm–Mar 10, 5:37 am	3rd	Scorpio
Mar 10, 5:37 am–Mar 12, 4:34 pm	3rd	Sagittarius
Mar 16, 10:30 pm–Mar 17, 1:30 am	4th	Pisces
Mar 17, 1:30 am–Mar 19, 1:41 am	4th	Pisces
Mar 25, 5:49 am–Mar 27, 1:04 pm	1st	Cancer
Apr 4, 12:35 am–Apr 6, 12:56 pm	3rd	Scorpio
Apr 6, 12:56 pm–Apr 8, 11:36 pm	3rd	Sagittarius
Apr 13, 11:38 am–Apr 15, 12:46 pm	4th	Pisces
Apr 21, 1:50 pm–Apr 23, 7:38 pm	1st	Cancer
May 1, 6:41 am–May 3, 6:47 pm	2nd	Scorpio
May 3, 6:47 pm–May 6, 5:21 am	3rd	Sagittarius
May 10, 7:31 pm–May 12, 10:19 pm	4th	Pisces
May 18, 11:38 pm–May 21, 3:56 am	1st	Cancer
May 28, 1:11 pm–May 31, 1:06 am	2nd	Scorpio
May 31, 1:06 am–Jun 2, 11:09 am	2nd	Sagittarius
Jun 7, 1:24 am–Jun 9, 5:26 am	3rd	Pisces
Jun 15, 9:45 am–Jun 17, 1:25 pm	1st	Cancer
Jun 24, 8:26 pm–Jun 27, 8:23 am	2nd	Scorpio
Jun 27, 8:23 am–Jun 29, 6:05 pm	2nd	Sagittarius
Jul 4, 6:52 am–Jul 6, 10:56 am	3rd	Pisces
Jul 6, 10:56 am–Jul 8, 1:54 pm	3rd	Aries

Date	Qtr.	Sign
Jul 12, 6:39 pm–Jul 14, 10:43 pm	4th	Cancer
Jul 22, 4:18 am–Jul 24, 4:29 pm	2nd	Scorpio
Jul 24, 4:29 pm–Jul 26, 11:21 pm	2nd	Sagittarius
Jul 31, 1:40 pm–Aug 2, 4:43 pm	3rd	Pisces
Aug 2, 4:43 pm–Aug 4, 7:16 pm	3rd	Aries
Aug 9, 1:36 am–Aug 11, 6:42 am	4th	Cancer
Aug 18, 12:13 pm–Aug 21, 12:44 am	1st	Scorpio
Aug 21, 12:44 am–Aug 23, 11:20 am	2nd	Sagittarius
Aug 27, 10:34 pm–Aug 30, 12:24 am	2nd	Pisces
Aug 30, 12:24 am–Aug 31, 1:35 am	3rd	Aries
Sep 5, 7:08 am–Sep 7, 12:59 pm	4th	Cancer
Sep 14, 7:37 pm–Sep 17, 8:21 am	1st	Scorpio
Sep 24, 8:55 am–Sep 26, 10:22 am	2nd	Pisces
Sep 26, 10:22 am–Sep 28, 10:17 am	2nd	Aries
Oct 2, 12:57 pm–Oct 4, 6:27 pm	3rd	Cancer
Oct 12, 2:13 am–Oct 14, 2:58 pm	4th	Scorpio
Oct 21, 7:02 pm–Oct 23, 9:24 pm	2nd	Pisces
Oct 23, 9:24 pm–Oct 25, 9:07 pm	2nd	Aries
Oct 29, 8:49 pm–Nov 1, 12:48 am	2nd	Cancer
Nov 8, 7:18 am–Nov 10, 7:59 pm	4th	Scorpio
Nov 18, 2:14 am–Nov 20, 6:24 am	2nd	Pisces
Nov 20, 6:24 am–Nov 22, 7:18 am	2nd	Aries
Nov 26, 6:07 am–Nov 28, 8:23 am	3rd	Cancer
Dec 5, 1:31 pm–Dec 8, 2:11 am	4th	Scorpio
Dec 15, 8:15 am–Dec 17, 1:52 pm	1st	Pisces
Dec 17, 1:52 pm–Dec 19, 4:38 pm	2nd	Aries
Dec 23, 5:18 pm–Dec 25, 6:52 pm	2nd	Cancer

Fire signs Aries, Leo, and Sagittarius are best for hunting. Water signs Cancer, Scorpio, and Pisces are best for fishing. See page 114 for more information about the best times for fishing.

Time Zone Map

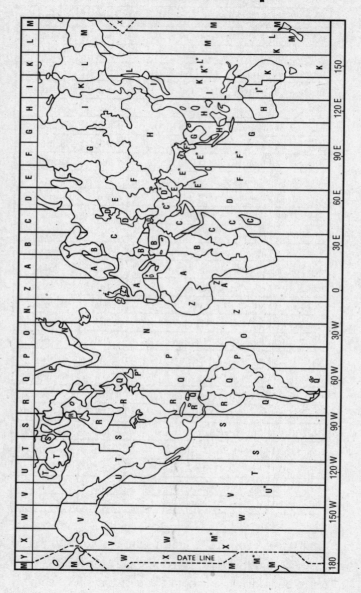

Time Zone Conversions

World Time Zones Compared to Eastern Time

(R) EST—Used in book
(S) CST—Subtract 1 hour
(T) MST—Subtract 2 hours
(U) PST—Subtract 3 hours
(V) Subtract 4 hours
(V*) Subtract 4½ hours
(U*) Subtract 3½ hours
(W) Subtract 5 hours
(X) Subtract 6 hours
(Y) Subtract 7 hours
(Q) Add 1 hour
(P) Add 2 hours
(P*) Add 2½ hours
(O) Add 3 hours
(N) Add 4 hours
(Z) Add 5 hours
(A) Add 6 hours
(B) Add 7 hours
(C) Add 8 hours
(C*) Add 8½ hours

(D) Add 9 hours
(D*) Add 9½ hours
(E) Add 10 hours
(E*) Add 10½ hours
(F) Add 11 hours
(F*) Add 11½ hours
(G) Add 12 hours
(H) Add 13 hours
(I) Add 14 hours
(I*) Add 14½ hours
(K) Add 15 hours
(K*) Add 15½ hours
(L) Add 16 hours
(L*) Add 16½ hours
(M) Add 17 hours
(M*) Add 18 hours
(P*) Add 2½ hours

Important!

All times given in the *Moon Sign Book* are set in Eastern Time. The conversions shown here are for standard times only. Use the time zone conversions map and table to calculate the difference in your time zone. You must make the adjustment for your time zone and adjust for Daylight Saving Time where applicable.

Weather Forecasting

By Kris Brandt Riske, M.A.

Astrometeorology—astrological weather forecasting—reveals seasonal and weekly weather trends based on the cardinal ingresses (Summer and Winter Solstices, and Spring and Autumn Equinoxes) and the four monthly lunar phases. The planetary alignments and the longitudes and latitudes they influence have the strongest effect, but the zodiacal signs are also involved in creating weather conditions.

The components of a thunderstorm, for example, are heat, wind, and electricity. A Mars-Jupiter configuration generates the necessary heat and Mercury adds wind and electricity. A severe thunderstorm, and those that produce tornados, usually involve Mercury, Mars, Uranus, or Neptune. The zodiacal signs add their energy to the planetary mix to increase or decrease the chance of weather phenomena and their severity.

In general, the fire signs (Aries, Leo, Sagittarius) indicate heat and dryness, both of which peak when Mars, the planet with a similar nature, is in these signs. Water signs (Cancer, Scorpio, Pisces) are conducive to precipitation, and air signs (Gemini, Libra, Aquarius) to cool temperatures and wind. Earth signs (Taurus, Virgo, Capricorn) vary from wet to dry, heat to cold. The signs and their prevailing weather conditions are listed here:

Aries: Heat, dry, wind
Taurus: Moderate temperatures, precipitation
Gemini: Cool temperatures, wind, dry
Cancer: Cold, steady precipitation
Leo: Heat, dry, lightning
Virgo: Cold, dry, windy
Libra: Cool, windy, fair
Scorpio: Extreme temperatures, abundant precipitation
Sagittarius: Warm, fair, moderate wind
Capricorn: Cold, wet, damp
Aquarius: Cold, dry, high pressure, lightning
Pisces: Wet, cool, low pressure

Take note of the Moon's sign at each lunar phase. It reveals the prevailing weather conditions for the next six to seven days. The same is true of Mercury and Venus. These two influential weather planets transit the entire zodiac each year, unless retrograde patterns add their influence.

Planetary Influences

People relied on astrology to forecast weather for thousands of years. They were able to predict drought, floods, and temperature variations through interpreting planetary alignments. In recent years there has been a renewed interest in astrometeorology. A weather forecast can be composed for any date—tomorrow, next week, or a thousand years in the future. Astrometeorology reveals seasonal and weekly weather trends based on the cardinal ingresses (Summer and Winter Solstices, and Spring and Fall Equinoxes) and the four lunar phases that occur monthly in combination with the transiting planets. According to astrometeorology, each planet governs certain weather phenomena. When certain planets are aligned with other planets, weather—precipitation, cloudy or clear skies, tornados, hurricanes, and other conditions—are generated.

Sun and Moon

The Sun governs the constitution of the weather and, like the Moon, it serves as a trigger for other planetary configurations that result in weather events. When the Sun is prominent in a cardinal ingress or lunar phase chart, the area is often warm and sunny. The Moon can bring or withhold moisture, depending upon its sign placement.

Mercury

Mercury is also a triggering planet, but its main influence is wind direction and velocity. In its stationary periods, Mercury reflects high winds, and its influence is always prominent in major weather events, such as hurricanes and tornados, when it tends to lower the temperature.

Venus

Venus governs moisture, clouds, and humidity. It brings warming trends that produce sunny, pleasant weather if in positive aspect to other planets. In some signs—Libra, Virgo, Gemini, Sagittarius—Venus is drier. It is at its wettest when placed in Cancer, Scorpio, Pisces, or Taurus.

Mars

Mars is associated with heat, drought, and wind, and can raise the temperature to record-setting levels when in a fire sign (Aries, Leo, Sagittarius). Mars also provides the spark that generates thunderstorms and is prominent in tornado and hurricane configurations.

Jupiter

Jupiter, a fair-weather planet, tends toward higher temperatures when in Aries, Leo, or Sagittarius. It is associated with high-pressure systems and is a contributing factor at times to dryness. Storms are often amplified by Jupiter.

Saturn

Saturn is associated with low-pressure systems, cloudy to overcast skies, and excessive precipitation. Temperatures drop when Saturn is involved. Major winter storms always have a strong Saturn influence, as do storms that produce a slow, steady downpour for hours or days.

Uranus

Like Jupiter, Uranus indicates high-pressure systems. It reflects descending cold air and, when prominent, is responsible for a jet stream that extends far south. Uranus can bring drought in winter, and it is involved in thunderstorms, tornados, and hurricanes.

Neptune

Neptune is the wettest planet. It signals low-pressure systems and is dominant when hurricanes are in the forecast. When Neptune is strongly placed, flood danger is high. It's often associated with winter thaws. Temperatures, humidity, and cloudiness increase where Neptune influences weather.

Pluto

Pluto is associated with weather extremes, as well as unseasonably warm temperatures and drought. It reflects the high winds involved in major hurricanes, storms, and tornados.

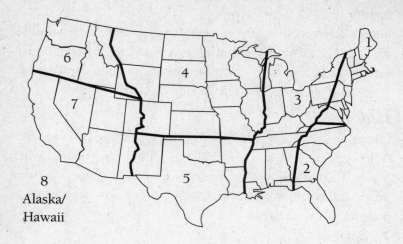

2007 Weather Forecast

By Kris Brandt Riske, M.A.

Winter (December 21, 2006 to March 19, 2007)

Zone 1: The zone sees many storms, predominantly cloudy skies, and cold temperatures.

Zone 2: Conditions are seasonal with precipitation abundant.

Zone 3: Eastern and western areas see abundant precipitation, and there are many storms in the central parts of the zone. Temperatures are seasonal to below.

Zone 4: Temperatures are seasonal to below, and conditions are windy to the west. Precipitation is average to above in some areas, especially east.

Zone 5: The zone is windy with average precipitation, cloudy more than fair skies, and temperatures range from seasonal to below.

Zone 6: Cooler temperatures and average precipitation prevail to the west, central areas are seasonal with below average precipitation, and eastern areas are cold with the most significant storms.

Zone 7: Northern coastal areas are windy with average to above precipitation. Southern coastal and central areas see below normal precipitation, and storms bring average to above precipitation to eastern areas, with temperatures seasonal to below.

Zone 8: Temperatures in Hawaii are mostly seasonal with average precipitation central and east and some significant storms with abundant downfall. Conditions are drier west. Eastern and central Alaska see more precipitation and storms, and temperatures are seasonal to below.

Full Moon, January 3

Zone 1: Weather is fair and seasonal west, with precipitation to the east. Temperatures are seasonal to below.

Zone 2: Much of the zone is overcast, cold, and windy with precipitation, which is heaviest in northern coastal areas.

Zone 3: Temperatures are seasonal to below across the zone. Fair skies prevail to the west, and central and eastern areas are windy, cold, and overcast with precipitation, some abundant.

Zone 4: Conditions are windy and an advancing front brings precipitation and cloudy skies to western areas and across the Plains. Low temperatures prevail, with eastern areas the coldest. Increasing clouds replace fair skies to the east, which sees precipitation at week's end.

Zone 5: Western areas are windy, and much of the zone is cold with precipitation.

Zone 6: Western and central areas see precipitation under cloudy, windy skies, as a front moves through much of the zone. Eastern skies are partly cloudy to cloudy and windy, with a chance for precipitation. Temperatures are seasonal to below.

Zone 7: Northern coastal areas are cold, while the southern coast sees precipitation that advances across much of the zone. Eastern skies are cloudy with a chance for precipitation. Temperatures range from seasonal to below.

Zone 8: Much of Hawaii is fair and breezy; a storm brings precipitation to the west, followed by cooler temperatures. Alaska is seasonal to cool central and west with precipitation, while eastern skies are mostly fair and seasonal.

> **Earth Note:** The Earth's axis is tilted 23.5 degrees to the plane of its orbit, and it is because of this tilt that we experience summer in the northern hemisphere while the southern hemisphere experiences winter.

Third Quarter Moon, January 11

Zone 1: Northern areas are overcast, cold, and windy, with fair to partly cloudy skies south gradually becoming cloudy. Much of the zone sees precipitation, and temperatures are seasonal to below.

Zone 2: Central and southern areas are windy and cold with precipitation. To the north, clouds increase, bringing precipitation at week's end.

Zone 3: Western and central areas are mostly fair and seasonal. Eastern areas see precipitation, some abundant northeast, with wind and temperatures seasonal to below.

Zone 4: Skies are fair to partly cloudy west, with seasonal temperatures. The Plains are windy, cold, and stormy with precipitation, as a front moves across the area.

Zone 5: Western conditions are fair and seasonal, while central and eastern areas are windy and cool with variable cloudiness.

Zone 6: Stormy weather prevails to the west, with wind, cloudy skies, low temperatures, and abundant precipitation. Central and eastern areas are seasonal to below, with increasing clouds bringing precipitation later in the week. Eastern skies are fair to partly cloudy.

Zone 7: Northern coastal and inland mountain areas are stormy and cold. Southern coastal and inland areas are partly cloudy and seasonal. Eastern skies are variably cloudy, with seasonal conditions and a chance for precipitation.

Zone 8: Hawaii is overcast and cool with precipitation, which is heaviest at week's end. In Alaska, cloudy skies and precipitation prevail in central and western areas; the east is fair and seasonal.

New Moon, January 18

Zone 1: The zone is mostly fair and cold with a chance for precipitation north.

Zone 2: Northern areas are fair to partly cloudy, and areas to the south are cloudy with precipitation. Temperatures range from seasonal to below.

Zone 3: Western and central areas are very windy, with a chance for precipitation west. Stormy skies prevail in central areas, with some abundant precipitation in southern areas. Fair to partly cloudy skies prevail to the north. Temperatures are seasonal to below.

Zone 4: Cold temperatures across the zone accompany fair skies west, while eastern and central areas are very windy with precipitation, which is abundant to the east.

Zone 5: Conditions are seasonal west under fair to partly cloudy skies, while wind accompanies variable cloudiness to the east. Stormy weather prevails to the east, with abundant precipitation and cold in some areas.

Zone 6: Clouds gradually increase west, bringing precipitation at week's end. Eastern and central areas are mostly fair and windy. Temperatures are seasonal to below.

Zone 7: Coastal areas are windy with a chance for precipitation later in the week. Central areas are fair and windy, and eastern parts of the zone see precipitation. Temperatures range from seasonal to below.

Zone 8: Hawaii is cool, breezy, and fair to partly cloudy. Alaska is cooler east, with wind and precipitation. Eastern and central Alaska is cloudy and seasonal with precipitation.

First Quarter Moon, January 25

Zone 1: Skies are fair to partly cloudy, and temperatures dip in northern areas, where there is a chance for precipitation.

Zone 2: Skies are mostly fair north with a chance for precipitation, and southern and central areas are fair and windy. Temperatures are seasonal to below.

Zone 3: Western and central skies are variably cloudy, windy, and cooler than the northeast, which is mostly fair to partly cloudy with a chance for precipitation.

Zone 4: Temperatures are seasonal to below across the zone, which is cloudy, very windy, and stormy as a front advances.

Zone 5: High winds and stormy conditions prevail in the western and central areas of the zone, while the east is fair to partly cloudy. There's a chance for precipitation later in the week.

Zone 6: Precipitation in western areas advances in central portions of the zone, while the east is cold and windy with precipitation.

Zone 7: Temperatures are seasonal to below, and skies are variably cloudy west. Central areas are stormy with abundant precipitation, while areas to the east are windy with precipitation.

Zone 8: Hawaii is windy, overcast, and stormy, with heaviest precipitation in central areas. Temperatures are seasonal to below. Central and eastern areas of Alaska are overcast and stormy, while conditions to the west are seasonal.

Full Moon, February 2

Zone 1: The zone is overcast, wet, and cold, with abundant precipitation south.

Zone 2: The zone is cloudy and cold, with precipitation south. Northern areas see significant precipitation.

Zone 3: Fair to partly cloudy skies prevail to the west, central areas are cloudy with precipitation, and the eastern part of the zone is overcast with abundant precipitation. The zone is cold.

Zone 4: Cold temperatures and variable cloudiness accompany precipitation across much of the zone.

Zone 5: Temperatures are seasonal to below, with cloudy skies and precipitation across much of the zone.

Zone 6: Precipitation and cloudy skies prevail across the zone, and eastern and central areas are cold and very windy.

Zone 7: An advancing front brings cloudy, windy skies, cold temperatures, and precipitation, some abundant, across the zone.

Zone 8: Hawaii is cloudy with precipitation, primarily central and east, with fair skies west. Alaska is windy and cold, with increasing cloudiness central and east that brings abundant precipitation to some areas.

Third Quarter Moon, February 10

Zone 1: Wind, variable cloudiness, and precipitation dominate, and northern areas are windy and cold.

Zone 2: Northern areas see precipitation, while areas to the south are windy, with seasonal temperatures and scattered precipitation.

Zone 3: Conditions are very windy and cloudy west with precipitation; stormy conditions prevail to the south. Eastern areas see precipitation, some abundant.

Zone 4: Skies are fair to partly cloudy west, and cloudy with a chance for precipitation central and east. Much of the zone is windy.

Zone 5: The zone is variably cloudy, and very windy east with a chance for precipitation.

Weather Fact: On Valentine's Day in 1987, severe thunderstorms spawned over Texas and Oklahoma and straight line winds gusting to 104 mph howled through Guadalupe Pass in West Texas. As the storm moved north into the Rocky Mountain Region, it produced heavy snows, with twenty-seven inches recorded at Telluride in Colorado.

—NATIONAL WEATHER SUMMARY

Zone 6: Abundant precipitation and cold temperatures prevail to the west, and central and eastern areas see downfall as a front advances across the zone.

Zone 7: Much of the zone is windy and wet, with abundant downfall in some areas. Temperatures are seasonal to below.

Zone 8: Hawaii is windy, with a chance of precipitation later in the week as temperatures range from seasonal to below. Central Alaska is fair to partly cloudy, while overcast skies and precipitation, some abundant, prevail to the west and east.

New Moon, February 17

Zone 1: Northern areas are overcast with precipitation, some abundant. Variable cloudiness prevails to the south, where there's a chance for precipitation. Temperatures are seasonal to below.

Zone 2: The zone is seasonal and fair to partly cloudy with a chance for precipitation.

Zone 3: Western areas have a chance for precipitation, while central parts of the zone are mostly fair and windy. Eastern areas are partly cloudy, windy, and colder, with a chance for precipitation.

Zone 4: Skies are mostly fair west, with variable cloudiness and a chance for precipitation in the Plains later in the week. Central and eastern areas are windy. Temperatures range from seasonal to below.

Zone 5: Eastern and central areas have a chance for precipitation. Skies are mostly fair to the west.

Zone 6: Temperatures dip to the west as skies clear and wet, windy weather moves into central areas later in the week. Eastern areas are cloudy with a chance for precipitation.

Zone 7: Northern coastal areas see precipitation that advances into central areas of the zone. Southern coastal areas are fair to partly cloudy, and eastern parts of the zone are windy and cloudy, with a chance for precipitation.

Zone 8: Hawaii is fair to partly cloudy, with seasonal temperatures and a chance for precipitation. Eastern areas of Alaska are cold and very windy, central areas are cold and wet, and western areas are variably cloudy and windy with a chance for precipitation.

First Quarter Moon, February 24

Zone 1: Temperatures are seasonal to below, and areas to the north are mostly fair and windy. Overcast skies to the south bring precipitation, some abundant.

Zone 2: Conditions are mostly fair to the south, with increasing wind and precipitation at week's end. Cloudy skies, wind, and precipitation, some abundant, prevail to the north.

Zone 3: Western and southern areas see precipitation, possibly thunderstorms with tornado potential. Areas to the north see precipitation later in the week. Conditions are windy and wet northeast, with some areas receiving abundant downfall.

Zone 4: Western areas are stormy, while central parts of the zone are mostly fair and breezy. Some eastern areas see abundant precipitation. Northern areas are cold.

Zone 5: Western areas are windy with rising temperatures, while central and eastern areas are fair to partly cloudy and windy with a chance for precipitation.

Zone 6: Conditions are windy and cold west and central, with precipitation west later in the week. A general warming trend prevails to the east.

Zone 7: Coastal areas are windy, with precipitation north, and a chance for precipitation south. Central areas are mostly fair, as are southern parts of the zone. The desert is unseasonably warm.

Zone 8: Hawaii is chilly, windy, and stormy east, and fair and seasonal west and central areas. Central Alaska sees storms and cold, while western and eastern parts of the zone are fair to partly cloudy and windy.

Full Moon, March 3

Zone 1: Much of the zone sees abundant precipitation; flood potential and severe weather to the south.

Zone 2: Seasonal to above temperatures with scattered showers in the south, while severe weather prevails to the north.

Zone 3: Temperatures are seasonal to above with precipitation and thunderstorms, some severe with tornado potential.

Zone 4: Western areas are overcast and cool. Expect precipitation, some abundant, with flood potential. Thunderstorms central and east could trigger tornados.

Zone 5: Central and western areas are overcast with abundant precipitation and flood potential. Tornados could accompany thunderstorms to the east. Temperatures are seasonal across the zone, but cooler to the west.

Zone 6: The zone sees scattered precipitation; western areas are windy and cooler.

Zone 7: Western and central areas are windy with a chance for precipitation, while eastern parts of the zone are fair to partly cloudy. Temperatures are seasonal to above.

Zone 8: Hawaii is fair to partly cloudy and breezy, with temperatures ranging from seasonal to above. Alaska is windy with precipitation central and east, and fair skies to the west with seasonal temperatures.

Third Quarter Moon, March 11

Zone 1: The zone is windy, with seasonal temperatures and precipitation to the north.

Zone 2: Temperatures dip; northern areas are fair and windy, while a chance for precipitation to the south could produce locally heavy downfall.

Zone 3: The zone is windy with temperatures seasonal to below. Western and central areas are overcast and stormy, with abundant precipitation and tornado potential. Fair to partly cloudy skies prevail northeast.

Zone 4: Cool temperatures accompany fair skies west and central, while areas to the east are windy and overcast with precipitation.

Zone 5: Temperatures dip under mostly fair skies and high winds.

Zone 6: The zone is windy and cool. Conditions are fair to partly cloudy west, partly cloudy central, and cloudy east with precipitation.

Zone 7: Variable cloudiness and cool temperatures prevail across the zone, while eastern areas are windy with precipitation.

Zone 8: Hawaii is fair and seasonal. Central and western Alaska are cold and stormy, while fair skies and seasonal conditions prevail to the east.

New Moon, March 18

Zone 1: Cloudy skies and stormy conditions prevail across the zone, with abundant precipitation south. Temperatures are seasonal to below.

Zone 2: The zone is stormy, cold, and cloudy, with heavy downfall in some locations, especially north. Tornados could develop in southern locations.

Zone 3: Western precipitation, some abundant, moves into central areas of the zone. Eastern and northern central areas are stormy with heavy precipitation and tornado potential. Temperatures range from seasonal to below.

Zone 4: Temperatures are seasonal to below with variable cloudiness and precipitation. Eastern areas are stormy with heavy precipitation and tornado potential.

Zone 5: Western areas see precipitation, while the central part of the zone is mostly fair and windy with scattered precipitation. Severe thunderstorms east could trigger abundant downfall and tornados.

Zone 6: Temperatures are cool across the zone. Stormy conditions west advance into central areas later in the week, and the east is windy with precipitation.

Zone 7: Northern coastal areas are stormy, and southern coastal and central areas of the zone have a chance for precipitation. Desert areas are dry and windy. Temperatures are cool north and seasonal south.

Zone 8: Hawaii is mostly fair and breezy with scattered precipitation. Western areas of Alaska see precipitation, eastern areas are cooler and stormy, and central areas see scattered precipitation.

Spring (March 20–June 20)

Zone 1: The zone sees average to above precipitation with some significant storms and below normal temperatures.

Zone 2: Severe thunderstorms with tornado potential and abundant precipitation dominate in central and southern areas. Temperatures are below normal north, with average precipitation.

Zone 3: Cloudy skies, below normal temperatures, abundant precipitation, and severe thunderstorms with tornado potential prevail in this zone.

Zone 4: Severe storms with tornado potential and abundant downfall accompany temperatures seasonal to above.

Zone 5: Temperatures are seasonal, with severe thunderstorms with tornado potential and abundant precipitation in some areas.

Zone 6: Central and eastern areas are mostly dry with temperatures seasonal to above. Western areas see average precipitation and seasonal conditions.

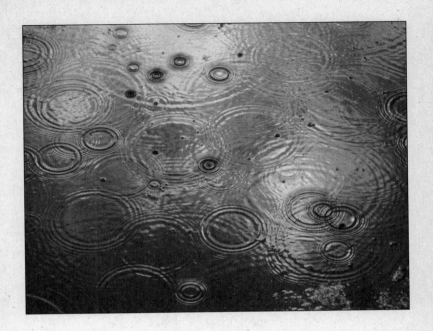

Zone 7: Northern coastal areas see average precipitation, and the rest of the zone is somewhat dry with seasonal temperatures.

Zone 8: Temperatures are seasonal in Hawaii with precipitation average to below. In Alaska, precipitation and temperatures are seasonal.

First Quarter Moon, March 25

Zone 1: The zone is windy and seasonal with scattered precipitation.

Zone 2: Fair to partly cloudy skies prevail; southern areas see scattered precipitation and scattered thunderstorms.

Zone 3: Some western areas see abundant precipitation from thunderstorms, which dominate the forecast for much of the zone, along with the potential for severe weather and tornados. Temperatures are seasonal to below.

Zone 4: Much of the zone is wet with thunderstorms, some severe with tornado potential, yielding abundant precipitation in some areas, especially central and east.

Zone 5: A front advances from the west, moving into central and eastern areas, bringing thunderstorms with tornado potential and heavy precipitation in some areas.

Zone 6: Conditions are fair to partly cloudy and windy west and central, with precipitation east. Temperatures are seasonal.

Zone 7: Much of the zone is fair to partly cloudy, with a chance for precipitation east, especially at higher elevations.

Zone 8: Hawaii is breezy with a chance for precipitation, with warmer temperatures to the east. Temperatures in Alaska range from seasonal to below, with abundant precipitation east, mostly fair skies west, and precipitation and wind in central areas.

Full Moon, April 2

Zone 1: Temperatures range from seasonal to below, with scattered precipitation north. To the south, severe thunderstorms with tornado potential bring significant precipitation to some areas.

Zone 2: Temperatures are cooler north, and warm and humid south, with scattered precipitation across the zone.

Zone 3: Much of the zone sees cloudy skies and some precipitation. Severe thunderstorms with tornado potential are in the central, north, and eastern areas. Temperatures are seasonal to below.

Zone 4: Thunderstorms could trigger tornados throughout the zone, along with abundant precipitation.

Zone 5: Western and central areas see severe thunderstorms with tornado potential and significant downfall. Eastern areas are warmer, with precipitation later in the week.

Zone 6: Eastern areas are mostly fair and seasonal, while the rest of the zone is wet and very windy.

Zone 7: Northern coastal areas are wet, while southern coastal are mostly fair, windy, and warm. Central and mountainous areas see scattered thunderstorms, and eastern portions of the zone are fair and dry.

Zone 8: Hawaii is fair to partly cloudy with scattered showers, some locally heavy. Windy conditions accompany downfall in eastern and western Alaska, while central areas are fair to partly cloudy. Eastern areas are cooler.

Third Quarter Moon, April 10

Zone 1: The zone is windy, with scattered precipitation south and heavier downfall north under cloudy skies.

Zone 2: Scattered thunderstorms throughout the zone are stronger south with high winds.

Zone 3: Variable cloudiness and scattered precipitation across the zone, with scattered thunderstorms and heavier downfall north.

Zone 4: Fair to partly cloudy west with variable cloudiness central and east, and temperatures seasonal to below. Central portions of the zone have a chance for precipitation, and eastern areas see scattered thunderstorms, some severe.

Zone 5: Central areas have a chance for precipitation, while fair to partly cloudy skies prevail west. To the east, high winds and cloudy skies yield precipitation.

Zone 6: Western and central areas see cloudy skies and precipitation, some abundant, and eastern areas are fair to partly cloudy and windy with a chance for precipitation. Temperatures are seasonal to below.

Zone 7: Western areas see cloudy and cool weather with precipitation, and the rest of the zone is windy and fair to partly cloudy with scattered precipitation.

Zone 8: Hawaii is fair to partly cloudy and breezy, with temperatures seasonal to above. Western Alaska is fair. Overcast skies in central Alaska yield abundant precipitation, which moves into eastern areas. Temperatures are seasonal to below.

New Moon, April 17

Zone 1: Temperatures are seasonal and skies mostly fair, with a chance for precipitation north.

Zone 2: Conditions are fair and seasonal north, with rising humidity and scattered thunderstorms south.

Zone 3: Western and central areas see scattered thunderstorms and showers, and fair and windy conditions prevail northeast. Temperatures are seasonal to below.

Zone 4: Western and eastern skies are windy and partly cloudy to cloudy with showers and scattered thunderstorms. Central areas are mostly fair.

Zone 5: Areas to the west are partly cloudy with scattered precipitation, central areas see scattered thunderstorms, and the east is fair and windy.

Zone 6: The zone is fair to partly cloudy with a chance for showers west.

Zone 7: Mostly fair to partly cloudy, northern coastal areas have a chance for precipitation, and temperatures are unseasonably warm in the desert.

Zone 8: Hawaii sees scattered showers east and central, and western areas are cloudy and cool with locally heavy downfall. Central Alaska is overcast with abundant precipitation, and areas east and west are mostly fair with scattered precipitation and seasonal temperatures.

First Quarter Moon, April 24

Zone 1: Areas to the north are fair, and southern locations are fair to partly cloudy with a chance for showers.

Zone 2: Fair skies prevail to the north, and southern areas are overcast with abundant precipitation and flood potential.

Zone 3: Western and central areas see thunderstorms, some severe with tornado potential. Flooding is possible central, where overcast skies yield abundant downfall. Skies to the northeast are mostly fair.

Zone 4: Thunderstorms, some severe with tornado potential, dominate the weather as a front travels across much of the zone.

Zone 5: Temperatures are seasonal to above, and much of the zone sees thunderstorms, some severe with tornado potential.

Zone 6: Weather is fair to partly cloudy west, with thunderstorms central and east, which is cooler and windy.

Zone 7: Skies are fair to partly cloudy in coastal areas and inland, with scattered thunderstorms in the central mountains. To the east, temperatures are seasonal to above, with partly cloudy and windy skies and a chance for precipitation at higher elevations.

Zone 8: Hawaii is mostly fair with scattered showers. Alaska is stormy east and fair central; western areas are overcast with abundant precipitation.

Full Moon, May 2

Zone 1: The zone is fair north, and fair to partly cloudy and humid south.

Zone 2: Fair to partly cloudy skies and rising humidity dominate the zone's weather, with scattered thunderstorms, some severe with tornado potential, to the south.

Zone 3: The zone is fair to partly cloudy with a chance for showers and thunderstorms, mostly north and east.

Zone 4: Western areas see scattered showers and thunderstorms, and eastern areas are fair to partly cloudy with a chance for showers. The central part of the zone is cloudy with abundant precipitation in some areas and severe thunderstorm and tornado potential.

Zone 5: Showers and thunderstorms, some severe with tornado potential, occur across the zone, first in western areas, and then central and east later in the week.

Zone 6: Skies are fair to partly cloudy west with a chance for precipitation, central areas are windy and cloudy with thunderstorms, and eastern areas are cloudy with severe thunderstorms, some with abundant downfall.

Zone 7: Northern coastal areas are mostly fair and seasonal with a chance for showers. Southern coastal and central areas see scattered thunderstorms, some severe. Partly cloudy skies are windy to the east with a chance of showers. Desert areas are hot.

Zone 8: Hawaii sees wind, showers, and thunderstorms across the zone, some locally heavy. Alaska is cool, windy, and wet in central areas, and overcast skies yield abundant downfall with flood potential east. Western areas are windy and fair to partly cloudy.

Third Quarter Moon, May 10

Zone 1: Southern areas are fair, humid, and windy with a chance for thunderstorms, and northern parts of the zone are overcast with abundant precipitation. Temperatures are seasonal to below.

Zone 2: The zone is partly cloudy to fair, with temperatures seasonal to above, and a chance for thunderstorms south.

Zone 3: The zone is mostly fair, windy, and humid, with temperatures ranging from seasonal to above. Central areas see precipitation, some abundant.

Zone 4: Western areas are fair to partly cloudy, and central and eastern areas see scattered thunderstorms, some severe. Temperatures are seasonal to above.

Zone 5: Most of the zone is fair to partly cloudy with temperatures seasonal to above, and precipitation west.

Zone 6: Western areas are windy with precipitation, some locally heavy, and high temperatures. Central areas see scattered severe thunderstorms, and eastern areas are variably cloudy with precipitation.

Zone 7: Northern coastal areas see precipitation, and southern coastal and central areas are windy and warm. To the east, skies are partly cloudy to cloudy with showers, thunderstorms, and abundant downfall in some areas.

Zone 8: Hawaii is overcast, seasonal to below, and windy, and significant precipitation could trigger flooding. Alaska is fair to the west, with a chance for precipitation east. Central areas are stormy with abundant precipitation.

New Moon, May 16

Zone 1: Humidity rises and temperatures are seasonal to above, with severe thunderstorms and heavy downfall north.

Zone 2: Northern areas are hot and humid with severe thunderstorms, and southern areas see scattered thunderstorms.

Zone 3: Weather is hot and humid across the zone, with severe thunderstorms, high winds, and tornado potential.

Zone 4: Temperatures rise and much of the zone sees severe thunderstorms with tornado potential.

Zone 5: The zone is mostly fair, hot, and dry, with a chance for precipitation east and severe thunderstorms west.

Zone 6: Stormy conditions with abundant precipitation could trigger flooding west and central. Eastern areas see variable cloudiness and some precipitation.

Zone 7: Western areas are stormy, with the heaviest downpour north and into central parts of the zone, where flooding is possible. Eastern areas have a chance for precipitation, and temperatures are high, especially in the desert.

Zone 8: Hawaii is mostly fair to partly cloudy, seasonal, and breezy with some showers. Alaska is stormy west, and fair and windy east. Central areas see precipitation.

First Quarter Moon, May 23

Zone 1: Mostly fair to partly cloudy with temperatures seasonal to below, the zone sees some scattered thunderstorms.

Zone 2: Northern areas are mostly fair with scattered thunderstorms. Southern areas are humid and breezy, with showers at week's end.

Zone 3: Northeastern areas are fair, and the rest of the zone sees showers and some thunderstorms. Temperatures are seasonal to below.

Zone 4: Skies are fair to partly cloudy west and in the western Plains with scattered thunderstorms. The central Plains are fair and dry, and eastern areas see showers and thunderstorms followed by cooler temperatures.

Zone 5: Western areas have a chance for thunderstorms, and central areas see some severe storms with tornado potential. Eastern areas are fair and dry.

Zone 6: Western and central areas are mostly fair and dry, with a chance for thunderstorms central, and eastern areas see severe thunderstorms. The zone is hot.

Zone 7: The zone is mostly fair to partly cloudy with some severe thunderstorms. Wind prevails to the east, and zonal temperatures are seasonal to above.

Zone 8: Hawaii is hot and fair to partly cloudy, with strong thunderstorms later in the week. Central areas of Alaska are fair and seasonal, eastern areas see abundant precipitation, and western skies turn stormy at week's end.

Full Moon, May 31

Zone 1: Temperatures are seasonal to above, with a chance for thunderstorms.

Zone 2: The zone is hot and humid with scattered thunderstorms.

Zone 3: The zone is fair to partly cloudy with high temperatures and a chance for severe thunderstorms.

Zone 4: Fair, hot, and dry conditions prevail west, with showers, thunderstorms, humidity, and high temperatures in the western Plains. Eastern areas are hot, humid, windy, and dry.

Zone 5: The zone is hot and fair, with a chance for thunderstorms.

Zone 6: Western and central areas are cloudy with abundant precipitation, while high temperatures prevail to the east, which is windy and fair.

Zone 7: Northern coastal areas are overcast and cool with heavy precipitation and flood potential. The southern coast and central portions of the zone have a chance for showers, and eastern areas are hot, windy, and dry.

Zone 8: Temperatures in Hawaii are seasonal to below under fair to partly cloudy skies. Eastern and western areas of Alaska are windy with precipitation, while central areas are partly cloudy.

Third Quarter Moon, June 8

Zone 1: Northern areas are cloudy with a chance for showers, and southern areas are mostly dry. Temperatures are seasonal to above.

Zone 2: Rising humidity and temperatures across the zone spark showers and scattered thunderstorms, some severe to the south.

Zone 3: Temperatures are seasonal to above across the zone. Dryness prevails to the west, and eastern areas see showers and thunderstorms, some severe.

Zone 4: Western skies are cloudy with scattered precipitation, and central and eastern areas are mostly fair and dry with a chance for showers. Temperatures are seasonal to above.

Zone 5: The zone is mostly fair to partly cloudy, hot, and dry, with a chance for showers west.

Zone 6: Eastern areas are cloudy with abundant precipitation and the potential for severe thunderstorms. Fair skies and

temperatures seasonal to above prevail central and west, with precipitation west at week's end.

Zone 7: Temperatures are seasonal to above in much of the zone, and eastern areas are cloudy and humid with scattered precipitation. The northern coast sees showers later in the week.

Zone 8: Hawaii is variably cloudy and humid with showers, some locally heavy. Central Alaska sees precipitation, some abundant, and eastern and western areas are mostly fair.

New Moon, June 14

Zone 1: Weather is fair and seasonal north, and windy with scattered thunderstorms south.

Zone 2: Areas north are fair, and central and southern parts of the zone see scattered thunderstorms. Temperatures are seasonal.

Zone 3: High temperatures trigger thunderstorms, some severe with tornado potential and heavy downfall, across much of the zone. Eastern areas are very humid.

Zone 4: Northwestern parts of the zone see scattered thunderstorms, some severe, and the western and central Plains are dry with temperatures seasonal to above. Eastern areas are more seasonal, with showers and strong thunderstorms.

Zone 5: Weather is fair with temperatures seasonal to above west and central, and eastern areas see showers and thunderstorms with high winds.

Zone 6: Showers and severe thunderstorms prevail across the zone, especially to the east. Temperatures are seasonal to above.

Zone 7: Western areas are windy with a chance for showers, and central areas see thunderstorms, some severe, and abundant downfall with temperatures seasonal to above. The desert is hot and humid.

Zone 8: Hawaii is fair with a chance for showers. Variable cloudiness and precipitation prevail across Alaska, with temperatures seasonal to below.

Summer (June 21–September 22)

Zone 1: Precipitation is average to above, and temperatures are seasonal to below.

Zone 2: The zone has high potential for hurricanes, tornados, and tropical storms central and south, and northern areas are seasonal with average precipitation.

Zone 3: Major storms, tornados, and the potential for hurricanes and tropical storms prevail west and central. Eastern areas are seasonal with average precipitation.

Zone 4: Major storms with high tornado potential prevail, and temperatures and precipitation are average to above.

Zone 5: Storms, precipitation, and temperatures are seasonal to above, with potential for hurricanes and tropical storms.

Zone 6: Conditions are seasonal west, and drier central and east with high temperatures.

Zone 7: Northern areas see average precipitation, while southern, central, and eastern areas are average to below, but with some severe storms and high temperatures east.

Zone 8: Temperatures are seasonal to above in Hawaii, with precipitation average to below. Alaska is drier west and central, and seasonal east, with higher temperatures.

First Quarter Moon, June 22

Zone 1: Stormy skies produce abundant precipitation and flood potential north. Southern areas see scattered thunderstorms.

Zone 2: Severe thunderstorms with tornado potential dominate to the south, while northern areas see scattered thunderstorms.

Zone 3: Western areas are mostly fair to partly cloudy with scattered thunderstorms and the chance for heavy downfall. Severe thunderstorms with tornado potential in central areas produce abundant downfall, and eastern areas see scattered showers and thunderstorms. Temperatures are seasonal to above.

Zone 4: Cloudy skies, abundant precipitation, and severe storms with tornado potential dominate the forecast for western and central areas. Eastern parts of the zone are cloudy and humid with scattered showers, some locally heavy. Temperatures are seasonal to above.

Zone 5: Much of the zone sees thunderstorms, some severe with tornado potential and abundant precipitation. Temperatures are seasonal to above.

Zone 6: Seasonal temperatures accompany thunderstorms, some severe, across the zone, with heaviest downfall in central areas.

Zone 7: Northern coastal areas see strong thunderstorms, and southern coastal and central areas are fair to partly cloudy. Scattered showers and thunderstorms east accompany temperatures seasonal to above.

Zone 8: Hawaii is variably cloudy with scattered showers and high temperatures. Eastern Alaska sees abundant precipitation with flood potential, and western and central areas are mostly fair to partly cloudy, with some precipitation central.

Full Moon, June 30

Zone 1: Conditions are fair and windy north, with temperatures seasonal to below. Abundant precipitation, cool, and cloudy weather prevails to the south, with the chance for strong thunderstorms.

Zone 2: Northern areas are cloudy and cool with abundant precipitation and potentially severe thunderstorms. Southern and central areas are more seasonal with scattered thunderstorms, some severe with tornado potential.

Zone 3: The zone is mostly fair and seasonal to above, with abundant precipitation and severe thunderstorms with tornado potential in cloudy eastern areas.

Zone 4: Areas to the west are fair to partly cloudy with a chance for precipitation. Central parts of the zone are hot, windy, and mostly dry, with a chance for thunderstorms. Conditions to the east are more seasonal and warming later in the week with a chance for thunderstorms.

Zone 5: Temperatures are above normal across the zone. Western areas are fair to partly cloudy, and eastern and central areas are fair with a chance for thunderstorms.

Zone 6: Western areas are windy with showers, and eastern areas are fair and seasonal. Overcast skies and stormy conditions in central areas produce abundant precipitation.

Zone 7: Central and coastal areas are cool with abundant precipitation, and eastern areas are fair and dry with temperatures seasonal to above.

Zone 8: Hawaii is fair, breezy, and seasonal, with showers west and central later in the week. Alaska is fair east, and zonal temperatures are seasonal to below. Western and central skies are overcast, with abundant precipitation and flood potential.

Third Quarter Moon, July 7

Zone 1: Northern areas are fair, dry, and seasonal, and areas to the south are warmer and fair to partly cloudy, with a chance for showers and thunderstorms.

Zone 2: Fair to partly cloudy skies prevail to the north, with a chance for showers and thunderstorms. Central and southern areas are windy, humid, and partly cloudy to cloudy with scattered thunderstorms, some severe.

Zone 3: Temperatures are seasonal to above across the zone, with scattered thunderstorms, some severe, west and central, which are windy and humid. Weather is partly cloudy northeast, with a chance for showers and thunderstorms.

Zone 4: Temperatures rise across the zone, and conditions are mostly fair and dry west. Central areas are partly cloudy, windy, and humid with scattered thunderstorms, and eastern parts of the zone are very windy and fair, with scattered thunderstorms, some severe.

Zone 5: Temperatures and humidity rise across the zone, which is mostly fair and dry with a chance for severe thunderstorms in the windy east.

Zone 6: Western areas see precipitation, central areas are fair and windy, and high temperatures east trigger thunderstorms.

Zone 7: Northern coastal areas are windy and cool with showers, and the rest of the zone is seasonal to above, with high temperatures in the desert and scattered thunderstorms central and east.

Zone 8: Hawaii is partly cloudy, seasonal, and breezy, with scattered showers. Alaska is fair to partly cloudy, with scattered precipitation across the zone and temperatures seasonal to above.

New Moon, July 14

Zone 1: Rising temperatures, wind, and humidity trigger scattered thunderstorms, some severe.

Zone 2: The zone sees scattered thunderstorms, with high humidity and temperatures seasonal to above.

Zone 3: Western and central areas are hot, humid, and partly cloudy with scattered thunderstorms, some severe with tornado potential. Skies are mostly fair east.

Zone 4: Conditions are fair to partly cloudy, with scattered thunderstorms and seasonal to high temperatures across the zone. Central and eastern areas are humid.

Zone 5: Scattered thunderstorms across the zone produce heaviest precipitation in central areas. Humidity and temperatures rise.

Zone 6: Much of the zone is windy with precipitation, variable cloudiness, and seasonal temperatures.

Zone 7: Western and central areas are windy and cooler, with variable cloudiness and precipitation. Eastern areas are windy with scattered thunderstorms, and the desert is hot and humid.

Zone 8: Hawaii is hot and windy, with thunderstorms. Alaska is windy and stormy east and central, and western areas are mostly fair. Temperatures are seasonal to below.

First Quarter Moon, July 22

Zone 1: Overcast skies produce significant precipitation with flood potential, possibly from a hurricane.

Zone 2: Abundant precipitation and flood potential accompany overcast skies, possibly from a hurricane. Tornado potential is high in central and southern areas.

Zone 3: High temperatures trigger scattered thunderstorms west and central. Northeastern areas are stormy with abundant precipitation and flood potential, possibly from a hurricane.

Zone 4: Western areas see showers and scattered thunderstorms, some severe with tornado potential, which are in the forecast later in the week for central and eastern areas. Temperatures are seasonal to above.

Zone 5: High temperatures trigger thunderstorms, some severe with tornado potential, across the zone, where humidity rises.

Zone 6: Thunderstorms in cloudy western and central areas produce locally heavy downfall and cool temperatures. Eastern areas see showers and scattered thunderstorms.

Zone 7: Northern coastal areas are stormy, with locally heavy downpour. Southern coastal and central areas are cloudy with precipitation, and eastern areas see scattered showers and thunderstorms later in the week. Temperatures are seasonal.

Zone 8: Hawaii is cloudy, with seasonal temperatures and abundant precipitation. Alaska sees cloudy skies and precipitation across the state, some abundant. Temperatures are seasonal.

Full Moon, July 29

Zone 1: Northern areas are mostly fair with scattered thunderstorms, and southern parts of the zone are windy with some severe thunderstorms. Temperatures are seasonal.

Zone 2: The zone is windy, with scattered showers and thunderstorms, some severe, and seasonal temperatures.

Zone 3: Stormy conditions produce abundant precipitation and increase flood potential to the west. Central areas are cloudy and stormy, and eastern areas see heavy downfall. The zone is windy, and a hurricane is possible.

Zone 4: The zone sees scattered showers and thunderstorms, with variable cloudiness and seasonal temperatures. Stormy conditions east, with high winds, abundant precipitation, and flood potential that could be the result of a hurricane.

Zone 5: The zone is seasonal, windy, and variably cloudy, with scattered thunderstorms and more precipitation to the east.

Zone 6: The zone is windy with scattered showers and thunderstorms, some severe with high winds, and abundant downfall, primarily west. Temperatures are seasonal under partly cloudy to cloudy skies.

Zone 7: Western and central areas see showers and thunderstorms, with heaviest downfall to the north. High winds accompany scattered thunderstorms east later in the week.

Zone 8: Hawaii is fair, seasonal, and breezy. Western Alaska sees abundant precipitation, eastern areas are stormy, and central parts of the state are mostly fair with scattered precipitation. Temperatures are seasonal.

Third Quarter Moon, August 5

Zone 1: The zone is fair to partly cloudy, with temperatures seasonal to above, scattered thunderstorms north, and high humidity south.

Zone 2: Northern areas are fair to partly cloudy with a chance for showers, and southern areas see thunderstorms, some severe. Temperatures are seasonal to above.

Zone 3: Conditions are windy and humid across the zone, with high temperatures, and a chance for thunderstorms central and east.

Zone 4: High temperatures trigger thunderstorms, some severe, west and central as a front moves through the zone, followed by cooler temperatures. Eastern areas are humid and fair to partly cloudy.

Zone 5: Humidity and temperatures rise, and much of the area sees thunderstorms, some severe with high winds.

Zone 6: Conditions are windy and cloudy west with precipitation, and mostly fair to partly cloudy central and east.

Zone 7: Coastal areas are cloudy with precipitation, and central and eastern parts of the zone are fair to partly cloudy and dry. Desert areas are hot and dry.

Zone 8: Hawaii is windy and seasonal, with fair to partly cloudy skies and scattered showers. Eastern Alaska is variably cloudy with scattered precipitation, and central and western areas are windy and fair to partly cloudy.

New Moon, August 12

Zone 1: Overcast skies yield abundant precipitation, possibly from a hurricane, and temperatures are below normal.

Zone 2: Precipitation is abundant, possibly from a hurricane, and tornado potential is high.

Zone 3: Western areas see scattered thunderstorms, as do central and eastern areas, where severe storms could trigger tornados, possibly from a hurricane. Temperatures are seasonal to above.

Zone 4: Areas to the northwest have a chance for precipitation, and scattered thunderstorms across the Plains produce abundant downfall in some areas. Eastern areas are mostly fair and windy, and temperatures across the zone are seasonal to above.

Zone 5: Severe thunderstorms central and east with tornado potential could be triggered by a hurricane, along with significant downfall. Temperatures are seasonal to above.

Zone 6: The zone is variably cloudy with scattered precipitation, which is heaviest to the east, where strong scattered thunderstorms are possible. Temperatures are seasonal to above, and western areas are windy.

Zone 7: Western and central areas are mostly fair to partly cloudy, with a chance for precipitation. Eastern areas are humid and windy, with thunderstorms. Temperatures are seasonal to above.

Zone 8: Hawaii is overcast, with high winds and abundant precipitation, possibly from a typhoon. Western and central areas of Alaska are cloudy and stormy with heavy precipitation, and eastern areas see scattered precipitation. Temperatures are seasonal to below.

First Quarter, August 20

Zone 1: The zone is mostly fair and seasonal, with scattered thunderstorms south.

Zone 2: Severe thunderstorms across much of the zone could be the result of a tropical storm or hurricane.

Zone 3: Abundant precipitation west could be triggered by a hurricane, along with severe thunderstorms with tornado potential in central and eastern parts of the zone. Flooding is possible.

Zone 4: Skies are mostly fair to the west, with some scattered thunderstorms. Eastern and central areas of the zone are cloudy and windy with abundant precipitation and flood potential, possibly from a hurricane.

Zone 5: Western areas are mostly fair and windy. Overcast skies and abundant precipitation central and east could trigger flooding, possibly from a hurricane.

Zone 6: Temperatures are seasonal to below with variable cloudiness and thunderstorms and showers, some locally heavy, across the zone.

Zone 7: Western and central areas are cloudy with precipitation, some heavy. Eastern areas see scattered thunderstorms and windy conditions. Temperatures are seasonal to below.

Zone 8: Hawaii is fair and seasonal, with scattered thunderstorms west. Alaska is wet, with variable cloudiness and temperatures seasonal to below.

Full Moon, August 28

Zone 1: Weather is fair north, and cloudy south with scattered precipitation. Temperatures are seasonal.

Zone 2: Areas to the south are cloudy and windy with thunderstorms, some severe, and northern parts of the zone are cloudy. Temperatures are seasonal to below.

Zone 3: A hurricane or tropical storm is possible, along with severe thunderstorms with tornado potential, wind, and abundant moisture west. Central and eastern areas are mostly fair. Temperatures are seasonal to above.

Zone 4: The zone sees showers and thunderstorms, some severe with tornado potential, and locally heavy precipitation under cloudy skies to the east. Temperatures are seasonal to above.

Zone 5: Western areas are variably cloudy and windy with a chance for precipitation. Much of the zone sees thunderstorms, some severe with tornado potential, as humidity and temperatures rise.

Zone 6: Scattered showers and thunderstorms across the zone accompany seasonal but windy weather.

Zone 7: Western and central areas have a chance for precipitation, and eastern areas see high temperatures and scattered thunderstorms, some strong with high winds.

Zone 8: Hawaii is fair and seasonal, with a chance of showers west. Alaska is stormy east with high winds, and fair to partly cloudy central and west. Temperatures are seasonal to below.

Third Quarter, September 3

Zone 1: Conditions are fair to the north, with strong thunderstorms south, and temperatures seasonal to above across the zone.

Zone 2: The zone sees strong thunderstorms and rising temperatures and humidity.

Zone 3: Temperatures are seasonal to above, and much of the zone is stormy with severe thunderstorms with tornado potential.

Zone 4: Western areas see showers and thunderstorms, and the western Plains are mostly fair and dry. Severe thunderstorms with tornado potential are possible central and east.

Zone 5: Central and eastern parts of the zone are cloudy with showers and thunderstorms, some severe with tornado potential, possibly from a tropical storm or hurricane. Western areas see scattered precipitation.

Zone 6: Western areas are stormy with high winds and heavy precipitation, and much of the zone is cloudy. Scattered thunderstorms, some strong with locally heavy downfall, and windy conditions prevail central and east. Temperatures are seasonal to above.

Zone 7: Northern coastal areas are stormy, southern coastal and central areas are partly cloudy and hot with a chance for precipitation, and eastern parts of the zone are variably cloudy with showers and thunderstorms, some severe.

Zone 8: Hawaii is stormy, cloudy, cool, and wet, with abundant downfall, possibly from a typhoon. Western and central areas of Alaska are cool, windy, and stormy as a front moves through and delivers abundant downfall. Eastern areas are mostly fair and seasonal.

New Moon, September 11

Zone 1: Abundant precipitation and cool temperatures across the zone could be the result of a hurricane or tropical storm.

Zone 2: The zone is wet with heavy precipitation, possibly from a hurricane or tropical storm; the tornado potential is high in central and southern areas.

Zone 3: Western areas see abundant precipitation and thunderstorms, some severe with tornado potential. Central and eastern areas are windy, with precipitation. A hurricane or tropical storm is possible.

Zone 4: Showers and scattered thunderstorms, some severe with abundant precipitation, prevail across the zone, possibly from a hurricane or tropical storm. Eastern areas are cooler and cloudier.

Zone 5: High temperatures trigger thunderstorms across the zone. Some are severe, with tornado potential, possibly from a hurricane or tropical storm.

Zone 6: Western areas are cloudy, with precipitation, and central and eastern areas are mostly fair and windy. Temperatures are seasonal to above.

Zone 7: Scattered precipitation prevails under cloudy western skies, mostly north. The rest of the zone is mostly fair and windy, and the desert is hot.

Zone 8: Hawaii is fair to partly cloudy, with high temperatures. Alaska is fair to partly cloudy, and cooler east with a chance for precipitation.

First Quarter Moon, September 19

Zone 1: Precipitation across the zone is accompanied by temperatures seasonal to below and high winds to the south.

Zone 2: The zone is wet with temperatures seasonal to below.

Zone 3: Cloudy conditions bring precipitation across the zone, with lower temperatures to the east.

Zone 4: Western areas see abundant precipitation with flood potential, and the eastern Plains are cloudy with precipitation. Central areas of the zone are mostly fair and windy, with a chance for precipitation.

Zone 5: Temperatures across the zone are seasonal to below, eastern areas are cloudy with precipitation, and central parts of the zone are windy with a chance for precipitation. Abundant downfall west increases flood potential.

Zone 6: The zone is variably cloudy, with scattered precipitation west and central, and heavy precipitation east with flood potential. Temperatures are seasonal to below.

Zone 7: Northern coastal areas are fair and cool, while temperatures rise to the south and in central portions of the zone, which also are windy. Eastern areas are overcast and windy with heavy precipitation.

Zone 8: Hawaii is cloudy with precipitation, some abundant, and temperatures are seasonal to below. Western Alaska is stormy with high winds, central areas are mostly fair and seasonal, and eastern areas see scattered precipitation.

Autumn (September 23–December 21)

Zone 1: Temperatures and precipitation are average throughout the zone, with some periods of cold, wet weather.

Zone 2: Seasonal temperatures and average precipitation prevail throughout the zone. Southern and central parts of the zone are windy, with periods of cold weather in central coastal areas.

Zone 3: Temperatures are seasonal and precipitation average to below across much of the zone. Western areas are cooler with more cloudiness and precipitation.

Zone 4: Eastern and western areas of the zone see precipitation average to above, with less downfall in some central areas. Temperatures are seasonal to below.

Zone 5: Western and some central areas of the zone see average to above precipitation, while conditions are drier to the east. Temperatures are seasonal.

Zone 6: Precipitation is average to above, with temperatures average to above.

Zone 7: Temperatures are average throughout the zone, and precipitation is average to above.

Zone 8: Hawaii is mostly seasonal, with average precipitation. Western and central Alaska are colder and stormier than eastern areas, which are seasonal.

Full Moon, September 26

Zone 1: Temperatures are seasonal to below and the zone is wet, with abundant precipitation, possibly from a hurricane or tropical storm.

Zone 2: Northern areas see abundant precipitation, and thunderstorms, some severe with tornado potential, are in the forecast for central and southern parts of the zone, possibly from a hurricane or tropical storm.

Zone 3: Cloudy skies bring wet weather to the zone, possibly from a hurricane or tropical storm. Heaviest downfall is to the east, along with the potential for severe thunderstorms with tornado potential.

Zone 4: The zone is variably cloudy, with some areas receiving abundant precipitation and the potential for severe thunderstorms with tornados. Temperatures are cooler east.

Zone 5: Temperatures are seasonal to above, with variably cloudiness and precipitation across the zone. Severe thunderstorms with tornado potential are possible to the east.

Zone 6: Conditions are stormy west and central, with some areas receiving abundant precipitation. Fair to partly cloudy skies dominate to the east, with a chance for showers later in the week.

Zone 7: Western and central areas are windy with precipitation, and areas to the north and east see scattered showers. The desert is fair and dry.

Zone 8: Hawaii is cloudy, windy, and wet, with abundant downfall. Eastern and central Alaska are cloudy, with the heaviest precipitation in central areas. Western parts of the state are mostly fair and windy.

Third Quarter Moon, October 3

Zone 1: Northern areas are stormy with high winds and abundant precipitation, and central and southern areas are windy with a chance for precipitation. Temperatures are seasonal to below.

Zone 2: Temperatures are seasonal, with scattered precipitation central and south, and windy with a chance for showers north.

Zone 3: The zone is windy, with variable cloudiness and a chance for precipitation.

Zone 4: Seasonal temperatures accompany fair skies to the east, while cloudy skies scattered precipitation conditions exist in west and central areas.

Zone 5: Western and central areas are cloudy with scattered precipitation, and eastern parts of the zone are mostly fair. Temperatures are seasonal.

Zone 6: Temperatures range from seasonal to below across the zone, along with variable cloudiness and precipitation.

Zone 7: The zone is windy, cloudy, and wet, with abundant downfall west and central, and temperatures seasonal to below.

Zone 8: Hawaii is breezy, with showers and temperatures seasonal to above. Eastern and central Alaska are mostly fair and seasonal, and western areas are windy and cloudy with precipitation.

New Moon, October 11

Zone 1: Areas to the north are fair to partly cloudy, while southern and central areas are cloudy with abundant precipitation, some abundant.

Zone 2: Northern areas are cloudy with precipitation, some heavy, and southern and central parts of the zone see variable cloudiness and scattered precipitation. Temperatures are seasonal to below.

Zone 3: Temperatures are seasonal to below across the zone. Thunderstorms, some severe with tornado potential, may develop to the west. Central areas are fair to partly cloudy, and the east is cloudy with precipitation, some abundant.

Zone 4: The zone is mostly fair and windy, but cloudy skies east brings heavy downfall to some areas.

Zone 5: Western and central areas are windy with a chance for scattered thunderstorms, and areas to the east have a chance for showers. Temperatures are seasonal.

Zone 6: Overcast, windy skies bring precipitation, some abundant, across the zone as a front advances west to east.

Zone 7: Areas to the east are fair to partly cloudy and seasonal, while western and central parts of the zone are cool, overcast, and windy with some areas seeing abundant downfall.

Zone 8: Hawaii is fair, breezy, and seasonal. Western Alaska sees precipitation, and central and eastern areas are mostly fair with a chance for precipitation. Temperatures are seasonal.

First Quarter Moon, October 19

Zone 1: The zone is windy, with fair skies north; and cloudy with precipitation to the south.

Zone 2: Areas to the north are fair to partly cloudy with scattered precipitation, while central and southern areas are stormy later in the week with some abundant downfall and cold temperatures.

Zone 3: Western areas are overcast, stormy, and cool with abundant downfall, which advances into central and eastern parts of the zone later in the week.

Zone 4: Variable cloudiness brings scattered precipitation west and central, and areas to the east are cloudy with precipitation. Temperatures are seasonal to below.

Zone 5: Central and western parts of the zone are fair to partly cloudy and windy, and eastern areas see scattered precipitation.

Zone 6: Temperatures are below average, western areas are windy with precipitation, and central and eastern parts of the zone are fair to partly cloudy.

Zone 7: Western and central areas of the zone are windy and cool with precipitation, and the same weather prevails to the east later in the week as a front advances.

Zone 8: Hawaii is windy, seasonal, and mostly fair. Western Alaska sees scattered precipitation, and central and eastern areas are mostly fair, with seasonal temperatures across the zone.

Full Moon, October 26

Zone 1: Precipitation prevails across the zone, with partly cloudy skies north and more cloudiness south. Temperatures are seasonal to below.

Zone 2: The zone is wet, with the heaviest downfall south, where some storms are severe with tornado potential. Temperatures are seasonal to below.

Zone 3: Much of the zone is cloudy, wet, and windy, with some areas to the east receiving abundant precipitation.

Zone 4: Precipitation, some locally heavy, centers over the east, while western and central parts of the zone are windy and fair to partly cloudy.

Zone 5: Temperatures are seasonal to above across the zone. Western skies are fair to partly cloudy and windy, and central and eastern areas are dry.

Zone 6: Western and central parts of the zone are cloudy, stormy, and cold, with abundant precipitation. Eastern areas see increasing clouds and wind later in the week, along with precipitation.

Zone 7: Stormy conditions west and central bring significant downfall, and areas to the east are windy and fair to partly cloudy. Temperatures rise in the desert.

Zone 8: Hawaii is cloudy and windy, with scattered precipitation. Much of Alaska is wet, with the heaviest downfall in eastern areas of the zone. Temperatures are seasonal to below.

Third Quarter Moon, November 1

Zone 1: Northern areas are cloudy with precipitation, and areas to the south are windy with scattered precipitation.

Zone 2: The zone is windy and fair to partly cloudy with scattered precipitation. Temperatures are seasonal, and areas to the south are humid.

Zone 3: Western areas see precipitation later in the week as a front moves in. Central parts of the zone are fair to partly cloudy, and eastern area is windy with precipitation. Temperatures are seasonal to below.

Zone 4: Conditions are cool and partly cloudy west, with precipitation central and east as a front moves through the area bringing clouds and precipitation, some abundant in the Plains.

Zone 5: Central and eastern areas are windy and seasonal with precipitation, some heavy, and western parts of the zone are cool and fair to partly cloudy.

Zone 6: The zone is windy, mostly fair to the west, and overcast central and east with precipitation. Temperatures range from seasonal to below.

Zone 7: Northern coastal areas are mostly fair and windy, while the southern coast and central parts of the zone are cloudy and windy with precipitation. Eastern areas are partly cloudy and windy, with a chance for precipitation north. Temperatures are seasonal to below.

Zone 8: Hawaii is windy with some severe thunderstorms and temperatures seasonal to below. Central and eastern Alaska see precipitation, and areas to the west are mostly fair. Temperatures are seasonal to below.

New Moon, November 9

Zone 1: Overcast skies bring abundant downfall with flood potential across the zone. Temperatures are seasonal.

Zone 2: Northern areas see abundant precipitation, while conditions central and south are windy and fair to partly cloudy.

Zone 3: Western and central areas are variably cloudy and seasonal with a chance for precipitation. Cloudiness prevails to the east, along with abundant downfall.

Zone 4: Western areas are wet, with the heaviest downfall south. Central parts of the zone are cloudy and very windy with precipitation, and eastern areas are windy and partly cloudy.

Zone 5: Central and eastern areas are variably cloudy with precipitation, while cloudy skies bring abundant precipitation to western parts of the zone. Temperatures are seasonal to below.

Zone 6: Temperatures are seasonal to below across the zone, and eastern areas are partly cloudy. Western and central parts of the zone see abundant downfall as a front advances through these areas.

Zone 7: Northern coastal areas see abundant precipitation, and southern coastal and central parts of the zone are partly cloudy with increasing cloudiness and precipitation later in the week. Eastern areas are windy and partly cloudy. Temperatures are seasonal to below.

Zone 8: Hawaii is windy and seasonal with scattered precipitation. Central Alaska is mostly fair zonal with seasonal to below temperatures. Eastern areas see scattered precipitation. Downfall is heaviest to the west.

First Quarter Moon, November 17

Zone 1: The zone is cloudy, windy, and wet, with heaviest downfall north, and temperatures seasonal to below.

Zone 2: Northern areas see abundant precipitation, and partly cloudy skies prevail central and south. The zone is windy with mostly seasonal temperatures.

Zone 3: Conditions are fair and cool west, and partly cloudy to cloudy central with a chance for precipitation. Eastern areas see precipitation, some abundant, and zonal temperatures are seasonal.

Zone 4: The zone is fair to partly cloudy and cool, with increasing cloudiness and precipitation west later in the week.

Zone 5: The zone is cool with variable cloudiness. Central areas have a chance for precipitation.

Zone 6: Western areas are partly cloudy with a chance for precipitation, central parts of the zone are windy with precipitation, and eastern areas are very windy and stormy, with some abundant downfall.

Zone 7: Areas to the west are partly cloudy. Central areas see precipitation and cloudy skies, which become clear as a front moves east, bringing windy conditions and precipitation to that part of the zone.

Zone 8: Hawaii is fair and breezy with a chance for showers and temperatures are seasonal to above. Eastern Alaska is mostly fair, central parts of the zone are cloudy with scattered precipitation, and areas to the west are cloudy with precipitation.

Full Moon, November 24

Zone 1: The zone is fair to partly cloudy, with a chance for precipitation north.

Zone 2: Northern areas are partly cloudy with scattered precipitation, and central parts of the zone see abundant downfall. Severe storms, some with tornado potential, developing in southern areas.

Zone 3: Conditions are fair to partly cloudy and windy with scattered precipitation in the west. Abundant precipitation falls in central areas, and skies are partly cloudy east with a chance for precipitation.

Zone 4: Central areas are mostly cloudy with precipitation, while the rest of the zone is generally fair to partly cloudy. Temperatures are seasonal to below.

Zone 5: Weather is fair to partly cloudy and windy west, and partly cloudy to cloudy, with some precipitation, in central and eastern areas. Temperatures are seasonal.

Zone 6: The zone is overcast with precipitation. Eastern areas are cold.

Zone 7: The zone is windy with temperatures seasonal to below. Central areas see scattered precipitation, and eastern areas are variably cloudy with a chance for precipitation. Western parts of the zone are cloudy, wet, and windy.

Zone 8: Hawaii is fair and cool with scattered showers. Temperatures are seasonal to below in Alaska, with scattered precipitation central and abundant downfall east. Western skies are fair to partly cloudy.

Third Quarter Moon, December 1

Zone 1: The zone is windy and cloudy with precipitation and seasonal temperatures.

Zone 2: Variable cloudiness accompanies windy conditions and scattered precipitation across the zone.

Zone 3: Weather is mostly fair and seasonal with scattered precipitation west and central, and cloudy skies and precipitation east.

Zone 4: Western and central areas are overcast and windy with abundant precipitation. Eastern skies are fair to partly cloudy, and the eastern Plains see precipitation and colder temperatures.

Zone 5: Precipitation dominates across the zone with the heaviest downfall west and central. Temperatures are colder east.

Zone 6: Variable cloudiness and a chance for precipitation prevail across the zone. Temperatures are colder west.

Zone 7: Cloudy skies yield precipitation across the zone with the potential for significant downfall. Eastern areas are very windy, and temperatures are seasonal.

Zone 8: Hawaii is windy with scattered precipitation and temperatures seasonal to above. Alaska is windy, stormy east, and mostly fair west and central, with temperatures seasonal to below.

New Moon, December 9

Zone 1: Northern areas are partly cloudy and windy with scattered precipitation, while areas to the south are stormy with temperatures seasonal to below.

Zone 2: Stormy conditions prevail to the north, and central and southern areas see precipitation with seasonal temperatures.

Zone 3: Temperatures are seasonal to below with stormy weather, some of which produces abundant downfall, across the zone.

Zone 4: Areas to the west are mostly fair, while central and eastern areas are cloudy, much colder, and very windy with precipitation, some abundant.

Zone 5: Temperatures range from seasonal to below, under mostly fair skies west and cloudy conditions central and east with precipitation.

Zone 6: Weather is cloudy west with precipitation, stormy in central areas, and fair to partly cloudy east, with temperatures seasonal to below.

Zone 7: Eastern areas are fair and windy, becoming cloudy with precipitation later in the week, while western and central parts of the zone are cloudy and wet. Temperatures are seasonal to below.

Zone 8: Hawaii is windy, wet, cloudy, and seasonal. Alaska is stormy central, and fair to partly cloudy in the rest of the zone.

First Quarter Moon, December 17

Zone 1: Areas to the south are cold with scattered precipitation, and to the north, temperatures are even colder under fair to partly cloudy skies.

Zone 2: The zone is cloudy and windy with precipitation and seasonal temperatures.

Zone 3: Overcast, windy skies bring precipitation across the zone, with temperatures seasonal to below.

Zone 4: Western and central areas are stormy, with some receiving abundant downfall. Temperatures are seasonal to below, and eastern areas see scattered precipitation.

Zone 5: Temperatures dip and stormy conditions with abundant precipitation prevail central and east. Western areas also see precipitation.

Zone 6: Western parts of the zone are partly cloudy and seasonal, while cold, windy weather with scattered precipitation is in the forecast east and central.

Zone 7: The zone is mostly fair to partly cloudy with temperatures below average. Areas to the east see scattered precipitation.

Zone 8: Hawaii is stormy, windy, and cool, with some areas receiving abundant precipitation. Conditions are fair over western Alaska, and cold and stormy conditions bring heavy downfall to central and eastern areas.

Full Moon, December 23

Zone 1: Southern areas are cloudy with scattered precipitation, and northern parts of the zone are cloudy and very windy with more downfall.

Zone 2: Temperatures are seasonal to below across the zone. Northern areas are cloudy with precipitation, and areas to the south see thunderstorms, some severe.

Zone 3: Eastern areas of the zone are stormy, and cloudy skies bring precipitation to central and western parts of the zone. Temperatures are below seasonal.

Zone 4: Western areas are stormy with abundant downfall, especially north; storms advance into central parts of the zone. Skies are cloudy to the east and then clearing.

Zone 5: The zone is mostly wet and windy, with cooler temperatures central and east.

Zone 6: Partly cloudy to cloudy skies west and central bring scattered precipitation, while areas to the east are stormy and cold with heavy downfall.

Zone 7: Eastern areas are stormy, with some heavy downfall north. Partly cloudy skies with scattered precipitation prevail west and central, and temperatures across the zone are seasonal to below.

Zone 8: Hawaii is fair, windy, and seasonal. Storms bring abundant precipitation to central and eastern Alaska, while western areas are mostly fair. Temperatures are cold.

About the Author

Kris Brandt Riske, M.A. holds professional certification from the American Federation of Astrologers (AFA). She's the author of Astrometeorology: Planetary Power in Weather Forecasting, *and she resides in Arizona.*

2007 Economic Forecast

By Dorothy J. Kovach

The handwriting is on the wall. Those people who do not get their financial act together may find themselves on a conveyer belt to nowhere. After years of being treated to what amounted to a virtual feast of easy money, the squeeze is on. While it may be tough to get ahead in this climate, it is not impossible. Wise investors observes the cyclical nature of the market. They know some months are just better for the market than others, and they posistion themselves accordingly. And an ever increasing number of investors look to the heavens to get the "real" scoop on the monetary future. If we want to look forward to a comfortable future, we might want to follow their lead. The coming year will surely reward those who do their astrological homework.

There are steps you can take—even if you don't invest in the market—to brighten your financial future. First, pay down debts. Debt is hanging over this country like a noose. The market is a place of speculation, and never play the market unless you can stand to lose. Know your limitations. In fact, it is wise to get to know everything there is to know about the sector or company you plan to invest in. If you do not have the time to do this, then make it a point to put as much energy as possible into those you chose to invest with. Remember that it is your money that's at risk.

The trend is always your friend. Remember, 70 percent of stocks move with the market. It can be a minefield out there, so the better prepared you are, the better your chances of making money. In good times stocks go up. In bad times, they go down. For the past few years we have been in a range bound market, but times have changed. We can't just park our money and watch it grow anymore.

Investing is no different from any other purchase. We want to shop for value. This means we should buy an item when it is at its lowest possible price and sell it when the value is high. This is, of course, easier said than done, because when a particular object or sector becomes "hot," like it or not, we become subject almost to a herd instinct. We saw this with the dot-coms in the 1990s, and that trend was followed by real estate. When bubbles result in each bull market, trouble follows. One can get ahead, but we cannot rely on luck alone. We need discipline. Until the time arrives when we can keep our emotions out of our purchases, we are best advised to avoid the marketplace.

Market Tip

Oil stocks may be too rich for our blood, but if we look around we will notice that solar companies will often do well right along with oil companies, and at much more affordable prices. Our favorite in the alternate energy sector is Evergreen Solar (trades on the NASDAQ under the ticker ESLR). The drilling and servicing companies are also less pricey than other energy related stocks, especially nuclear suppliers.

As long as we as a nation are unable to supply the bulk of our own energy domestically, we will witness the energy sector become "hot" intermittently. When energy is high, everybody but the richest suffers because there is less money to go around. As a result, the economy often falters.

Jupiter and Saturn

There are two basic emotions that drive business: greed and fear. Once we understand this, it becomes far easier to navigate through the constantly fluctuating world of finance. If we learn a little about the contrasting natures of Jupiter and Saturn, we have a leg up on most of the competition. In essence, markets can be likened to a pendulum that swings between the emotions of these two celestial Titans. Since our object is to make money, the quicker we learn their dance, the better.

Jupiter puts the "bull" in markets. He's the planet with the Midas touch, expanding all sectors he touches. Jupiter entered Sagittarius on Thanksgiving Day in 2006 and he stays in that sign for approximately one year. Unfortunately, Jupiter is combust (traveling very close to the Sun) at this time so there will be much happening behind the scenes, which infers that it will be wise to keep a low profile and keep everything on the up and up. Morals become a big issue when Jupiter is in Sagittarius. The centaur (symbol for Sagittarius) is dual in nature, being half man and half beast, and it tends to arouse religious feelings. Because the centaur's lower half is animal, Jupiter here can be problematic, from a fiscal point of view, because it tends to expand the extremist elements. There may be a rise in terrorist threats worldwide as a result of Jupiter's placement in Sagittarius. Since Jupiter is heading toward Pluto, threats that do occur may become ever more deadly. The climate of the cold war era is back in place, with the nuclear card played with ever more frequency.

Sagittarius is one of the three signs ruling energy. Expect energy, and those companies that explore, service, and drill, to do well in the coming year. Look to see nuclear energy make a comeback.

The Titan's Impact on the Year Ahead

We can expect to see some real discoveries in the year ahead, and if we follow the path of Jupiter, we will always get ahead.

- The race for deep space is on (The Jupiter-Saturn combination has to do with the rise of foreign powers.)
- Necessity is the mother of invention and the car is a mechanical horse (perhaps some discovery can aid the long-troubled American auto industry), and we can expect to see hybrid autos become more mainstream
- Horses and all things equestrian will be on the rise
- Look for major mergers and acquisitions in the energy industry as those flush with cash take risk, which has its reward
- Game shows featuring poker and other forms of gambling continue to be in vogue

As we know, in the real world, markets do not stay up forever and fortunes are lost. Loss, and its accompanying bear markets, are Saturn's domain. The transition between Jupiter and Saturn could be likened to the evolution from pie-eyed optimism to hard-nosed realism. Where Jupiter is kindly and fun loving, Saturn is all business. Where Jupiter is all about ample supply,

Saturn is all about shortages. When there is abundance of supply, prices stay relatively cheap. When supply tightens, demand increases and prices go up. When Saturn is in Leo, things connected with royalty will always go up. In this category we have both gold and her cousin, black gold, or oil.

Where Saturn Goes, Trouble Follows

Saturn, the planet that diminishes all it touches, will remain in Leo until September 1, 2007. Therefore, we will see increased resentment toward the rich and highly placed. Leo is the sign of royalty, so get ready to see some crowns come tumbling down from those lofty perches. Saturn rules business, and while Saturn is in Leo, the wealthy are targets, as the "have-nots" rebel. Unfortunately, when Saturn is in this sign, people become averse to taking on risk, making venture capital less available and small businesses falter. Saturn always brings sectors that have lost touch with reality back to Earth. In the case of real estate, buyer-beware! With increasing oil and energy prices people are more worried than ever. Markets hate uncertainty.

There are silver linings in every market that we can take advantage of, though. Unlike the radical hikes in gas and oil over the past couple of years, when Jupiter and Saturn were in a challenging relationship to one another, they are now in an easy-going relationship. We can expect to see steady increases in energy throughout the cycle. While Jupiter and Saturn are in fire signs there is still money to be made, but the risk environment is greatly increased for the little guy, so be very careful. And, more than that, be smart.

- Take opportunities to purchase gold when the market turns down in March, and sell off each year in late October.
- Jupiter is strong in his own sign, Sagittarius, while Saturn is weak in Leo. Look for bargains in faraway places. There is money to be made in foreign shores. If you can afford the risk, take it.

- Tech has taken many years of retrofitting. Add more, and check hpc. Consider doing some bottom feeding.

Jupiter and Pluto

With the cost of energy skyrocketing, watch for the grim reaper of all energy forces to rise again from the ashes of Chernobyl. The nuclear industry quietly makes a comeback! With Jupiter and Pluto coming together in Sagittarius during the second half of the year, we might consider placing some of our bets on the nuclear industry as natural gas suppliers and oil supplies remain tight. The big boys have been buying up small nuclear plants. Watch for those companies that build and maintain nuclear plants to be the makers of money in the years to come.

Jupiter and Pluto are the "big boys" of our solar system. They are even more imposing now because Jupiter is in his own sign. The time is quite ripe for mergers and acquisitions. Keep your eye out for profitable small companies—like tech companies—that have been beaten up because of the times, to be gobbled up. When Jupiter and Pluto are together, deals that are made will be made in secrecy. Therefore, those who do their homework and can keep their lips sealed about what they find stand to do best

in the year ahead. Given the combined effects of the diminishing supplies of greenhouse-gas-producing oil, its ever increasing price, and Jupiter's expanding effect on radioactive Pluto, it becomes a no-brainer that the nuclear industry can only thrive in such a climate.

Everything about Pluto is extreme, from its placement at the far end of the heavens to its contrary orbit. Given that Pluto is the most secretive of planets, insider trading will be the rule, not the exception, in 2007.

A word to the wise: Get your financial house in order while Pluto is still in Sagittarius, because once Pluto enters Capricorn, debtors are in for a radical alteration that will not be pleasant! This goes doubly for the federal government.

Saturn and Neptune

Remember back in 1989, when the Berlin Wall came down and they said we had won the cold war and that communism was dead? Well, guess again. The pendulum swings both ways. This combination has long been connected with left-leaning causes. China tends to flex her muscles. With this year's contact, we may see a return of the cold war mentality, but this cold war may be economic in nature. As of this writing, China has a $90 billion trade surplus. The U.S., on the other hand, has a whopping $782.6 billion trade deficit. Unless something can be done to mitigate this imbalance, we will see our dependence on foreign goods cripple our power and effectiveness globally, as David becomes Goliath.

The wake of a Saturn and Neptune combination has been known to bring scandal that is brought about by paranoia. This aspect is known to create victims, tarnish reputations, and expose liars. We will get glimpses into the inner workings of government and what we will see will not be pretty.

One way or another, this contact is never good for business. It brings with it major bankruptcies and governmental interference, and it hurts speculators. Keep a close eye on your own debt level. Those who are free and clear stand to profit in such times. The underdog claws his way to victory when Saturn and Neptune oppose each other. Since Saturn is in Leo, it will bring shortages in energy and rising fuel prices. Saturn and Neptune have been historically tough on the seated party. It is not surprising that the abuses stemming from the McCarthy Hearings took place when these two were together in the early 1950s. The Republicans could lose the House.

The Nodes

The North Node is in Pisces, the sign associated with drugs. In recent years, we have seen the giants in the pharmaceuticals lick their wounds, from litigation to fewer drugs in the pipeline. The good news is for the young, newer pharmaceuticals, especially those involved in research and development. The bio-tech industry is very promising at this juncture. Stem cells may be among the many breakthroughs in medicine that stand to take place in 2007. Look for a lot of new jobs in North Carolina, when Castle and Cook, the developer end of Dole, breaks ground for an enormous bio-tech facility there. Energy stocks and innovation will continue to run sky-high.

The South Node has to do with draining, and its location shows where the draining will occur. In the year ahead, the South Node will traverse the sign of Virgo. One place you don't want to go to this season is the hospital. Hospitals in the U.S. will suffer greatly due to cost-cutting measures over the past ten years that

Market Tip

Necessity is the mother of invention. Look for new inventions that will cut down our dependence upon gasoline, like bio diesel. Hybrid cars will become commonplace as we try to get around the high cost of getting around.

have squeezed every cent out of the industry, leaving medical personnel shorthanded and non-profitable hospitals to close at a time when illness is on the rise.

This is going to be a tough time for health care workers and their patients. The average doctor sees a patient for less than seven minutes. Given their crushing schedule, and an aging population, health care workers may be at the brink. Overworked and under-paid, fewer will want to enter this profession, and there will be an overall malaise in the nursing and care giving industries. Look for strikes in our nation's hospitals as managed care comes head to head with healers.

The Tech Industry Drain

The South Node in Virgo will bring troubles to the tech indus-try, too, as not only support but also programming is shipped overseas. Silicon Valley is on shaky ground, as not only the tech industry but all of California (a Virgo-ruled state) may become more seismic under these conditions. We can look forward to more clouds hanging over those who are not scrupulously hon-est in doing their books. Aggressive accounting may be exposed for what it is—white-collar fraud.

2006–2007 Ingresses

For centuries, wise astrologers have drawn charts based upon the moment that the Sun enters each season. These quarterly solar beginnings are known as Ingress charts. Those who want to make their money grow can find all they need to know about the upcoming season's financial promise, or lack thereof.

Fall 2006

Worry and uncertainty brought about by high energy prices and dwindling supplies eats any gains in the economy at the begin-ning of the season. There may be a very active weather pattern headed for the East Coast and those in the east will have to pre-pare to batten down the hatches. Storm threats put pressure on the market due to mounting fears of a Katrina repeat, when oil and gas were shut out driving supplies down and costs up.

As energy prices soar, the market flattens, but we cannot hope to build a solid financial future out of fear. Avoid tech stocks in the beginning of the quarter. We might see some new bottoms with no less than seven planetary idioms in the Fourth House. Gold may go up under these circumstances. Driving costs continue to rise and with them the ability for commerce to satisfy the needs of the people. The enemy right now is the high cost of energy, as oil and gas prices close out any ability for prosperity in the marketplace.

Potential trouble in the housing market could spell trouble in the coming year. There could be a deepening slowdown in real estate as wages fail to cover the amounts projected in homes. Troubled times have brought bargains to the markets. Tough times call for stiff remedies and stiff remedies are good for distillers, in both the booze and the oil industries. Watch for the stock market to gain from an overpriced real estate market. For some reason, foreign markets look volatile and pricey. Saturn in Leo does not bode well for incumbents. The House may turn blue.

Winter 2006-07 Overview

With Neptune prominent, the story is oil and fear. We will have some very stark reminders of the damage and troubles due to ravages left behind from the hurricanes, and there is more rough sailing ahead for the Bush administration. A hearing about the Katrina disaster may be planned at this time. As long as oil prices stay at record numbers, and we produce so little of it, we are going to be forced to make some tough decisions in order to keep warm. People want government to become accountable. Gas prices have been through the roof and there is talk in many circles about rationing this highly valuable resource. With so much of our money going to rent and energy, there is less and less to go around.

Smart investors are putting their money into foreign funds. There does not seem to be any reverse of the downward cycle, not just for the overly oil dependent U.S., but for all developed countries. As long as Saturn is in Leo, the people in those countries are going to have to get used to doing without as much of the world competes for dwindling resources. The problem for the developed world is that it is very fixed in its way of handling things.

The proliferation of gambling shows on TV over the past few years has made its mark; the gambling industry has made a comeback. There is a "devil may care" attitude. Some people believe that taking risks is the only way they can get ahead in the world, but the odds are stacked in favor of the house. With Neptune in aspect with Saturn, it is easier than ever to lose one's shirt. Gamble and speculate with care.

Those in the know should keep an eye on all insider trading during the winter months. This could be a sign of renewed mergers and acquisitions. The large corporations, especially in the energy sector, have been socking away money for a while. This year they will be in a purchasing mood, and keen investors can profit in a rough market.

There are more than four planets in the sign of Sagittarius. When prominent, this constellation raises the religious zeal in fanatics everywhere. Terrorism can be a real threat this holiday season and right on into January. The government and the people of the U.S. should be prepared to take appropriate measures to ensure safety against potential terrorist strikes. Local governments should be especially sure that they know what to do in a disaster.

Spring 2007 Overview

This spring echoes words from an old Rolling Stones' song, "You can't always get what you want." The days when dollars burned a hole in our pockets are gone. Debt and bankruptcy is on the rise, and those who have lived on credit are the hardest hit. Look for a rise in foreclosures as high energy costs crash head-on with rising interest rates.

Dark clouds always have a silver lining, though. Look for growth in businesses that help others to reorganize debt. This includes everything from auctioneering to the legal industry. We'll see a lot more consolidating in the communications industry.

This may not be an easy season for women. The star known as the Widowmaker rises over Washington at the first moment of spring. When women suffer, it throws a shadow on retail and other household industries. Oil continues to dominate conversations as prices continue to rise. Casualties may continue to plague our armed forces abroad. With a dwindling supply of domestic oil and natural gas, and Jupiter heading toward Pluto, smart investors are getting ready to watch the nuclear industry make a comeback. Look for profits in those companies that service and provide safety equipment to this industry. As long as we remain dependent upon foreign oil, the rest of the economy will falter. When there is uncertainty about the future, the market reacts accordingly.

"Get Rich" schemes abound. Some folks can charm the birds from the trees during this combination; make certain they don't charm you out of your wallet. Gambling continues to be a growth industry as more folks dream of quick riches. Lotteries and all forms of online betting companies make money.

Worry about the potential sudden rise in contagious illnesses borders on paranoia. In this climate, we need to take proper precautions. Investors should always be mindful that what goes up must come down, and vice versa. Despite some darlings, like Google, the tech sector as a whole has been beaten to a pulp since the turn of the millennium. No sector stays down forever. While it may not be time yet to invest in tech heavily, there are many undervalued tech and communications stocks out there right now. This is the time to do our homework.

Again, this is not the time to follow the pack. Only the strong survive in this climate, and this is doubly true in technology. Rewards come to those who know how to copy the big boys, and wise traders keep abreast of insider trading.

Look for growth in industries that serve to investigate people, and for colleges to begin to offer majors in spying. But all industries that run checks on individuals will stand to gain in this season of espionage.

Summer 2007 Ingress

Worries about more gas shortages and high gas prices persist. If we cannot curb our desires and start living within our means, we will be our own worst enemy.

Oil and gas will continue to dominate the market, while the Federal Reserve will keep raising rates. Markets are based upon supply and demand. With demand high and supply low, this can only spell trouble for the little guy. Don't pin your expectations on energy prices coming down. When uncertainty runs the market, it can only adjust downward. But oddly enough, despite shortages looming and the fear of higher gas prices, people are out driving. Perhaps it is because they feel it might be their last chance. We want to go places, but we need to have the ability to pay for it.

Global nerves are frayed and the U.S. may have become a credit problem. International lenders, like China, may use this as leverage against our better interests. Watch for trouble on the high seas. The costs associated with rebuilding the damaged Gulf Region while also fighting a foreign war may drive the dollar down.

Where's the Silver Lining?

With Jupiter present in the Third House of the Ingress chart, the wise will keep a close eye on mergers and acquisitions. One can always make some money on companies about to be bought. Do your homework.

- Tech companies have taken a beating in the past decade, and many good tech and communications companies are selling well below their actual value. Look for these companies to be swallowed up by bigger fish.
- It is still a good time to be a pharmaceutical company. Look for new breakthroughs in this industry, although there may be more incidents of miracle drugs linked to death.
- The health care industry is in trouble. Americans are paying through the roof for medical coverage. The cost of caring for an aging population may be highlighted this season.
- We could see some ease in the strains on trucking. The shipping industry will thrive despite rising fuel costs, perhaps brought about by innovation.
- The sectors that shine are nuclear and security.
- Insurance, private surveillance companies, high tech identification companies, and all manner of spyware will be doing well in the third quarter of 2007. Unfortunately, this country will continue to have trouble in the realm of diplomacy.
- Our trading partners may change their minds about taking our money. Look for questions about the long-term bond market.

Market Watch

October 2006

The market is still jittery, but a collective sigh of relief makes traders cautiously optimistic the second half of the month. Semi-conductors are up, and tech companies show promise. The market is still driven by the high cost of getting around and fears about a sluggish economy spawn rumors that thwart the housing market.

November 2006

As more vie for diminishing commodities, like oil and other raw materials, tensions between nations mount. This is hard on the market, especially around November 8–9. Keep your friends close by and keep your enemies even closer. Look for mergers and acquisitions to lead the way as the big boys make their plays. Look for tech and energy to come into play. Resume signing important documents after November 20, when Mercury turns direct.

December 2006

We may see a rise in religious fanaticism. Higher prices combine with terrorist threats to keep shoppers at home more than in Christmas seasons past. Look for Internet businesses and energy to be the big winner this month

January 2007

The market reacts negatively to the news of the growing deficit, and Americans will have to learn to live within their means. Look for large swings as volatility rules when Mars conjoins Pluto in mid-January. The market bounces back around January 24. Those who are in the know keep one eye always open. The big boys are hungry, and good opportunities follow their lead. Mergers and acquisitions are the name of the day in the money rich oil companies.

February 2007

Market thrives and we think everything is coming up roses thanks to Mars in Capricorn. Get all papers signed by Valentine's Day or watch those agreements turn to dust, and postpone major decisions until next month. Regardless of Mercury's backwards drift, this may be the best month of the quarter. Consider locking in your profits now. The rising oil prices will damper gains but cause weakness to set into the market after this time. Foreign stocks will do best during this cycle.

March 2007

Lots of action and with it, lots of uncertainty. The market hates uncertainty. Gas may move up this month, putting a drain on stocks. For best results, position yourself defensively. Look for gold to rise on global concerns. Jitters may also arise in the currency market. For the most part, with Mars heading toward Neptune oil stocks are on fire. In general, look for stocks to sour. Pluto turns retrograde, dragging business down with it.

April 2007

Look for the market to sour on news that Big Brother is going to be keeping a closer eye on business. Inflationary effects do not sit well with investors. Global tensions mount, taking the wind out of the sails of the electronic markets. Jupiter turns retrograde on April 6. Those heavily invested abroad may want to take profits. Bankruptcies and foreclosures are on the rise. As the market readies for adjustment, position yourself accordingly

May 2007

Global tensions mount, taking the wind out of the equities markets. Those heavily invested abroad may rethink the risks. Bankruptcies and foreclosures are rising. Trouble looms in the shipping industry midmonth. Oil controls it all. New cures bring smiles to those invested in bio-techs and distilleries. High energy and commodity prices take their toll. Earnings are nowhere near projected, while bankruptcies are on the rise. The growing divide in income levels between the "haves" and "have-nots" is hard on the little guy.

June 2007

Global tensions mount. High gas prices make telecommuting a more viable choice for the wise company. With shortages looming, everybody feels the pinch. By the time the check comes we have already spent it. We may hear of trouble to our troops abroad as the nuclear card seems to be ever in the news. Get important papers signed by midmonth, when Mercury makes words not worth the paper they are written on. Positive breakthroughs and some surprise good news in tech lifts the markets toward the end of month.

July 2007

This is a worrisome month. Take proper precautions. Lay off making any commitments, especially in writing, until after the 10th. High costs of gas and global tension dog us as we embark on our Independence Day holiday. There is some good news at the end of the cycle from new-home-building numbers (mostly in the south), which are keeping the slowing real-estate market alive. Earnings disappoint investors in the third week. We can't always get what we want. Look for fear of terrorism and uncertainty about energy to spill into the marketplace around July 25.

August 2007

The mounting trade imbalance and piling debts will come home to haunt the markets in August. The energy sector thrives, as driving season is in full swing. With so many planets in Leo, could there be any doubt that gold will be heading higher? One needs fortitude in such a market. Consumers question each purchase with Venus retrograde. Markets turn inward as memories of hurricanes past linger. Pluto is at the eclipse point. Taking risks may not guarantee rewards at this time.

September 2007

It is this month that has always proven to be the toughest month on the market and this year is no exception. Caution is the watchword. Saturn enters Virgo on September 2 and brings trouble to the battered technology sector. Trading partners are getting impatient. Energy brings on the speculators in force. Look for gold to climb and stocks to drop. The brave can count their money at the end of the month.

About the Author

Dorothy J. Kovach is a practicing astrologer, writer, and timing expert based in northern California. She acts as a consultant to both businesses and individuals interested in finding the very optimum time to start projects for successful outcomes. She advises on the best timing for those wanting success in their business and private endeavors. Her specialty is horary astrology, the branch of astrology that answers specific questions. She has been writing the economic outlook for the Llewellyn Moon Sign Book since 2001. She is best known for having called the end of the bull market to the year and the month, five years in advance. Her clients hail from around the globe. To contact Dorothy via Internet, go to Dorothy@worldastrology.net and her Web site: www.worldastrology.net

Your Cosmic Planting Guide

By Maggie Anderson

One of the earliest uses of astrology was to help categorize the natural world. Since ancient times, each known plant species has been associated with a particular planet or luminary. Some plants were assigned according to their affinity with a quality or expression of a planet. For instance, those with a pleasing fragrance were given to Venus, which governs beauty and lovely aromas.

The cosmic associations of herbs were determined according to their ability to cure ailments or assist the functioning of particular parts of the human body. The names of some herbs reflect their healing specialty. Boneset, an herb that was said to speed healing of broken bones, was identified with Saturn because this planet is the astrological ruler of the skeletal system.

Other botanicals were assigned to a heavenly body because of color or the utility of their seed heads. The golden sunflower reflects the qualities of the Sun in its shape, size, and color, and so it belongs to the Sun. The Moon governs the tides, and therefore most water plants are naturally part of the Moon's domain.

This system of planetary governance was an evolving science sometimes complicated by the assignation of a co-ruler. Astrologer-physicians frequently debated these rulerships. In 1643 Nicholas Culpeper wrote of plantain:

> "It is true, Mizaldus and others, yea, almost all astrological physicians, hold this to be an herb of Mars, because it cures the disease of the head and privities, which are under the houses of Mars, Aries, and Scorpio: the truth is, it is under the command of Venus, and cure the head by antipathy to Mars, and the privities by sympathy to Venus."

Another method used to classify the plant world related to particular qualities of the planets that were well understood by the public at the time. Plants that tolerate shade were given to Saturn because it represented limitation and restriction. Mercury, a mutable (changeable) planet, is ruler or coruler of variegated plants.

In their strong desire to live in harmony with the natural cycles of the Earth, our ancestors planted and harvested not only by the phases of the Moon but also by the planetary ruler of particular plants. Plants ruled by Jupiter would be picked during a Jupiter day and hour and various concoctions from the plant made when Jupiter was strong (astrologically prominent).

As you consider what plants to want in your garden, look first to the traditional ruler of your Sun sign (in the following chart) because it's likely that you will be drawn to these. Or perhaps you'd like to manifest all planetary possibilities on your little piece of Earth and plant at least one specimen each for the Sun, Moon, and seven planets. (Note that the modern planets Uranus, Neptune, and Pluto are not included in this system.)

Plants of the Sun

The Sun governs the will and ego in humans, and plants associated with Old Sol are seldom accused of being modest. Those

Zodiac Sign	Planet Ruler
Aries and Scorpio	Mars
Taurus and Libra	Venus
Gemini and Virgo	Mercury
Cancer	Moon
Leo	Sun
Sagittarius and Pisces	Jupiter
Capricorn and Aquarius	Saturn

that cannot stand out in a crowd need not apply to the Sun for rulership, for the Sun has authority: it governs the rhythms of our days. Sun-ruled plants display such grand exuberance and vitality that they must sit at the center of our gardens.

Colors of the Sun—bright yellow and orange, and the deeper colors of gold, honey, sand, and sienna, like the colors you notice streaking across the sky at sunset—reflect its core energy and dynamism. Fortunately, nature has replicated these colors in many forms.

Herbs that belong to the Sun strengthen the heart and increase circulation and metabolism. Foxglove, which contains digitalis, is now a modern standard in treating heart disease. The circulatory systems of our ancestors were kept in good condition through massages with rose oil. The Sun is also connected with human fertility and some scented geraniums were believed to increase and support fertility.

Sunny botanicals are usually larger and more showy than those ruled by other planets. They need more space around them in order to stand out from the crowd. Above all, they need to be rooted in a place where their owners and other people can admire them.

The zodiac sign of Leo is governed by the Sun and both have connections with drama and the theatre. If they could speak, plants of the Sun would ask you to add a bit of stagecraft to your gardening skills. A sunflower does stand out better when in front of red barn board, and a lemony Honey Locust can upstage a simple pine tree for at least three acts of our four-season entertainment.

Solar gardens declare who we are as individuals. Take a walk in mid-July and note the unique botanical statements of your neighbors. Whether they garden on a rooftop in New York or on acreage in Minnesota, each planting will tell you something special about the gardener that he or she wants you to know.

Consider which part of your personality you wish to share with the world. A stand of merry daffodils in your front yard tells those passing by, "I'm happy and friendly and I hope these flowers brighten your day! Even if your space is limited, one large amaryllis placed in a prominent spot in your apartment window becomes a small Sun Garden that says, "I'm beautifully in touch with the natural world and hope that you can be too!" The table below lists some trees, shrubs, and plants that are Sun-ruled.

Trees	Shrubs	Flowers	Herbs
Gold medalion	Brachychiton	Black-eyed Susan	Eyebright
Larch	English yew	California poppy	Burnet
Sunburst "honey locust"	Spiraea	Cup-of-gold	St. John's wort
Western red cedar	Vicary golden privet	Morning glory	Wild angelica

Plants of the Moon

Our nearest and dearest cosmic companion is the Moon. As ruler of the night, her light is reflected after her heavenly partner sets in the west. Luna's monthly waxing and waning controls the rhythms of biological life on Earth and all watery elements, like the tides. Astrologically, the Moon rules our inner life of the emotions.

The Moon regulates the everyday affairs of individuals and groups. She also represents the public or common people and the private domains of the public—our homes. The Moon invites us to come home again in the evening and reflect on the events of our days. As keepers of the household, mothers are also associated with the Moon. Whether Mom is there in person or not, her spirit remains in the small ways we nurture others and ourselves.

The Moon governs the tides, water, and other liquids. All plants that thrive in the water or marshes, as well as water gardens and those with small fountains and streams, are assigned to Luna. However, since the light of the Moon is reflected, it is not uncommon for its plants to have a coruler. Another expression of Moon gardens is flowers that open in the evening, such as evening primrose and nicotiana.

The wild wall-flower, a Moon-ruled herb, "helps the hardness and pains of the mother." Clary, another herb with lunar connections, helps to expel afterbirth. A mother might also apply clary to her child's skin to draw out a tiny sliver.

Colors of the Moon include the colors of the Moon itself: white, silver, pearl, silvery gray, and white-gray; and colors of the sea that it governs: aqua, silvery green, blue, turquoise, and yellow-green. Many Moon plants have a luminous or iridescent quality that mimics the Moon's reflective quality.

Gardens of the Moon usually contain at least a few old-fashioned plants. Your own Moon Garden might center around plants grown from seeds that have been passed down in your family for many generations. Even if your great-grandpa didn't leave you prized zucchini seeds as an inheritance, the Seed Savers Exchange (http://www.seedsavers.org/Home.asp) in Decorah, Iowa, will be happy to assist you (and they have more than one variety of zucchini).

Your Moon Garden will preserve heritage variety plants by growing older varieties of seeds out regularly. By doing this, you are following the Moon's tradition of valuing our ancestral roots.

The Moon is most strongly reflected in English cottage gardens, cutting gardens, and kitchen gardens. These gardens provide blooms, herbs, and produce that can be brought into our living quarters for decoration or become part of the evening meal. They all have a certain utility and a small but important part to play in our daily lives. Above all, these plants revive memories of our childhoods and those who nurtured us.

Trees	Shrubs	Flowers	Herbs
Coconut palm	Aronia	Dusty miller	Motherwort
Poplar	Elderberry	Cicely	Clary
Water oak	Euonymus	Narcissus	Water cress
Weeping silver pear tree	Wild rose	Money plant	Red raspberry leaf
Willow	Sea buckthorn	Water lily	Water chestnuts

Plants of Mercury

Mercury never moves far from the Sun. It sometimes acts as Old Sol's messenger, preceding him in a stately procession through the zodiac. At other times, it trails behind, acting more as a servant. Both of these cosmic jobs make good use of Mercury's flexibility and skillful adaptation to its environment. This planet governs two "dual" signs of the zodiac, Gemini and Virgo. It is the natural ruler of all forms of communication, children, and youth.

Mercury's herbs strengthen the parts of the body connected with Gemini and Virgo: the lungs, shoulders, arms, hands, the nervous and digestive systems, and the mind. They are used to cure weakness in the lungs, stomach, and bowels, and some airborne conditions, such as hay fever.

This very adaptable planet governs growing things that acclimate easily to their surroundings. Mercury-ruled plants tolerate a variety of growing conditions, with some doing well in either sun or shade and a wide variety of soil conditions. You can easily transplant them to a new spot in the garden, or dig them up and take them with you to a new home.

Plants associated with Mercury often display two or more distinct colors. They can be variegated or striped, or contain flowers that turn an interesting succession of colors. The climbing rose, Joseph's Coat, with its magnificent display of yellow, orange, and red blooms, belongs to Mercury with Venus as its co-ruler. Mercury rules patterns—stripes, spots, and checkers—so the guineahen flower (checkered lily) belongs to Mercury, along with the striped squill.

A Mercury Garden is one that adapts easily to its surroundings, but it also adapts its surroundings to the garden. It contains many visual surprises and is imaginative and playful. You might see a bean teepee for the little ones to hide under, an autumn corn maze, or a vine-covered swing set in the middle of a stand of wild grasses. Mercury is a good recycler too: an old bicycle holding a market basket of petunias, or a child's riding toy car turned flower container, express this planet's lighthearted nature.

If you decide to bring Mercury's best qualities into your garden, consider establishing at least two separate areas—and maybe more! There may be one place that delights your senses, that is filled with botanical and man-made surprises and curiosities. Its plants would make subtle visual statements and invite stroking. The other could be a place to calm your nervous system at the end of a busy day. The calming garden corner might feature a bench set so that you

can face east in the morning and west at dusk for your daily meditation. Or perhaps you would prefer a rocking chair or gliding chair.

Your Mercury Garden will remind you daily to remain young at heart, flexible, and imaginative. It will call out to your friends and neighbors, to cats and dogs, and especially to small children, who may wander in and out, delighted at your Mercury Garden.

Trees	Shrubs	Flowers	Herbs
Common hackberry	False cypress	Azalea	Caraway
Desert willow	Germanders	Gayfeather	Catmint
Mulberry	Siberian peashrub	Lily of the valley	Fennel
Pomegranate	Smoke tree	Santolina	Horehound

Plants of Venus

The aptly named Venus de Milo is a show-stopper, even in her old age. This planet of balance and harmony sets the standard for beauty in every culture on the globe. Venus governs fruit trees, including that tempting apple tree in the Garden of Eden, and Venus-ruled flowers, like the lilac, perfume the air, sometimes entire neighborhoods, in springtime.

Venus' colors are subtle, pale pastels of every hue. Pink roses naturally belong to her, and so do light blues, greens, and purples. Her colors are lightly brushed on flowers like rouge on a pretty cheek. (Is it any wonder these tones invite pollination?) Whenever you notice butterflies or hummingbirds kissing a plant in your garden, assume that the specimen belongs to Venus.

Since Venus is the astrological ruler of love, baby's breath and every other stalk in bridal bouquets are in her domain, and any bloom that a young maid tucks behind her ear to invite romance falls under the guardianship of Venus. The same is true of flowers given to a true love on Valentine's Day, or the single rose on a table set for two.

As the natural ruler of young women, Venus is associated with herbs that are used for perfumes or in potpourris, like delicate violets, lemon balm, and sweet woodruff. Others, such as chamomile and ginger, promote health during pregnancy.

There are several approaches to establishing a Venusian Garden. You can go for the romance of flowers in bloom or perhaps a butterfly garden. After love finds you there, you may also want to engage the down-to-earth, practical qualities of Venus and plant a few fruit trees and shrubs. When you share a homemade cherry pie made from the fruits of your own tree with your sweetheart, Venus will send her ambassador, Cupid, to host the party for two.

There are ways to combine romance and utility for a lovely Venus Garden. One way is to construct a grape arbor with a garden bench for two. Another is to plant a bed of Venus herbs in a "Lover's Knot" pattern. Let your romantic imagination be your guide. Of course, if you already have someone in your life to hold hands with, you will want to plant his or her favorites there too, as a sign of your affection. See the following table for suggestions about botanicals to include in your Venus Garden.

Trees	Shrubs	Flowers	Herbs
Apple, peach, pear, cherry	Currant	Candytuft	Selfheal
Birch	Gooseberries	Carnation	Soapwort
Black alder	Flowering quince	Gaillardia	Lady's bedstraw
Dwarf elder	Jostaberries	Yarrow	Lady's mantle
White poplar	Roses	Tansy	Violets

Plants of Mars

"Ouch! That hurt!" is a common complaint when gardeners are around Mars-ruled plants, because they seem to reach out and attack us with thorns and other prickly parts. Blackberry bushes and stinging nettles are among those plants governed by Mars, and so is the peppery-hot, eye-watering Jalapeño.

Why does the botanical world contain these difficult expressions of Martian forms anyway? One reason is that our food would be very dull without them. Like the red light at a street crossing or red flag waved in front of a bull, Mars' red color produces a bit of excitement. Its flowers and fruit run from the brightest shades of fuchsia to the deepest purple-black. It's their less desirable qualities that help them survive in difficult environments. Animals are unlikely to graze very far into a bramble patch or munch on a bed of wild nettles. Many herbs assigned to Mars produce heat in the body and are favorites of humans only. Ginger, mustard, leeks, and chives are but a few Martian edibles. Bitter, sharp-tasting vegetables, such as onions and radishes, are members of this plant family.

Astrologers associate Mars with taking risks. To take a risk is to invite change, and change sometimes produces hostility from others happy with the status quo. Perhaps Martian plants developed some of their assertiveness in self-defense. How many wild thistles have been allowed to grow in a well-tended garden because it just hurts too much to pull them?

Not to take chances invites stagnation and boredom. If we ignore the scorn of neighbors and allow a few thistles to grow in our gardens, they eventually attract hummingbirds, a welcome novelty. Like sticky personal situations, Mars and its plants occasionally demand that we do something bold in order to reach the good things, like wade through brambles for a handful of luscious red raspberries.

Some gardeners feel we'd be better off with only user-friendly plants, but we need Martian plants to add spice to our lives. Flowers of incredible beauty grow on the stems of thorns. The rose is a lovely metaphor for the reality of love, and a perfect expression of committed relationships. A thorny Martian stem holds up the beauty of Venus. In the botanical world, Venus and Mars seem to have worked out their problems well enough. Beautiful partnerships can be the result of working through difficult times.

Trees	Shrubs	Flowers	Herbs
Hackberry	Japanese maple	Pincushion	Dame's rocket
Hercules club	Bittersweet	Red hot pokers	Hedgeweed
Mexican palo verde	Blackberries, raspberries	Salvia	Red valerian
Tamarisk	Firethorn	Snapdragon	Wild onions
Saguaro cactys	Myrtle	Watsonia	Wild garlic

Plants of Jupiter

Jupiter is one of the social planets. It has affinity with our life in community and the common ground we share, including libraries, city halls, and universities. In countries with a ruling monarchy, Jupiter's influence may be seen in the formal gardens near the homes of royalty. In lands of democracy, officials seem cosmically inspired to plant Jupiter's oak and chestnut trees in public parks and around government buildings.

The plants associated with Jupiter always make a grand public display. They are big and colorful and they demand to be noticed. Like royalty, these plants are often clothed in purple, blue, yellow, and sea green. Who can ignore a group of flowering canna bulbs or a blooming redbud tree?

Jupiter is the eternal optimist. Its plants never become discouraged, even when growing conditions are less than ideal. They are extremely hardy, able to survive a crowded urban environment and even inclement weather. If you've seen a bed of tulips persist through a late spring snow, you can understand how Jupiter's hope and enthusiasm overcomes many obstacles.

Our faith communities come under the domain of Jupiter, so those heavenly floral arrangements that accompany worship services are also connected with this planet. The flowers that adorn our altars—gladiolas, dahlias, and passionflowers—have an affinity with this planet. No rite of passage, like a wedding or funeral, would be complete without an exhibit of Jupiter's flowers.

Jupiter is also the most bountiful of planets. Annuals that continue to produce flowers all summer, such as petunias, belong to Jupiter, as do many species of evergreens. Out of this bounty comes great generosity and kindness toward others. This planet assures we'll always have enough daisies and delphiniums to share with friends and family.

Herbalists are familiar with the beneficial effects of Jupiter's herbs. In the body, this planet governs the liver and lungs. Its herbs are considered beneficial to these organs and to all diseases that stem from corruption of the blood. Liverwort, lungwort, and selfheal are three Jupiter herbs used to promote healing of these kinds of infirmity. Plants of borage, sage, and chervil bring Jupiter's beneficial influence into our herb beds and our salads.

Jupiter is known as the Great Benefic, the planet of extreme good fortune. Where Saturn sets limits and boundaries, Jupiter expands them. It invites us to go beyond our limits, to stretch and expand our horizons by doing something entirely different. Jupiter insists that we don't become rigid or stale. Gardeners who experiment by planting even a few new varieties of plants each year are paying homage to Jupiter. Those who share their harvest with others are living in accordance with the highest principles of this bountiful planet.

Trees	Shrubs	Flowers	Herbs
Crabapple	Juniper	Columbine	Lungwort
Cedar	Red twig dogwood	Globe thistle	Selfheal
Redbud	Spicebush	Heliotrope	Speedwell
Scarlet maple	Viburum	Iris	Purple loosetrife

Plants of Saturn

Saturn plants grow in woodlands, obscure valleys, high elevations, and abandoned, neglected locations unfit for human habitation.

Most shade-loving and mountain wildflowers fall under the dominion of Saturn. Wispy, pale flowers that bloom for only a short time distinguish Saturn-ruled plants. Solomon's seal, hosta, and members of the nightshade family fall under the dominion of Saturn. These wildflowers grow where nothing else will, but deliberately establishing them in a garden can be a challenge. Like good habits, Saturn's plants are difficult to stabilize but easy to maintain once they've become part of the daily landscape.

In astrology, Saturn signifies mountains and rocks. Plant forms that can take hold in the small crevices of a rock wall or thrive in rock gardens, such as carpet bugle and alpine poppies, belong to Saturn. Saturn-governed herbs include sage, thyme, and comfrey. Many Saturn plants, such as mullein and amaranth, produce unusually large numbers of seeds. Other Saturn plants spread quickly through shallow root systems. Gardeners fear the very Saturn Creeping Charlie as much as astrologers dread a Saturn transit.

Gardeners can enhance their horticultural experience through Saturn in several ways. The first is to choose plants assigned to Saturn for shade, rock walls, and high elevations where other plants won't thrive. Its energies are also well used during all forms of cultivation by weeding out "volunteer" Saturn plants.

This planet encourages us to maintain good boundaries by blurring our tidy rows of green beans with pigweed. There's no guarantee that understanding Saturn will make garden chores more fun; however, gardeners who work in harmony with Saturn can embrace its energy when they plan their garden and with each tug on a weed.

Saturn is known to astrologers as the Great Teacher, the planet of karma. Saturn's cosmic job is to invite humans to take control of their lives through self-discipline and responsible conduct. If we don't take up the challenge, Saturn introduces challenges that won't go away until order is restored.

Gardeners who lose control of their gardens reap an instant weedy karma. Saturn fills bare, mulch-free spots with its own choice of plant life, one much less attractive than the pictures in seed catalogs. Humans who take charge of their own lives don't have to worry about someone else doing it. A garden gone to weeds is a metaphor for a life become unproductive due to lack of discipline and control. A well-tended garden is a real-life representation of a responsible and productive life.

Trees	Shrubs	Flowers	Herbs
Balsam fir	Canada hemlock	Brunnera	Goat's beard
Cedar	Boxwood	Coral bells	Gentian
Cyprus	Tree ferns	Glory of the snow	Stonecress
Katsura	Sweet bay	Hellebore	Maserwort
Tamarisk	Privet	Sulphur flower	Sandwort

About the Author

Maggie Anderson makes her home in Mount Vernon, Iowa, where she maintains a full-time astrological practice and teaches astrology. Maggie specializes in "all affairs of the heart," which allows her to utilize her experience as a family therapist when counseling clients. You can see more of her writings on her Web site: www.astromaggie.com.

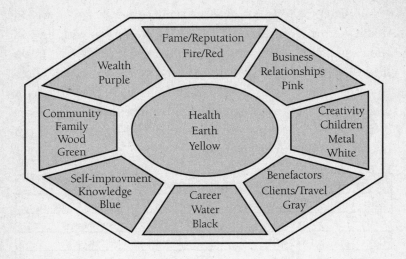

Fame/Reputation
Fire/Red

Wealth
Purple

Business
Relationships
Pink

Community
Family
Wood
Green

Health
Earth
Yellow

Creativity
Children
Metal
White

Self-improvment
Knowledge
Blue

Career
Water
Black

Benefactors
Clients/Travel
Gray

Feng Shui for the Garden

By Christine Ayres

Feng Shui Basics

> *The water is clear, the trees are lush,*
> *the wind is mild, the Sun is bright.*
> —From an OLD CHINESE POEM

Feng shui, which translates "wind/water," is one of the oldest forms of garden cultivation in the world. Legend has it that this name for the art of placement came from an old Chinese poem about the attributes of the ideal place to live.

Feng shui is a technology to insure that we live in harmonious relationship with our environment. This is especially true when we apply it to the garden. Feng shui can be used in the garden to improve the general flow and balance, which reflects back to our own well being, and also to unblock, enhance, and uplift particular life areas, such as health, wealth, and career.

Garden Bagua Energy Map

"Ba" means eight and "gua" is section or area. This octagonal pattern is a time-honored guide to how energy lays out in a space. Let's take a quick trip around the bagua and define these life areas just a bit more. This will help when deciding plant colors and elements as we continue below.

The far left corner, extending into the center of the garden, is the "gua" (area/section) for Wealth and Abundance. Moving in a clockwise direction, the next gua is Fame. This relates to your face to the world and how you wish to be seen by others, as well as the energy of being recognized for who you are. The far right gua is that of Relationship. This is the love relationship with a spouse, partner, or boyfriend/girlfriend. Continuing our journey around the bagua, we have the gua for Children and Creativity. This is creative love and can manifest as children or can be expressed as artistic endeavors, creating a business, or anything tapping into creativity. Next is Benefactors, or helpful people, in life. These are friends and mentors, and extend into all realms of creation including angels. As we move along the front line of the bagua, we come to Career. This represents your life's work or dharma. Knowledge is the near left section and is twofold in its energy. One aspect is that of education and learning. The other aspect is that of spiritual growth and development. This will make for some interesting garden enhancements as we move along. The next gua is Family. The feng shui definition of this area is mothers, fathers, brothers, and sisters. Last, and certainly not least, is the center gua for Health. All aspects of health can be addressed in the center area, the core of the bagua. It is the balance point of the bagua.

Our first step in feng shui for the garden is the correct placement of the bagua energy map to your lawn or garden. Lay the bagua over a bird's-eye view sketch of the area under consideration. The front edge of the bagua aligns with the front boundary of your yard or garden. That is, the line indicating Knowledge, Career, and Benefactors will be where you enter the area.

Many people have both front and rear yards. This provides a few choices in how to use the bagua. If the front and back yard are entirely separate, then there are two separate energy grids, or baguas, to enhance and uplift life in a feng shui way. This is especially true if there is a fence dividing the front from the back yard. If side yards link the front and back areas, then one big bagua will cover the entire space. That is, the front line of Knowledge/Career/Benefactors will be at the front property line. It is important to note the life areas designated in the bagua energy map are not just corners; they are guas that meet in the center Health gua.

Feng Shui Garden Tools

Now that we know where these areas are, the next step is to decide what kind of chi or energy is desired in each. There are feng shui tools to seed specific energies in the garden.

Stability

Is your relationship a bit shaky? Are your finances uncertain? Then a feng shui garden enhancement for stability would be in order. This consists of placing heavy objects, such as large rocks, heavy garden statuary, or a garden structure, in the shaky area of the bagua. A big, heavy bench can ground the chi in any area.

Movement

Movement is used to address life areas that are stuck or stagnant. If your career seems to be on hold, then using a movement cure, such as a windsock, whirligig, or flag, can tickle the chi in the Career gua. Planting ornamental grasses or trees that move in the wind, such as aspens, can cure the stagnation of a property situated in a cul-de-sac.

Sound

Wind chimes will also draw attention and bring life to an area that needs some uplift through the agency of sound. Hang a chime in the Benefactors area of the garden to call in help and support. The sound of moving water is a great feng shui enhancement to calm or lift your spirits.

Light

Bringing light into the garden can literally bring an area of your life out of shadow. For example, if you're not sure what is going on with a family member, bring the issue out by placing light in the Family gua. This can be a torch or any kind of outdoor lighting. Reflected light in mirrors, ponds, and fountains are wonderful ways to incorporate light. Thinning dense foliage and clearing out debris will also allow more sunlight into the garden.

Bamboo

Bamboo is the powerful, traditional feng shui cure that can be used in any area of the garden. If you can't decide what to use in a particular area, use bamboo. You can't go wrong. Its secret is that it is a hollow tube that channels earth energy up and out into the garden. There are many types of bamboo suitable for different planting areas.

Symbols

Symbols are a unique feng shui tool for the garden because they have strong, personal resonances within the psyche and can be used to great effect. Select your symbols according to your personal traditions. You can utilize simple yet strong symbols such as hearts in the Relationship Gua, a Sun in the Fame area, or a statue of Buddha or St. Francis in the Knowledge area of the garden.

Color

Color is easy and fun to use in the garden and always uplifts chi. This can be done with foliage, blossoms, or objects. Red or rainbows can both be used almost everywhere for a big punch of chi. Feng shui suggests specific colors for each area:

Wealth	Purple, red, gold
Fame	Red, orange
Relationship	Pink, white, red
Children/Creativity	White, silver
Benefactors	Gray, white
Career	Black, gray, blue
Knowledge	Bue, green
Family	Green, blue
Health	Yellow, earth tones

Life Force

Life force encompasses all of your plant material, birds, fish in ponds, even healthy pets. Placing a bird feeder or birdbath will bring the charming chi of birds to enliven your garden. Fish ponds are fantastic feng shui and are best used in Wealth or Career guas. Even your healthy pets embody life energy and loving chi.

Elemental Harmony and Balance

For flow and harmony in the garden, a key factor is the balance of the five feng shui elements of wood, water, fire, earth, and metal. You can create a perfect balance by incorporating all of these in some form into the yard. Each element has a color and a shape associated with it, which creates more possibilities for its use in the garden.

Element	Color	Shape	Manifestation
Wood	Green	Columnar	Trees, shrubs, plant material
Fire	Red	Triangular	Fire pits, barbecues, torches
Earth	Yellow	Rectangular	Ceramic pots, stone pathways/patios
Metal	White	Round	Metal sculpture, wind chimes
Water	Black	Irregular	Fountains, pools, birdbaths

For example, if you are lacking the metal element, plant shrubs with round, white blossoms like the common snowball or hydrangea. The best location for metal is the Children/Creativity area of the garden. A solution for a lack of fire is planting a triangular shaped evergreen. The ideal spot for this is in the Fame gua of the garden.

Use the element of water to promote financial abundance in the wealth gua. Water features flowing out of this gua toward the home promote cash flow, as water symbolizes money.

A great way to support good health is to use the earth element in the center of your garden. This could be anything from a patio to a large terracotta pot planted with healthful herbs. Create a healthy heart to your garden space that draws you in to linger there.

Another consideration when using the five elements is that they each have distinctive qualities of chi. You can promote a particular energy by using the corresponding element. Generally speaking these are:

Wood	Upward growth and movement
Fire	Expansion and uplift
Earth	Stability and reliability
Metal	Contraction and condensation
Water	Fluidity and movement

For example, if your life feels a bit out of control, you could benefit from giving your garden more of the earth and metal elements. This would create both grounding and calming effects. If you have difficulty moving ahead in life, then fire, wood, and water would all be beneficial. Use the element chart above for quick reference.

Cycles of the Elements

There are two ways the five elements interact: the Creative Cycle and the Destructive Cycle. The Creative Cycle depicts how elements are created from each other:

- Water feeds wood, wood feeds fire, fire creates earth (think of ashes), out of earth comes metal, and metal precipitates water (picture beads of water on a metal container).

As depicted in the bagua, the home of water is in Career. Therefore, one way to support career chi would be to place an irregularly-shaped pond there along with a metal sculpture, thus combining water and the element that produces water (metal) in the Career qua. However, do take care in placing the elements. For example, water is not desirable in the Fame area, as water here would put out the fire of fame and dampen your reputation.

The other relationship of the elements is seen in the Destructive Cycle. The Destructive Cycle depicts how elements destroy each other:

- Water puts out fire, fire melts metal, metal burns wood, wood diminishes earth (think of a tree drawing nourishment through roots in earth), and earth obstructs water (like an earthen dam holding water back).

When there is an overabundance of a particular element, the Destructive Cycle demonstrates how the elements can diminish each other. How is this cycle of the elements useful in the garden? Perhaps you live in a wooded area and do not want to cut any trees on your property. Trees represent the wood element, of which you would have an overabundance. To bring things into balance, introduce more of the fire element by introducing more red plant material such as coleus, spirea, heather, or ribes. If you have a swimming pool or large pond that dominates your garden, bring harmony to the space with the addition of large terracotta pots (nine is a great number) planted with yellow or red flowers.

Structure and Direction

Paths, gates, and bridges give a garden structure and direction and add coherence and purpose to the space. Paths direct chi flow to specific areas. Consider which element to use for your pathways, such as gravel (earth) or wood chips. Have your garden paths mirror the natural flow of chi, which is like a meandering stream. Garden gates and arches make strong "mouths" of chi to inhale vitality and life into the garden. They also can set apart areas of the garden where chi can gather. To create a feeling of sanctuary and of crossing into another dimension in your garden, use a decorative bridge or traditional Moon gate.

Specialty Feng Shui Gardens

A way to unleash your creativity in the garden and provide super support for a particular life area is to design a specialty garden. You can place it in the appropriate gua or use a theme for the entire garden space to really pack a punch.

Abundance Garden

An Abundance Garden will really put the emphasis on wealth and abundance. This garden should use flowing water in fountains or waterfalls, taking care that all water flows toward the house. The best colors for plant material are purple, red, green, and gold. Mass plantings reflect the concept of abundance. A grouping of purple lilacs will have a much greater impact than a single purple iris in this garden. Fruit trees also say something about your desires coming to fruition, and don't forget to hang a metal wind chime to call in the cash!

Good Reputation Garden

This garden is best placed in the rear center of the yard. Feed the fire of fame with reds. This is the place for barbecues, fire pits, and garden torches. A ceramic Sun on the back fence can symbolize the fire element. If you have a totem or animal symbol that says something about who you are, set it in the garden of Good Reputation.

Relationship Garden

Let love bloom in your Relationship Garden. Harmony is important here, so use your favorite chimes. To demonstrate a harmonious relationship, this area should be planted in pairs: two pink rosebushes, two flowering cherries, and don't forget a love seat bench for two! Pink, white, and red all support relationship chi. Stay away from cactus or weeping plants in this gua. Instead, go for heart-shaped leaves and romantic fragrance in your plant material.

Playful Children's Garden

This garden is all about fun and creativity. White is the color to emphasize and round is the shape. Use daisies for their shape and color, or pussy willows for their fun, soft texture. A round sandbox or a round play table will uplift children's chi. Your local garden shop has decorative metal elements to use in the garden:

suns, moons, animals, etc. A butterfly bush or a bird feeder will encourage fun visitors for the kids.

Friends' Garden

To boost the energy of benefactors in your life, plant a Friends' Garden. Use favorite flowers of your friends and mentors. Perhaps Aunt Mabel loved violets, while your best friend Sue is crazy about honeysuckle. Planting their favorites will honor these people and bring them to mind as you spend time in this garden. Silver mound, dusty miller, and other plants and shrubs with gray or white foliage work wonders here.

Uplifting Career Garden

As you may have gathered, water is the best element for an Uplifting Career Garden. If you cannot have a water feature, then use ornamental water animals such as frogs and fish. A birdbath is a great way to incorporate water, and you won't need to maintain a pond. Flower beds in non-geometric shapes are also recommended in the Career gua. Blue flowers are best here, as well as in our next garden, the Garden of Knowledge.

Knowledge Garden

The Knowledge Garden is well-suited to a more contemplative garden. Place a Buddha, Green Man, or goddess statue in the Knowledge gua. Choose appropriate personal symbols to add. Place a bench for meditation and peaceful contemplation of your garden in this area. Construct a rock labyrinth or lay out a medicine wheel as tools for spiritual growth. This is a power spot in your garden for generating spiritual chi. The color blue belongs in the Knowledge Garden, so don't hesitate to use your favorite blue flowers like delphinium, lupine, bachelor buttons, or forget-me-nots.

Family Fun Garden

The best place to encourage group activity is the Family Fun Garden. Wood is the element here, so picnic tables and wooden chairs are perfect choices. Trees, especially those with columnar shapes like poplar or Italian cypress, support family chi. Planting in groups of three or more will also promote family harmony. How about a bocce ball court or a horseshoe pit? Encourage family gatherings and play in the Family Fun Garden. Green is the color of the wood element, so the entire garden provides uplift for the family.

Good Health Garden

The center of the yard is the place for a Good Health Garden. Herbs and veggies for your health and well-being belong here. Ceramic pots and ornaments bring in the earth element, so a tile or flagstone patio in the Good Health qua can help create an earthy center. Sunflowers and other yellow bloomers promote healthy chi. This is also a great place for crystals—beautiful pieces of the earth element—to magnify positive energy.

Enjoying Feng Shui for the Garden

Using feng shui to adjust the energy flows and create balance in your garden is a creative and fulfilling experience. It assists you with being a conscious gardener. You can begin to perceive chi flow and build in the different areas of your garden. Adjustments can be made as your life and priorities change from season to season.

It is important to note that feng shui in the garden is not just placement and planting. It is also energy work. You need to pace yourself and complete bagua areas where you need the most support first. Then, as you see results and your fulfillment grows, you will breeze through your garden activities with renewed energy. The garden is an extension of yourself. With feng shui in the garden, it will reflect a lifetime of joy and happiness back to you.

When you have a sense of completion about the feng shui in your garden, invite friends and family over to bless the garden with their presence. This is a great opportunity for a ceremony or ritual to set your intention for the garden. One suggestion is to place each of the five elements in the center of the garden to symbolize completion and wholeness. Create your own celebration and enjoy!

About the Author

Christine Ayres is a feng shui consultant and avid gardener. Her firm, Feng Shui Services, is based in the Lake Tahoe region of the Sierra Nevada. Ms. Ayres has been working with feng shui since 1991, when she moved to Hong Kong for four years of work and study. Ms. Ayres writes a regular column on feng shui and her articles have appeared widely over the last ten years. She has appeared on television and radio in the U.S. and Asia, and has a worldwide clientele. Christine Ayres can be reached at aalchemy@sbcglobal.net.

A Potpourri of Herbal Goodies

By Sally Cragin

When I was a child growing up in New England, I found the subtle and beguiling smells of spring flowers fascinating. I began to notice that the flowers popped up in the garden in a specific order. First came the pink, purple, yellow, and white crocuses, which had a subtle floral scent. They were followed by the snowdrops and bluettes, tiny six-petalled blooms that carpeted the newly greening woods. Next came the daffodils, with their strong and pungent aroma. Daffodils were followed by the flowers that truly meant spring had arrived and we were done with snow—the lilacs. Those generous sprays of bunched flowers—each bough drooping with dozens of elf-sized bouquets—were marvelous.

Wanting to save and savor the odor, I crushed flowers in my fist, wrapped them in handkerchiefs, I even pounded the blooms onto paper. My efforts were all futile, but even if the results weren't always satisfactory, doing-it-myself was actually a lot of fun.

My interest in homemade health and beauty products continues today. The essential raw ingredients—almonds, basil, chamomile, dandelions (when in season), lavender, rosewater and oil, oatmeal, honey, yogurt—are always in my house. It's astonishing how inexpensive homemade products are, and how easy it is to make them up.

I'm sure you've known women who get into that "gotta buy something" mode in department stores or pharmacies. High-end designer cosmetics and products are the result of many really smart people doing brilliant work—starting in the lab. Lab work is followed by product design, an advertising campaign, and the budget. You, the consumer, end up paying for all that overhead. But many simple products are at your fingertips, so let's start with some basic ingredients and see what you can make at home. The directory below lists numerous common plants and substances.

Plants, Herbs, and Leafy Things

Basil

The botanical name of basil derives from the Greek words *okimon* (perfumed plant) and *basilicon* (royal). The first-century naturalist Pliny the Elder advised farmers to use the herb as a fertility enhancement for asses. In the medieval period, people believed that if you crushed basil under a stone, it would transform into a scorpion. In the eighteenth century, French doctor Nicholas Lemery prescribed basil tonics to help women with sluggish menstrual periods. It was also thought to work as a digestive, and to help with flatulence.

Basil Heath Drink

Make a health drink by pouring a cup of boiling water over a teaspoon of crushed basil leaves. Let stand for ten minutes before you drink it.

Basil Skin Lotion

Macerate a tablespoon of leaves and infuse in five tablespoons of non-fruity olive oil. Let stand for five days and then filter. This makes a pleasant massage oil for sensitive skin.

Bay Laurel

I love the smell of this herb, which has fabulous mythological origins. When the beautiful and chaste nymph Daphne was unable to escape from amorous Apollo, she begged the gods to transform her into a laurel. Distraught and thwarted, Apollo made the tree his emblem. From then on, his priestesses, victorious athletes, and poets were honored for their triumphs with a crown of laurel leaves. The oracles of Delphi chewed this leaf before making prophecies, and when the Romans adopted the custom, they planted avenues of laurel trees alongside their palaces. It had medicinal value for early doctors, and was thought to be a brain stimulant and panacea for asthma. Along with thyme and other herbs, it is an essential ingredient of the "bouquet garni" used in soups.

Bay Remedy for Flu

When the very first symptoms of the flu or a virus appear, a bay leaf tonic may be helpful. Crumble five leaves in a cup of cold water; then, boil for three minutes. Let this stand for ten minutes, filter, and drink.

Lavender

For me, there is no more soothing smell than lavender oil, and one of my treasures is a small vial of essential oil that I received from thoughtful relatives who had visited Provence, France. The Romans used lavender for their bath and laundry water. (The name comes from the Italian, *lavanda,* which relates to washing.) During plague epidemics, it was used with the aromatic, antiseptic plants in those picturesque long black "nose cones" worn by doctors.

Lavender Tea

Infuse a tablespoon of flowers in a cup of boiling water. Let it stand for ten minutes, filter, and drink.

Parsley, Sage, Rosemary, and Thyme

One of the most beautiful refrains in the folk music canon of Simon and Garfunkel links these four disparate herbs. You could combine all four (in their dried leaf form) to make a facial steam. Put equal parts with boiling water in a metal or glass bowl; stir and cover for five minutes. Uncover and steam your face by draping a towel over the back of your head. You can buy an electric steamer, but the first method works fine. Just make sure you're in a comfortable chair and don't have to lean over too far.

Parsley Garnish

Yes, the scruffy little leaflet alongside your entrée has a purpose, although it should actually be served before the meal, as parsley is said to encourage the appetite and aid digestion. Parsley can also be used to help with bladder infections, and it has natural antihistamine properties. Crush a leaf and apply to a bug bite.

Sage

The name derives from the Latin word *salvare* (to heal). The Greeks offered bouquets of sage to the gods before asking oracles for prophecies. Nineteenth-century botanist Joseph Roques told his readers to grow sage in their gardens: ". . . it will not stop you dying, but will revive you when you are weary, increase your appetite, and stimulate your stomach."

Sage Decoction

Add a generous handful of leaves to a quart of cold water. Boil for fifteen minutes, infuse for twenty minutes, and then filter. Use warm as a mouthwash or gargle, or cold as a daily scalp rub.

Rosemary

Egyptians noted that this herb was an evergreen, and considered it the symbol of immortality. The Romans viewed it as Jupiter's herb and burned sprigs of it in purification rituals. In Shakespeare's day, people used rosemary "for remembrance." These days, rosemary can be an aromatic addition to a bath.

Rosemary Bath Water

Take three handfuls of herbs and boil in two quarts of water for ten minutes. Let stand for twenty minutes. Filter the liquid before adding it to bath water.

Thyme

This has a beautiful Greek root word *thumos*, which refers to the soul. Thumos derives from the Egyptian word *tham*, which describes aromatic plants used for embalming. The Romans viewed it as a stomach tonic, and its distinctive sharp flavor can range from sweetish to savory.

Thyme Tea

Add one teaspoon of dried leaves to one cup boiling water and infuse for ten minutes. The tea can be helpful for breathing difficulties and various forms of fatigue.

Raspberry Leaf

Raspberry Leaf Tea

Raspberry leaf tea is a staple in my kitchen. The leaves are both astringent and tonic and are thought to have a special function for the female reproductive system. For centuries, women have drunk raspberry leaf tea as they prepared for childbirth, and it's also thought to help reduce a heavy menstrual flow. You can buy bags of the leaf tea, but it's absurdly easy to make it yourself. Since raspberries grow wild in waste places, you won't have too much difficulty finding the plants. Simply cut leaves from the stems (we have so many plants at our house, I just thin the branches), and let them dry on screens or in baskets. In a pinch, I've used an open pizza box, since the leaves curl up when they dry. It can take up to two weeks for the leaves to dry. Put the dried leaves in a blender, or simply crush them in your hands. I put a tablespoon in a two-cup microwaveable glass-measuring cup and then fill with water. Raspberry leaves are amazingly waterproof, so it's good to stir the blend to integrate the leaves. I microwave the tea for three minutes and then let it stand for about a half hour, or until the water is tepid and the liquid is a strong yellow color. Filter and drink. The longer this tea sits, the better.

Backyard and Woodside Beauties

Raspberry and thyme probably belong here also, but I wanted to put a small list together of very common plants (some would say weeds) that are available to most folks. If you're reading this in the warm weather, chances are you can easily find some of the following:

Dandelion

Who does not love the dandelion—the always-cheerful ornament of lawns? *Dents de lions* (the teeth of lions) describes the spiky leaves, which ooze bitter, white milk when broken. Before the flower blooms and the leaves turn bitter, pull the very young shoots to add spice to a salad. The roots may be baked and chopped and used for a decoction that has diuretic and mild laxative properties. As an adult, I have not found this delightful weed to have cosmetic applications, but as a child, I was fascinated by the bright yellow pollen that could be rubbed off the flower onto the skin.

Red Clover

This familiar perennial (sometimes biennial) plant is the state flower of Vermont. It's traditionally been used as an expectorant, mild sedative, blood purifier, and antispasmodic. I've also read that it can be helpful for problems with eczema and psoriasis. Though it grows everywhere, avoid picking clover that is on roadsides or near cars (lead will be an unwanted extra additive).

The native tribes sometimes dried the flowers and smoked them, and clover can add a sweetish aroma to tobacco. You can gather the flower heads when the plant is blooming, although blooms that are dry or faded should be avoided. Pluck the blossoms and spread on a screen, or dry in brown paper bags that are frequently turned. Store the flowers when they are crumbly to the touch, and keep them away from sunlight or direct lighting.

Red Clover Tea

This can soothe a cough or help with chest congestion. Add two teaspoons dried flowers to a cup of boiling water. Let steep for five minutes, and then cool to room temperature and drink. I've also read in a variety of folklore sources that clover tea can be helpful with skin ailments.

Queen Anne's Lace

Warning: I have not used this plant, but some folklore associated with it sounds interesting. This bristly-stemmed biennial is the most elegant of waste-lot flowers. With its flat disk of minute white flowers, it is immediately recognizable in its resemblance to a white cotton doily. It's a European import, and the root tea was traditionally used as a diuretic and to help avoid and eliminate

urinary stones and worms. Who would have thought this delicate and dazzling bloom had such an interesting story?

Wintergreen

If you walk in the woods on the East Coast, you will find this low-growing plant with glossy oval leaves and, in the fall, a bright red berry. Also known as teaberry, it has highly aromatic leaves and can be found under winter snow. Its essential oil is methyl salicylate, the basic component of aspirin, so if you have allergies with aspirin, this should be avoided. The plant is both analgesic and astringent. You can dry the leaves and make a tea that can help with pain or with bladder irritations. Oil of wintergreen (available in most health food stores) can help with tooth or gum pain if used very sparingly. Don't swallow: it's toxic.

Other Essentials

Honey

Books have been written about honey, which is both a sweetener and healer, but here are some highlights. As a sweetener, honey is a simple sugar (fructose and glucose), so it's easily absorbed in your digestive tract, but it's slightly more caloric than white sugar (sixty-four calories per tablespoon versus forty-six). If you suffer from hay fever (honey contains minute grains of pollen), you may be able to desensitize reactions by consuming honey that has been produced locally in your region. Honey can also be used as an antiseptic.

Yankee Drink

Add boiling water to a cup that contains one tablespoon each of honey and cider vinegar. Drink hot or cold.

Ginger Honey Tea for Colds

Put in a saucepan an inch of ginger (sliced or grated), half a lemon (sliced and unpeeled), a couple of garlic cloves, and two cups of water. Bring to a boil, simmer for twenty minutes, strain, and put in mugs. Add a tablespoon of honey to each mug.

Honey-Yogurt Mask

A spoonful of honey added to a spoonful of yogurt makes an astringent mask. Leave on for twenty minutes, until dry, and you'll notice the skin-softening results.

Almonds

Ripe almonds have a slight bleaching action when ground into a moist powder in the blender. Add this paste to a variety of liquids for interesting and useful products.

Almond Meal Mask

Blenderize a handful of almonds and add just enough yogurt to make a paste. Apply to the face and wash off when dry.

Almond-Oatmeal Bath Scrubbie

I made these as presents for years and years and probably will again now that I'm advising you to do the same. Mix equal parts almond meal and ground-up oatmeal on a square of cheesecloth, tie into a ball, and use as a scrubber in the bath. Be sure you squeeze this out when you're done (these are organic materials, so there is no preservative). For variety, add dried orange peel that's been blenderized. To dry your orange peel, just let it dry in a warm windowsill until it's hard.

Best-ever Sun Tea

Put two chamomile tea bags and one peppermint tea bag in a glass container (this works for quart or 1.5 liter). Fill with water, and let sit in the sun until pale yellow. Remove bags, and refrigerate for a completely refreshing drink.

Last words

I love granola bars and I'm always happy to try a new brand, but frankly, you can get as much nutritional value in a plain old yellow banana. Of all the fruits, bananas come closest to being a meal in that they are a low-fat, high-potassium source of complex carbohydrates. You'll find vitamins B, B-1, B-2, B-6, B-12, and vitamin C, yet they're just 120 calories. The U.S. Food and Drug Administration has announced that, if eaten, bananas could keep blood pressure within healthy limits. The fruit also stimulates mucous and cells in your stomach lining that protect your digestive system from acids associated with heartburn, indigestion, and diarrhea. They're also a good source of soluble fiber. Those B vitamins are important, especially B-6, which can help reduce swelling and increases tendon flexibility. If your arms are sore from working at a keyboard, or if you have full-on carpal tunnel syndrome, trying eating more bananas. Athletes might also enjoy bananas, which can alleviate muscle cramps and pain after a workout.

About the Author

Sally Cragin writes "Moon Signs," an astrology column for the Boston Phoenix newspaper in New England. She also writes about theater- and arts-related topics for the Boston Globe. Her Web site is www.moonsigns.net.

Venus, Goddess of Gardens

By Janice Sharkey

> *Fairest Isle, all isles excelling*
> *Seat of Pleasures and of loves;*
> *Venus here will choose her dwelling,*
> *And forsake her Cyprian groves.*

—DRYDEN SONG OF VENUS

Venus exists across many cultures. She maybe called Aphrodite, Athena, Persephone, Demeter, or Hera to name but a few. She is even associated with the Moon, as she embodies femininity and fertility. She is linked with Themis, goddess of law and equity, so aptly symbolized by the scales of Libra. It was the Roman poet Varro who hailed Venus the true "Goddess of gardens." Go into any garden center today and it is guaranteed to have at least one Diana or Venus statue for sale. She symbolizes not just beauty but the bounty of life itself.

Librian Fauna

Astrologer and herbalist Nicolas Culpeper suggested that Venus-ruled plants have "a gentle cleansing nature." (One plant with very feminine undertones is motherwort.) Culpeper also wrote of Venus-ruled plants: ". . . it makes women joyful mothers of children, and settles their wombs."

The Victorians believed it was a good omen for newlyweds to plant a myrtle tree in their garden so their marriage would be fruitful. Fruit trees, from plums to pears to peaches, and the ubiquitous apple—abound under Venus. The yielding of seeds into fruit to be savored, not just for their taste but was also a symbol of love, falls under Venus, too. All saplings come under the sway of Libra due to their tender state.

The theme of love is never lost in a Libran garden. All those plants that belong to the rose family, including blackberry, silverweed, and even wild strawberry, are truly Libran. The heady essence of old damask roses is in itself an image of summer and romance.

It is no surprise that a Libra Moon is the best sign for planting flowers. Yet, there is a drawback to planting for the express purpose of producing beautiful flowers: overflowering can produce seeds or bulbs that are poor germinators. So, if its flowers you want, plant in Libra. She is concerned with the blossom and petals of a plant, in particular the *perianth* (the outer part of the flower). With Libra being an air sign, it is interesting to note that petals are the only part of the plant that needs and absorbs oxygen from the air.

> **Think Sensual:** The essence of a Libra plant is its sensuality. Even the wildflower, tansy, with its fern-like foliage, falls into this category. Add tactile qualities to your garden to your Venus Garden.

Soft pastels abound in the Libran Eden, from pale blue to ultramarine (dusky blue delphinium), to pink (damask rose), and pale greens (Bells of Ireland). And somewhere in between are the deep pastel tints of foxglove—the spectrum of color and floral range is momentous.

Planting a Bed for Venus

Reflecting in my back garden, on a forlorn, empty patch of ground, a glint of an idea came to me. As I gazed at the dormant seed heads of a clump of tansy, I remembered that Nicholas Culpeper believed in the popular philosophical doctrine of affinity: as above, so below. Although I was not standing in a medieval garden, I was aware that the cosmos was making closer waves in our world. The year was now 2006, and it was common knowledge that Venus had transited between the Sun and Earth in June 2004, and that the Voyager spacecraft had taken its final glimpse of Venus and attempted to pass through her poisonous gases to land on Venusian ground. What had that unearthed? Had they found evidence of living matter, I wondered as I reflected upon my own growing space, imagined it dug out—a fresh canvas on which to plant a "bed for Venus."

The decision to design a border with the theme of Venus meant grounding myself in the site practicalities as well as learning from the past. Following the golden rules of good garden design, I reacquainted myself with the fundamentals of my own back garden. It had a south-easterly aspect with a long rectangular shape, half in shade, with the remaining half receiving sometimes only glimpses of the patchy sunshine that favors us in the southwest of

Scotland. I kept reminding myself that out of every disadvantage there is an advantage and shade brought its own opportunities.

My soil is neutral to alkaline and relatively free draining. The chosen border had a sorry, skeletal selection of plants that had either become too woody, or needed ruthless thinning.

I soon got down to the back-breaking task of clearing the plot for my new border. As I dug and sieved each chunk of rubble, I wondered how roots could bypass half bricks of sandstone excavated from some post-war patio wall. I let my subconscious ruminate over what form the eventual design should take. I shoveled the brown crumbly earth and added a good portion of homemade compost in a semi-trance state, and allowed my mind to reflect upon books I had treasured. *Medieval Flowers* is one such book. It shows ancient illustrations from the Hours from the Duke of Burgundy, where gardens were designed as enticing love nests but also tiny *hortus conclusus* (closed-off garden, or orchard). A garden made for courtly love but protective of virginal untouchability, with admittance limited to those vetted upon entrance or chaperoned. Trellises were ideal structures for scented enclaves to veil would-be lovers from the eyes of the onlooker, as well as offer functional shade and shelter against the elements.

My design was to be more open than a hortus conclusus, but I wanted it to be a "room" within other garden rooms. It would be next to the kitchen garden and adjacent to the partially shady border running alongside a native wildlife hedge. All the plants chosen could certainly be traced back to our own native species during medieval times. Although medieval gardens tended to have a sparse choice of plants, mine would be stuffed with diverse planting that had to deliver all year round interest and withstand wintery temperatures to minus 10° Celsius. Above all, I wanted this border to reflect the ancient in modern times.

As a garden room it had to stand out independently, yet also blend into the surrounding areas. I poured over ancient herbals such as *Culpeper's Complete Herbal, The English Physitian,* and even the Elizabethan *The Gardener's Labyrinth.* All of these ancient texts lead me back to Virgil's *The Georgics*, which eulogized the influence of the cosmos upon flora and fauna.

To Culpeper, any plant that was governed by Dame Venus had to have healing attributes for women's ailments (such as menstrual cramps or fainting), whereupon he advised using rose hips or motherwort. Tansy, with its florets of golden buttons held upright by ferny foliage, was associated with childbirth, but also with the awakening in the soil. It was a custom to celebrate springtime's "opening" by baking a tansy cake.

Venus embodies the feminine principle, as opposed to the warrior Mars. Her charm and beauty bestow the joys of love, and it is her task to unify and balance—characteristics that are necessary is any herbaceous border, but in mine she had her work cut out.

My final planting choice had to have plants that would have more than one season's interest. Spring would be heralded by primrose and cowslips, followed by jonquils. The viola, a leftover winter attraction, would still create a purple splash to contrast and offset all that lemony luminosity. I chose the buttercup yellow cowslip *primula veris*, and I left some yellow-leaved feverfew and catmint, giving bursts of yellow and sky-blue, to fill any vacant space in summer.

In early summer, Nora Barlow *aqualegias* would pop up to help disguise the depleating daffodils. Aqualegias have a reputation for licentious self-seeding, which may lead to a future abundance of columbine cousins. They will be given free reign only to the extent of producing the right color and plant combination. Each still had to work overtime in this smallish border. Meanwhile, the summer border would have some biennial daisies (*bellis*) with their red pompons sprinkled here and there to fizz up the border. To give height and a seasonal focal point I chose *malus sargentii*, one of the smallest crab apple trees available that has masses of scented white flowers in spring. By autumn it has bright red, currant-like fruits, while its leaves turn wonderfully yellow. I chose Foxy (*digitalis purpurea*), a new dwarf variety of foxglove, that would flower the first year, to plant near the crab apple tree.

By mid- to high-summer, the roses would be in bloom, companion planted with tansy at their feet. Spoilt for choice, I finally decided upon *rosa gallica officinalis*, known as the apothecary's rose. It produces semi-double, fragrant, cerise-red flowers in abundant clusters, and it would climb the willow arch. Ideally suited even in poorer soil, it also had the added generosity of producing large autumnal scarlet hips. To wind up the rustic espalier at the other side of the border, I opted for rose Graham Thomas, with its yellow, fully-double, cupped flowers, that would waft some scent to those sitting nearby. I gave both roses plenty of organic matter and underplanted them with catnip. In the spring, they would get an ample helping of well-rotted manure.

As the summer moved to autumn, the roses would produce hips while the crab apple would add splendor and color to the season of mists and mellow fruitfulness and, hopefully, there would be enough tiny apples to produce some homemade preserve.

Winter would see the skeletal Miss Wilmott's Ghost (*eryngium giganteum*), giving her aluminum exclamations with silvery bracts bristling in the frost. Variegated vinca minor mixed with violas would add spectacle on cold winter's day.

After the last primula and nepeta had been bedded in, and the apple staked and anchored, I stood back in trepidation to gaze at my handiwork. My hands were, by now, callused and smeared brown by the earth. The cowslips nodded their dew-eyed approval with their necks above and behind the frontline display of variegated vinca. The spectacle was tantalizing!

Increased light and warmth signalling spring soon moved into summer, and my Venus border erupted into life. A walk underneath the willow arch sent heady scented rose to one's senses. Emerging from the other side, sweeps of tubular spotted foxgloves created pastel landing "towers," and added the drone of bees to the cacophony of summer sounds from welcome pest devourers such as hoverflies. The sweet aroma from Madonna lilies and lilium regale mixed with musky scented feverfew and rubbed shoulders with achillea 'Moonbeam.'

The whole border paraded in a diversity of Venusian sun to partial-shade lovers. Offering a welcome pause between the blaze of color, Miss Wilmott's Ghost bristled statuesque, her steely blue bracts glinting in the sunlight.

By autumn, the color harmony had reached a rich autumnal crescendo, with Venusian apple, rose hips, and sprinkles of contrasting aluminium silver blue of *eryngiun*, with shades echoed by catmint. On a crisp December day, I ventured out, my eyes acclimatizing to the cold air and light of late afternoon. The border was drenched in a December drizzle and the fine wet air highlighted remaining cobwebs clinging to Miss Wilmott's Ghost. Had the border finally been put to bed, I wondered?

I spied a glint of yellow as violas mixed with the luminous variegated yellow of vinca stirred in the light breeze. As I trod back into the warmth of my electric lit, centrally-warmed world, I wondered what a New Year on Venus would be like and whether it would turn out to be as welcoming as Venus on my Earth.

About the Author

Janice Sharkey is a dedicated astrological gardener and she practices both lunar and organic gardening. She studied and gained a certificate from the London Faculty of Astrological Studies. She designs gardens to reflect a client's individual birth chart. She lives in the United Kingdom with her husband William and two kids, David and Rose. She can be reached by e-mail at astrologygarden@aol.com.

Cultivating Your Garden of Soul

By Robert Ayres

Sometimes, when we can pause in a peaceful forest or get lulled into reverie by the rolling waves crashing on the beach, we feel as if we have reconnected with something deep inside of ourselves that has been neglected. Our experiences in nature often leave us feeling refreshed, revitalized, and more alive.

Most of us have lived in cities, where the natural environment has been transformed into paved streets lined with glass and steel buildings. Our urban environments disconnect and insulate us from the underlying reality of nature. We may feel unfulfilled and alienated, and there is a need to fill the emptiness inside.

It is our soul that cries out to us for attention. Our soul, this deep inner aspect of our being, is not fulfilled by our fast-paced, hectic lives. We need to improve our quality of life and give the feeding of our soul a higher priority on our agenda of activities. Gardening is one way to feed one's soul.

Gardening

Gardening is an activity that has long defined the working inter-relationship between man and nature. In the past, gardening was more of a necessity for survival, but it also kept us connected with nature's laws and rhythms. Today, for most people, gardening is a choice. We may live in apartments or condominiums where there is no yard in which to garden. However, we can still have house plants, window boxes, or container plants on the patio, balcony, or window sill. We may have a house with a yard.

If we are not gardening, we are missing a significant opportunity for personal fulfillment. There is nothing quite as healthy and good for us in getting rid of the stress, conflict, and the troubles of modern life as digging in the dirt, watering the plants, cutting the flowers, and harvesting the vegetables. It is a nurturing and healing activity for one's body and soul.

Nature and Soul

Nature is where the sacred is manifest in physical form. It provides us an opportunity to interact with and learn from it. By studying nature with the right attitude, humanity can gain deep insight into the basic laws and rules that govern life. Nature is our teacher. She embodies within herself all of the cosmic forces, powers, and intelligences of creation. Through soulful interaction with and observation of nature, we come to understand how life works and the laws and principles that govern our existence.

We have spoken of nature as feminine. It is the Mother aspect of the divine whose role is to create, nurture, and heal all life. The fundamental energy behind all of this activity of nature and soul is love. Through the soul's expression of love, everything is held together in the unity and harmony of life. There is a reciprocal relationship of mutual nurturing intended between humanity and nature. When we grow and enliven our souls, we enliven nature. When we cultivate and nurture nature, we also cultivate and nurture our souls. As we destroy nature, we destroy our souls.

Cultivating the Garden of Soul

Cultivating the garden of soul is analogous to traversing the spiritual path in order to return home. The soul is multifaceted and very rich in its contents. There is tremendous opportunity to unfold consciousness from within ourselves—to actualize a beautiful garden of possibilities.

The Kabbalah and other spiritual traditions differentiate between five levels of soul. The lowest and most primitive level of soul is known as the *nefesh* (animal soul). This aspect of the soul is ruled by the lower instinctual passions and drives of survival, reproduction, and personal power. The instinctual unconscious soul needs to be cultivated to a more enlightened level.

We can compare this to taking a wild, natural tract of land and turning it into a beautiful garden. The mineral, plant, and animal kingdoms are all represented by the soil and rocks, the incredible variety of plant life, and the animal world from insects to squirrels and birds. All are naturally present and have established a balance and harmony through time. These are the natural resources provided by nature. It is like a fresh palette for the painter to paint upon.

Now, if we add man to the equation, we have inserted a catalyst for potential change. The human, through his thoughts and actions, will implement intention to realize his own chosen goals. If there are trees producing fruits that are desirable to eat, we will clear away the brush and vines that block the flow of sunlight, air, and water to the tree. We can divert water from a nearby stream so that it irrigates the tree, enhancing the conditions of the tree so that it will grow and prosper and produce more fruit. From that point, we slowly expand out to cultivate the entire area so it provides us with what we want. Our life is the raw material that we each have to cultivate, nurture, and grow in order to manifest what we want.

Most people today place their attention on cultivating and developing their outer material life and tend to neglect the development and growth of their inner life. Spiritual law tells us that the outer is based on the inner; the material is based on the spiritual. How high a tree will grow is dependent on how deeply its roots penetrate into the earth. The roots are hidden from view, but are the source of life for the tree. The same is true of the design of the human being. The inner life of soul is the immediate source of our outer activity and life expression. To the degree that we cultivate, feed, and water the roots of the tree, it will live and produce abundantly.

The same is true of the soul. When we understand its needs and provide for them, the soul unfolds its full potential as it was originally intended to do. But, it takes conscious effort and intention and action in order to realize the full potential of the soul.

The Rhythms of Growth

When we want to consciously develop our relationship with nature and the soul, it is important to put ourselves in touch with these forces in a correct manner. Nature and the soul express in a cyclic manner. Time expresses in cycles, which establish specific rhythms to the growth process. These rhythms condition all life. Each day, month, and year has its cycle.

All of these cycles contain within them the alternation of rest and activity, inner and outer, and spiritual and material. For example, the seasons of the year have the predictable sequence of spring, summer, fall, and winter. The seasons relate to the relationship of the Sun to the Earth. The spring is a time of rebirth and a bursting forth of life. In summer, the light and heat are at their greatest strength and support maximum growth. Fall is traditionally harvest time, when we reap what we have sown. Winter is the time for rest and turning within, in preparation for the next cycle.

The process that is unfolded through the seasons is that of birth, growth, decay, and death, respectively. Death is a preparation for rebirth. This same rhythm is demonstrated on a monthly basis in the lunation cycle of New Moon, first quarter, Full Moon, and third quarter. We can see this cycle reflected in the twenty-four hour day by sunrise, noon, sunset, and midnight. These are the rhythms of growth that condition every moment in time and determine what activity is most appropriate. Being in right timing is crucial for achieving success in growing our inner and outer gardens.

Growing Your Inner and Outer Gardens

While gardening is an excellent form of recreation, it can also be a valuable spiritual discipline for the development of the inner life of soul. We have to cultivate the soil that we are going to plant in. We loosen the soil and remove the rocks so that it is not hard and compact. We want the roots of the plants to be able to grow in a supportive environment and we want to eliminate any blockage or resistance to their growth. Developing a good growing medium is an ongoing, long-term process. We add compost and fertilizer in order to provide abundant food and nutrients to the plants. We plant seeds or transplants into the prepared soil, making sure that the plants will get the appropriate sunlight that is needed.

After we plant our garden, we need to water and feed it on a regular basis. Weeding is also necessary. There is always an ongoing attempt by primitive, wild nature to reclaim its space. If we become complacent, our garden can revert back to the wild jungle or barren wasteland that it originally was. We must also prune the growth so that it follows our intention. Particular plants can get too large and begin to take over. They become out of proportion and upset the balance and harmony of the overall garden.

We are striving for balance and harmony in both our inner and outer gardens. All of the vast diversity of life must be honored and supported. This adds to the richness of life that we want to live and experience. We want to cultivate an inner and outer garden that includes the full spectrum of the multifaceted nature of life.

Of course, we must also harvest the fruit and flowers that our garden produces. We must remember that nature is here to give and we are here to receive. Harvest is that time of fulfillment when we are rewarded with the bounty that life has to give in return for all our conscientious hard work. But it has been a labor of love if it has been done with the correct attitude. In our outer garden, our harvest of fruit and flowers helps to nurture and feed our soul and our body.

In the cultivation of our inner garden of soul, we must first prepare the ground in which we will plant. This phase of cultivating the soul has to do with placing our awareness in an inner directed way through meditation and contemplation. Inner-directed attention on a daily basis creates the conditions and prerequisites for the growth of soul. We are cultivating and preparing the ground for our garden of soul to grow. For most of us, there is a hardness and rockiness of heart and soul, which makes it difficult for our soul life to grow. Meditation softens the hardness and helps us to dissolve the rocks of bitterness, disappointment, and hurt. The result is an increased flexibility and openness to life. Gone is the rigidity and crystallization of negative patterns of thinking and feeling.

Just as we are careful in our selection of the plants to use in our garden, so must we be selective in terms of the thoughts and ideas that we are going to cultivate in our soul garden. The standard, which the spiritual traditions established thousands of years ago and are still appropriate today, are the cultivation of "the Good, the True, and the Beautiful." We want only the best, because we want to create our own inner and outer Garden of Eden. We are going to actively create our own paradise that we can retreat to any time we want. We are creating our own sacred space.

The watering of our garden of the soul consists of daily meditation and prayer that nourishes new, growing consciousness. Weeding our inner garden involves the conscious rooting out of negative thoughts and feelings. We must starve them by having the mental and emotional self-discipline to not give them energy or attention. The inner pruning of our soul garden is to not let ourselves become obsessed with one aspect of the divine, or one particular approach to the spiritual. This is limiting and can result in an inner imbalance that can manifest in the extreme expression of fanaticism.

In our inner garden we harvest happiness and fulfillment. We harvest the good, the true, and the beautiful, which elevates our quality of life significantly. We have consciously chosen to re-establish our individual life in harmony and cooperation with the Divine. We are no longer in resistance to it or in conflict with it. There is a flow to our life that was not there before.

Heaven on Earth

There is an objective and real Garden of Eden, or Paradise, in the celestial worlds. In fact, there are many. We remember this Garden of Eden deep within our soul. It is not fantasy. This is the archetypal Garden of Eden—the prototype or model for all gardens—whether they are manifested in the inner or outer worlds. But we have to realize our deeper mission and destiny, which is to create a Garden of Eden here on Earth or Heaven on Earth. This is not something that God must do, but what mankind must do. We are to consciously co-create with God a Heaven on Earth.

This is the realization of the perfection that we have mentioned. We have been given all the raw materials, the natural and spiritual resources, to create it. The paradigm is hidden within our souls. We must bring this into conscious awareness through cultivating our inner garden of soul. Then, we put this into action to manifest it in concrete reality. It is a process of manifestation from the celestial to the terrestrial and from the inner to the outer. With each year of ongoing cultivation and work in our garden, it grows in fullness and perfection. Correspondingly, our personal qualities of life of joy, happiness, and fulfillment continue to expand.

As each one of us grows in consciousness of love and wisdom, then our influence on our environment increases in positivity and harmony. Through our personal growth we add to the collective growth and we add our individual contribution to the overall good of society. When you improve the part, you automatically improve the whole. Society and community grow toward the light. In the process we re-establish a correct, conscious relationship with nature. Good gardening!

About the Author

Robert Ayres is a professional astrologer and spiritual teacher living at Lake Tahoe, California. He has been a student and teacher of the spiritual traditions of the East and West for forty years. His main areas of expertise are astrology, Tarot, Kabbalah, the Vedic tradition, and meditation. For further information, please visit his Web site at www.astrologicalalchemy.com.

Living in Harmony with Urban Wildlife

By Judy Carman

It was late May when Mary brought six baby bluebirds into the local wildlife rehabilitation center and told this unforgettable story. Mary had been watching the mother and father bluebirds as they built their nest in the nesting box Mary had provided. She watched as they faithfully fed their growing babies. One day, however, Mary noticed that the mother bluebird was no longer coming to the nest. The father was left to feed the hungry youngsters. Then suddenly, he also disappeared. After waiting twenty-four hours just to make sure the parents were really gone, Mary approached the nesting box, fearing the worst. There she found the father bird fatally wounded, having been attacked by a predator who was trying to reach the babies. The father's wings were stretched out fully over the nest, and when Mary lifted him, there beneath his body she found all six babies protected and alive. Thanks to their father's courage and sacrifice, all six little ones survived and were released when they were ready to fly and sing.

Above the noise of traffic, street repairs, sirens, televisions and CD players, there are bluebirds caring for their little ones. Just past the sight of cars, houses, buildings, and bridges, there are brilliant yellow butterflies sipping nectar. Indeed, there are whole nations of beings, under our feet and over our heads, sharing the urban environment we have created. How blessed we are that they have found ways to adapt to our urban world.

As *Moon Sign Book* readers, we seek to live consciously and harmoniously within the natural world. We feel our connection with the Moon, the stars, the Earth, and the elements of life and spirit. Yet those of us who live in urban areas often feel disconnected from nature and long for the simplicity and beauty that it brings into our lives. It is becoming clearer to us all that stress, depression, anxiety, and many other ailments are significantly reduced by having regular contact with animals and nature.

I believe we are witnessing a dramatic movement away from the centuries-old paradigm that human beings are here to dominate and exploit nature. This movement, which we might call conscious living, is an exciting awakening. In these days of cultural transformation, millions of people are waking up to and embracing a wisdom world-view that regards all life as sacred and interconnected.

Some years ago, Teilhard de Chardin predicted a "new humanity coming into new form." Within that "new humanity" we find compassion being extended to all creatures and an awareness that animals and nature are not here for us to use however we wish.

Indeed, within such a paradigm, we find that true joy arrives when one lives in a state of awe and wonder at the mystery and magnificence of all living beings. When we leave behind our notion of human superiority and begin to feel our oneness with all life, there comes a great sigh and a deep sense of peace.

Knowing this, many of us long to live closer to the wild places, but for various reasons must content ourselves with living in the cities. So it is important for us to find ways to connect with the natural world right where we live. By doing so, we benefit ourselves, the natural world, and other people as well. By learning to connect and live harmoniously with our wild neighbors, we return to the Earth a sense of peace.

There are many elements involved in creating this harmony. One involves actively defending wildlife and their quickly disappearing ecosystems through education, legislation, and various forms of activism. There are hundreds of local and national groups to join and support in this effort. In addition, if you wish to help injured wildlife return to their homes, you may be able to find a wildlife rehabilitation center near you and volunteer to help.

In this chapter, we'll touch on two other important elements. The first will include activities designed to attract wildlife to our yards, parks, and neighborhoods. The other covers the subject of dealing compassionately and peacefully with the conflicts that arise between human beings and wildlife. Deer in the garden, goose poop on the lawn, rats in the birdseed, squirrels in the attic, and many other "problems" have created an entire "pest control" industry designed, in most cases, to lethally eradicate these "problem" animals. Yet, as we know, it is we who have intruded into their territory. As it turns out, these non-human species are not pests at all but rather fellow travelers on this earthly journey with us. Fortunately, as we continue to create this new, more compassionate culture, we are learning many non-lethal ways to deal with the conflicts.

Attracting Wildlife

Animals, like us, need food and shelter. Piles of branches create homes for rabbits and other small mammals and birds. Dead branches, fallen trees, and stumps provide a gold mine of food for birds, squirrels, and raccoons. Tall grasses, wildflowers, bushes, and trees all provide cover, shelter, flowers, nuts, seeds, and berries for animals. Your local nursery can advise you on the ones that attract butterflies, hummingbirds, and other critters as well as which ones are suited for your climate.

Birdfeeders, birdbaths, and small ponds are a welcome sight for hungry and thirsty critters. However, if you fill your feeders regularly, your visitors will become dependent on them. If you cannot guarantee that you or a neighbor can fill the feeders every day, especially through the cold months, it is better not to have them. An option is to put only a half cup of birdseed a day in several feeders. That way when you are gone, the food won't be missed. Another option, if you can be consistent throughout the winter, is to feed them in the cold months when they need it so much and then cut back to a small amount in the warm months, thus encouraging the animals to find natural sources of food that are available in the neighborhood. Remember to periodically clean the feeders and the ground beneath them to prevent disease.

If you have a birdbath or small pond, be sure to keep sticks, rocks, or some device by which small insects and other little guys can escape from the water. That goes for window wells also, as many animals can become trapped in them.

Providing nesting boxes and housing for birds, bats, squirrels, etc. is another way to invite wildlife into your area. Be prepared, though, to clean these each year.

If a tree is in danger of falling on your home and needs to be cut down, it should be done when you are sure no one is nesting in it. Pesticides and herbicides must be avoided entirely, not just for the animal visitors but for your own pets and children as well.

Several more tips for protecting wildlife include using only non-toxic antifreeze and cutting up six pack holders and containers in which animals' heads could get stuck. Clean out and smash tin cans before recycling. Keep trash cans securely covered. Animals can drown or starve in dumpsters and uncovered trash cans, so make sure there is a branch or other means of escape for them.

Also be sure to cap your chimney so that animals and birds do not take up residence in it. If it happens that one day you hear the chirping or murmuring of babies in your chimney, close the damper and wait, if at all possible, until they are grown and gone and then cap the chimney so that it can't happen again. If you cannot wait, however, and if they are mammals, you can prompt the mother to move her babies to another nest if you place a radio on a talk show station in the fireplace and shine a light down into the chimney. It may be necessary also to hang a rope down the chimney to help Mom get a foothold while carrying her babies. If the babies are birds, however, there is not much Mom can do, but it won't be long before her little ones are ready to fly.

To learn more about living in harmony with urban wildlife, see www.Audubon.org, www.nwf.org (National Wildlife Federation), www.hsus.org (Humane Society of the U.S.), www.Api4animals.org (Animal Protection Institute), www.peta.org (People for the Ethical Treatment of Animals—click on fact sheets) and www.wildneighbors.org.

Conflicts With Wildlife

There are many ways to deal with wildlife conflicts. For example, here is the story of Paula and a little mouse. Paula had inadvertently left an open box of crackers in her cupboard, and Mr. Mouse had located it and was noisily chewing away. It happened that Paula had a cat who was very good at catching mice, and as she was very tired, she went to bed thinking the cat would take care of the situation. But as she lay there, she began to think about that tiny mouse and how vulnerable he was. So Paula got up and went to the cupboard with a shoe. She told the mouse that if he climbed into the shoe, she would take him outside away from the cat. Amazingly, the mouse went right into the shoe and stayed there until she had laid the shoe down in the yard. Now this could all be explained away as a weird coincidence except that Paula forgot to remove the crackers, and the next night Mr. Mouse was back in the cupboard. Believe it or not, she talked him back into the shoe and rescued him once again. (For similar stories of communication with flies, dogs, snakes, and many others, read *Kinship With All Life* by J. Allen Boone. You will love it.)

And then there are those of us who, try as we might, are not able to coax an animal out of the house or garden with flowery words alone. For situations such as these, there are many solutions available. Here are a few tips and resources to help us all live in harmony with our wild brothers and sisters who share the city with us.

Mice

Mice will often leave on their own if you seal all food in chew proof containers, place cotton balls soaked in peppermint oil in drawers and cabinets, and plug up holes with steel wool. That failing, most hardware stores sell ultrasonic high frequency emitters which annoy mice enough to make them want to go elsewhere. There are also humane mousetraps available, but be very careful with these. If they are not checked every several hours, the mice could die in them. Never use glue traps or poison as the suffering they cause is severe for these innocent creatures and, of course, the poisons can also harm children and pets.

Ants

As with mice, we have invaded their homes, and it seems only fair that they would enter ours to search for food and water. The first step is to eliminate all sources of food, such as sticky juice on the floor or sugar on the counter. Then, place near their entrances to your home any of the following: cinnamon sticks, cayenne pepper, lavender, garlic, peppermint, or lemon juice.

Rabbits

As precious and adorable as rabbits are, there are some plants and flowers that humans don't want them to touch. There are many lethal methods that are used routinely and are extremely cruel. Many poisons can cause rabbits severe pain and suffering for days before they die. When they are then eaten by a predator or a family dog or cat, those animals also die from the poisons. Lethal traps likewise cause terrible suffering and often catch other animals and pets instead. Live trapping and removal may separate mothers from babies or cause so much stress that the rabbits die from fright.

Here are some ways to share your space with the bunnies in the neighborhood and protect your plantings at the same time. One inch wire mesh fencing can be placed around gardens and trees. The fence needs to be at least three feet high. The bottom of the fence must be buried in the ground at least six inches so that they will be discouraged from digging into the garden.

As with most other animals, reflective tape, flapping flags, bird-shaped kites, balloons, and other scary items can be placed around the garden. Also, there are repellent pepper and capsicum sprays that can be used on plants that you're not going to eat. You can also make a spray with mashed garlic and water to apply to any of your plants.

Rabbits are very vulnerable little guys. They need the protection of thick brush, bushes, or tall grass. If you grow your garden out in an open space, a good distance from their cover, they will be less likely to visit your garden. If you let a portion of your yard grow and only mow it once a year after the babies have grown, that will provide them with cover and food. You could even plant some bushes in among the grasses and make a brush pile for extra protection. This will give them a safe haven and they will be less tempted to brave the open space between them and your garden.

Gophers and Moles

As with all animals, these two have important work to do within a healthy ecosystem. Because they burrow in the ground, they help to aerate it. While underground, gophers eat some roots and moles eat insect larvae. Nevertheless, some homeowners would rather not have the mounds of dirt appearing in their yards and gardens. Once again, poisons, traps, and other lethal methods are often used to kill them. And again, many non-target animals, including pets, often perish along with them. As with all the others, these animals are innocently carrying on the same activity that their ancestors did prior to suburbs and cities taking over their territory.

Non-lethal, more peaceful methods include the same wire mesh fencing as for rabbits. Also, they do not like wet soil, so keeping your soil moist discourages them. In addition, there are commercial sound emitters that repel gophers and moles as well as other animals and insects. Some can be found in the Harmony catalog at www.gaiam.com.

Geese

Geese love short grass, open water, and no predators. Many suburban housing developments, golf courses, and business areas surround lakes of various sizes. The lawns are neatly clipped, and predators are few. Many communities are finding that geese have taken up year-round residence on their lakes and ponds. As the goose populations grow, some residents complain about the excrement problem and the noise, as geese are full of personality and very talkative. Sadly, many lake communities have killed the geese, but there are many non-lethal and very effective alternatives. The organization known as Geesepeace (www.geesepeace. org) has saved the lives of many geese by educating and helping people with the issues.

Some of their strategies include destroying eggs and nests in order to prevent overpopulation of the geese. However, this can only be done by an expert with a permit. According to the Animal Protection Institute (www.Api4animals.org) this is a last resort effort, but it is certainly preferable to killing the adult birds. If the birds are not permanent residents and have travel plans, this is definitely not an option.

Border collies are very effective at encouraging the birds to leave a certain area, and there are individuals who can bring their trained collies to the location to help with the goose problems. However, if the birds are molting (have lost their flight feathers), border collies should not be used until the birds can fly again after six to eight weeks. Border collies should also not be used to frighten the geese between November and mid-May. During that time, geese should not be disturbed.

Feeding geese, of course, encourages them to stay, and if the quality of the food is poor, such as white bread, it will negatively impact their health. Feeding geese, therefore, is a big no-no.

Of course, fencing is effective at keeping geese off certain areas. It must be at least thirty inches high. In addition, there are some scare devices that work to deter geese, such as strobe lights; shiny, reflective streamers on poles; scarecrows; kites or flags shaped like eagles; firecrackers; horns; and radios.

Geese are beautiful, fascinating, intelligent birds. To be in the presence of a pair of devoted parents and their goslings is a rare privilege indeed. I wish for you that happy experience and peace with geese.

Beavers

Beavers create valuable habitat for fish, mammals, birds, and amphibians. Because of their importance to the web of life, Native Americans called them the "sacred center." Their dams help purify water before it goes into our ponds and lakes, and the beauty they create with their wetland creations is a source of amazement and serenity for us. Nevertheless, Europeans have killed so many beavers since arriving in the U.S. that they number only 5 percent of their original population. In urban areas, residents worry about beavers causing flooding and the loss of trees, and often neighborhoods and governments opt to destroy the dams and the beavers.

Fortunately, trees can be protected from beavers with wire fencing or by painting a sand/paint mixture up the first three feet of the tree trunk. Flooding can be completely prevented by installing wire enclosures around culvert openings and other places where beavers tend to plug up flowing water. A wealth of information can be found at www.beaversww.org, or write to Beavers Wetlands and Wildlife at 146 Van Dyke Rd., Dolgeville, NY 13329.

Deer

Deer populations have grown over the last century from about a half million to around fifteen million. There are several reasons for this. Many of their main predators have been killed by people. Ironically, though, their top predator, the American "sport" hunter, is the primary cause of their population expansion. In order to insure what the hunters call a good "crop," state wildlife agencies and hunting groups clear-cut forests and plant food to encourage population growth.

The Humane Society of the U.S. (www.hsus.org) and other groups are working to perfect a deer contraceptive, which shows great promise in limiting deer populations. As individuals, we can protect our gardens and shrubs from deer with fencing and many of the scare devices mentioned above. Keeping a radio on a talk show station and placing it in the garden does a good job also. The Fund for Animals, at www.fund.org and 212-246-2096, has a wealth of information about the suffering that hunting inflicts on animals as well as ways to live in harmony with wildlife.

Squirrels and Other Critters

These little guys can become unwelcome guests that you hear when they're running around the attic. The basic rule of thumb in this situation is to wait until babies are grown. If they are animals who are active during the day, wait until the entire family leaves, and then cover their entrances so they cannot re-enter your house If a baby is left inside, parents can do a lot of damage trying to get to their little one, so it is best for all concerned to wait for the whole family to vacate. If the animals are nocturnal, such as raccoons, then you must cover their entrance at night while they are out of the house. Live trapping is an absolute last resort because it separates animals from their loved ones and places them into unknown territory.

Flies, Spiders, and Wasps

I keep a cup and a piece of cardboard handy so that any time I see a spider, wasp, fly, or other tiny one, I can catch them (yes, even flies if you sneak up behind them) and release them outside unharmed and happy. If you use a transparent cup to trap the little guy and then slide the cardboard in under the cup, it works like a charm, and it's a great way to give children an up-close look at their tiny neighbors as well as at your compassionate and respectful treatment of them.

John Muir once said, "When we tug on a single thing in nature, we find it attached to everything else." Gandhi, Albert Schweitzer, Einstein, and many others expressed the wisdom that we will not and cannot have world peace among human beings until we stop killing, eating, and causing suffering to our fellow beings. Gandhi challenged us all to "Be the change you wish to see in the world." Living in harmony with urban wildlife is just one of the radical notions, along with veganism, environmental protection, feminism, peace, and justice, and many others, that is bringing about this transformation of humanity from the most violent species on earth into a species of kindness, compassion, and peace. May we grow in numbers and in wisdom, and may we bring peace to all beings.

About the Author

Judy Carman is an animal rights, environmental, and peace activist. She is founder of the Circle of Compassion Initiative, cofounder of Animal Outreach of Kansas (www.animaloutreach-ks.org), and cofounder of the Prayer Circle for Animals (www.circleofcompassion.org). She is author of Peace to All Beings: Veggie Soup for the Chicken's Soul, *published by Lantern Books. This book explores in depth the coming transformation of the human world-view from one of domination and exploitation to one of cooperation and living in harmony and with respect for all beings.*

Raising Poultry

By Tammy Sullivan

More and more, people are turning to their own backyard when it comes to food production. The commercial production of poultry items relies heavily on the use of chemicals, growth hormones, and ill-kept birds. This is not what nature intended.

While tending a home flock is usually a simple matter of remembering to feed the birds and gather the eggs, there can be a bit more to it. I consider the following information to be essential when it comes to producing and maintaining healthy poultry.

Raising your own poultry has extra benefits besides just the purity of the food products. The birds also help to control the insect population, and the resulting waste material is an excellent fertilizer for the lawn or garden. Plus, fuzzy little baby chicks are just flat-out cute!

Stocking A Flock

The first step is choosing the type of bird best suited to your needs. There are two primary breeds of these birds: egg-laying and broilers. You can, of course, consume the egg-laying type, but it is usually a small bird with a large laying capacity, while the broiler is a larger bird with a poorer egg output. The Rhode Island Red breed is especially popular for folks who like brown-shelled eggs, while Cornish Game Hens are well known for the juicy meat they provide. Other popular breeds for eggs are the Pearl-White Leghorn, Golden Comet, Red Star, and the Black Star. The most popular breeds for meat production are the Delaware and the Black or White Jersey Giant.

Chicks with red earlobes normally produce brown eggs, while those with white earlobes produce white eggs. The Araucana breed lays eggs with a blue-green shell.

If you are raising your chickens for their egg-laying capabilities, a rooster will not be necessary. Curiously enough, if a rooster is not provided a hen will often step up and mother the flock. Most breeds will begin to lay eggs at around six months of age. The eggs will start out small but increase in size as the chick matures. A mature, healthy hen will lay approximately one egg per day. Egg production increases when the temperature is maintained between 45° and 80° Fahrenheit.

If there is no local source of birds available, many people obtain their flocks from hatcheries that operate on the Internet. It is completely safe to ship baby chicks once they are hatched, as the leftover yolk provides them with sustenance for several days.

Unfortunately, there are some hatcheries out there that still practice debeaking—an operation where one-half to two-thirds of the chick's beak is cut off with a hot blade, ostensibly to reduce pecking deaths among the flock. Thankfully, most hatcheries have discontinued this practice. You can always request that your chicks not undergo this procedure. Pecking can be avoided provided that each chick has enough room to move around and free access to food and water. More importantly, if you are planning to allow your chicks to free-range (wander about and forage for extra food) on your land, they will need their beaks to defend themselves.

The Home Nest

Chickens are easily raised in a backyard setting, even in urban areas. You need only to construct a pen allowing for about one and one half square feet of living area per bird. Any less than this and the chicks will peck at each other nonstop. As the chicks grow, they will need more room, preferably about three square feet each. Half of the pen should be made of chicken wire and the other half of plywood (or similar materials). This allows for shelter from rain and snow.

Nesting boxes are small compartments built into the enclosed section of the pen. They are normally one foot off the ground, 1 foot deep, and 1.5 feet tall and wide. There should be one nesting box per four hens.

The floor of the chicken pen can be either dirt with a layer of chick litter over it, or grass. The best litter to use is wood shavings.

A small warmer light will also be needed to keep the birds warm during the colder months, as well as for light year round. Keep in mind that heat adversely effects chickens faster than cold will, so don't overdo it with the heat source. With proper care, a chicken can live up to fifteen years.

In addition to warmth, chicks must also be provided with light. The duration of light you should provide depends on the age of the chick. Pullets (hens under one year of age) need a minimum of fifteen hours of light each day. Any change in the lighting schedule of the chickens can cause delays in egg production and other problems. Check with your local extension agent to determine the correct light duration for your birds and supplement the natural light accordingly.

Chicks also enjoy taking dust baths. The dirt on their feathers helps to keep away lice and mites that can irritate their skin. A shallow dish filled with dry, loose dirt can serve as their bathtub.

One of the easiest mistakes to make is to assume that chickens need a spotless coop. They don't, but they do need a clean one. Clean the coop at least once a week.

Feeding The Flock

Providing the right kind of diet for your chicks is also important. Chicks must have ready access to food, grit, and water at all times. Chickens have no way to flush their internal system out, as they do not urinate, so a build-up of too much salt or other electrolytes can be toxic. For this reason, certain dietary measures are practiced.

Baby chicks should be fed a starter formula (you can buy this with antibiotics included) that contains a higher protein level than the food fed to fully developed birds. The diet varies according to purpose. For instance, you would not feed an egg layer the same as you would a broiler chick.

Meat-type birds require high protein foods in order to gain weight quickly. They consume starter feed until six weeks of age, then high protein thereafter.

Once a hen begins to lay eggs, she will need added calcium in her diet to strengthen the eggshells. Also, when rearing the chicks for egg production, the dietary measures are threefold. Begin with a starter feed until six weeks of age, follow with a developer feed until twenty weeks of age, and finish up with a feed specifically suited to egg-laying hens.

Grit is a mixture of sand and small pebbles that the birds hold in the gizzard to help them grind their food. Including oyster shell in the grit mixture is said to help thicken the eggshells once the hens begin to lay.

The Meat Option

If you are raising the birds for meat you will want to build your stock. How many roosters you need depends on your beginning hen count. One rooster can tend to fifteen hens. If you had two roosters for such a small number of hens, more than likely only one rooster would survive. Roosters are highly territorial and will fight to the death over their hens. That said, you also don't want to overtax your rooster. When one rooster tends to too many hens on his own, he grows weak. One sign that this could be happening is eggs that remain clear or have no visible sign of an embryo.

Once fertilization occurs, the incubation period for the egg is twenty-one days. These eggs must be placed in an incubator or underneath a broody hen. A broody hen is a hen that will sit on the eggs, keeping them warm until they hatch. The eggs should be "candled" to assure fertilization did indeed take place. Candling is a simple matter of backlighting the egg with an intense light in order to see through the shell. If you see shadows and dark areas it is due to the development of the embryo inside the shell. You should clearly see spidery red lines. You can keep an eye on the eggs and candle them again if you are unsure of what you see, but it is best to disturb the nest as little as possible.

If you see shadows but no spidery red lines, be aware that that particular egg just may be rotting. It if is, the egg will explode. As the smell of a rotten egg is horrid, it's better not to chance it and throw any suspicious eggs out.

Also if you are raising the chickens for meat, you must be prepared to butcher them when the time is right. Speak with your local extension agent to learn all applicable laws for your area.

Special Care For Baby Chicks

It's best to keep the younger chicks separate from the older chicks. They can all join together once they are all of laying age, but it is wisest to keep the flock at the same age. The risk of disease among poultry runs high, and any time you introduce birds from different flocks the risk increases. Ideally, all new birds should be isolated for at least thirty days.

It's unwise to handle the baby chicks, so keep handling to a minimum. They are extremely vulnerable to viruses (they can catch the common cold!) and one rough move could injure them severely. Give them a few weeks before handling. Also, be sure that the environment you provide for the first few weeks of their lives is rounded. An old plastic wading pool works great for this! When chicks are placed in a square box, they tend to huddle together for warmth; and quite often, one or more chicks will be trampled upon and smothered. Keep this temporary pen in an area that is free from drafts.

Health Care
When you raise your own chickens you can ensure that both the meat and the eggs are organic and chemical free. However, there will be certain treatments you may need to apply to keep your chickens free of parasites. Tending to the health of the chickens is important, as one sick bird can infect the entire population in a short time. If your hatchery provides vaccination for a small fee, it is well worth the investment. Many hatcheries today use vaccines that are certified organic and completely safe.

If one of your birds shows signs of being diseased, it must be removed from the pen immediately. The signs are: sneezing, wheezing, coughing, mucous drainage, diarrhea, a drop in egg production, thin eggshells, swelling, blood in the stool, lesions, droopiness, depression, and paralysis.

If you are building your stock of birds, you can tend to the vaccinations yourself in order to keep the flock healthy. It's a simple matter of buying the medicines and following a schedule, or buying the starter food with built-in antibiotics. Personally, I think an ounce of prevention is worth a pound of cure.

Don't Waste The Waste

The waste material is valuable as an additive to the compost pile, or it can be aged separately for use in the vegetable garden as a fertilizer. You may add both the droppings and the used litter to the compost pile.

Let's Eat

It's wise to abide by safe handling rules at all times when dealing with poultry products, so the manner in which you tend to the bird after butchering does matter substantially. Always assume that the meat has traces of salmonella bacteria on it and treat it accordingly. It must be refrigerated or frozen. Raw chicken will keep in the refrigerator for two to three days. If frozen, it must be thawed in a refrigerated environment.

Wash the meat under warm running water. If needed, use a plastic cutting board and soak it in bleach immediately after. Be sure the meat is thoroughly cooked. All of the meat's juices should run clear.

When it comes to handling eggs safely, things are much more simple. Gather the eggs two to three times a day. Throw out any cracked eggs. Keep the eggs refrigerated. They will last in the refrigerator for at least three weeks.

Once you gather the eggs it is not necessary to wash them, but if the shell is dirty you may want to. Use a soft washcloth and hot water. If the water is not hot enough, it could penetrate the shell of the egg and this will cause it to age faster. Keep in mind that bad eggs float, and get rid of any floaters right away. The eggs will last longer if they are not submerged for longer than two minutes and immediately refrigerated after cleaning.

There is a sanitizing spray on the market that makes cleaning eggs even easier. Simply spray and wipe.

Useful Information

Once a chick reaches the molting age, egg production will stop during the molting process (shedding of feathers), which can take up to four months. This is a natural function and laying will resume after molting. The normal molting season is late summer through early fall.

I've yet to mention the final benefit to raising your own chicks—the one that keeps backyard flocks thriving. Chickens make fantastic pets! Their silly antics provide comedic entertainment all year long. Once you taste true, farm-fresh eggs, you will never want another store-bought one. But, once you experience the personality of a chicken, you will see why people tend to home flocks for many years.

Helpful Tips

- Providing lukewarm drinking water in the winter helps increase egg production.
- Provide fresh water several times a day in warm weather.
- Yellow corn meal added to the food or litter will darken the yellow of the yolk.
- To get your baby chicks drinking, dip their beak in water; and do this one at a time.

About the Author

Tammy Sullivan is a full-time writer who writes from her home in the foothills of the Great Smoky Mountains.

Under a Northern Moon

By Nancy Bennett

For a long time those who did not know the North called the Inuit "Eskimos." Inuit no longer find this term acceptable. They have always been known to themselves as Inuit, which means "the people" in their own language, Inuktitut. Within the barren landscape of the Northwest Territories their own mythology and calendar evolved, following a lunar cycle and based on the survival needs of the people.

The Inuit divide the year into thirteen lunar periods of twenty-eight days each. Though local customs, availability of animals, and unique Inuit groups (such as the Arctic Inuit, the Copper Inuit, and the Mackenzie Inuit) offer variations on the following, all were more comfortable with the lunar cycle of thirteen months. Beginning with the January Moon, as recorded by historians in 1800s, this is one of their calendars.

Kah-pid-rah—It Is Cold

Everything is in total darkness. This is the last full month, when only the Moon sheds light on the North. To live this way for some would be depressing, but not for the Inuit. It was a time to tell tales and to socialize. During the winter, each camp had a large ceremonial igloo used for games and festivals. Drum dancing and singing, throat singing, storytelling, contests that tested the strength such as wrestling, made the long dark days go fast.

Hir-ker-maun—The Sun Returns

According to custom among the Igulik people of Northwestern Hudson Bay, the children would put out the flames on their lamps and then relight them to welcome the Sun. The traditional Inuit rite of Winter Solstice was the Bladder Festival (sometimes still observed). During this time, the hunters undergo a purification ritual in a hut that is filled with the inflated bladders of all the animals they've killed that year. After five days, they cast the bladders into a hole cut in the sea ice. Then the hunters leap through a bonfire, engage in contests of strength, and take a final sweat bath. In modern times people still celebrate the Festival of the Return of the Sun, or Qaggiq, as it is called.

Ik-ke-ar-par-roon—The Sun Is Rising

This was often a lean time and hunters looked forward to filling their family's larder once more. Seals and walruses were the first to arrive. For the Inuit, the seal was a major source of food, oil, and skins. Before the seal hunt, a shaman would be sent into the water to ask the goddess Sedna to release the sea animals the Inuit were dependent on. Sometimes a shaman would take a comb to comb out Sedna's hair because she had no fingers. Sedna's father had chopped them off and left her to drown. From her severed digits rose common seals, walrus, and bearded seals.

A-von-eve—Baby Seals Are Born

The Inuit never hunted the baby seals, despite rumors and bad publicity given to present day hunts of other nations, who are only interested in the white coats. The Inuit honored the seals, for they knew without them they would not survive. They allowed them to mature and then hunted them throughout the year. Sometimes this could be dangerous. "You do not know who is your friend or enemy until the ice breaks," is an old Inuit saying.

Neoh-e-a-ler-roon—Seals Take to Water

Traditionally, when a seal was brought into a house for butchering, certain rituals had to be followed. A lump of snow was dripped into the seal's mouth to quench the thirst of the soul. It was believed that the soul of the seal would reside in the harpoon that killed it for that first night. After butchering, women were not allowed to sew or do any other work for that day. Whale hunts, consisting of 200 or more kayakers, were organized in the ice-freed areas. The blubber and meat would be dried to last into the dark days, and dances were performed after successful hunts to give thanks to the whales.

Kav-ah-roc-vik—Time Seals Shed Their Coats

In olden times, the people would break winter camp and move in smaller groups to forage and gather wild berries, small game, and fish. Prayers are sent to help with the hunt. While Sedna was the goddess of the sea, the Moon was the god who directed the tides, storms, eclipses, earthquakes, and falling snow, and who also took care of game and wild fowl. He also took care of the souls of dead animals, and he watched over the behavior of humans. Sins would rise up to him as pungent smoke, hurting his eyes and angering him. The people often confessed their sins to the Moon, and promised to follow the rituals more closely so he would not be displeased.

Nook-rah-hah-le-yoon—The Fawn of the Caribou Are Born

This time coincides with the Summer Solstice in the North (June 21). The Inuit, especially the Copper Inuit, calculated the Summer Solstice by referencing certain fixed landmarks in relation to the Sun, or by the position of the star Altair, when it rose just before dawn. A large boulder, or a cairn of stones, was sometimes used to align with a point on the horizon. The Inuit believe in the reincarnation of the animal soul. When a caribou gets killed, the hunter must sever its head from the body. The caribou's living soul leaves and goes to the other caribou. Because the other caribou know of this death, they surround this living soul and clothe it, making it a caribou once more.

Mun-cha-le-yoon—The Birds Are Nesting

For this short time, eggs will be gathered to add to the family's diet. Special trips are organized out to the small islands where birds such as eider ducks lay their eggs. Traditionally it is forbidden to camp on these small islands, and those who gather eggs today still follow this belief which serves to keep the birds nesting area from being disrupted. Most ducks will lay a second clutch, and the gatherers make sure to leave the nest and down lining intact. In olden times the people would have moved inland to follow the caribou and to gather the plants in their brief growing season. Despite the harsh climate, over 800 plant species still survive in the North.

Ich-yah-yoon—The Young Birds Are Hatched

Birds are hunted and used for food. In one area, when the caribou disappeared, the people made a coat of the eider duck skins, which is warm, but fragile. Birds are taken for food and for magical purposes. A stuffed raven may be used as a shaman's tool. Amulets made from owls' claws, or bird skulls were worn to give strength. Evenings are sometimes spent sky watching. In the past, the Moon was associated with disease during a lunar eclipse. Shamans were often called to avert an epidemic. During a lunar eclipse, women are not supposed to leave their houses. During a solar eclipse, it is the males who are supposed to stay inside.

Ah-mer-ral-yoon—The Caribou Migrate

The best coats made from the caribou are taken in fall when the coats are thick. Hunters would dress in caribou skins and imitated the animal's sounds to lure them close enough to kill. Another hunting technique was to build Inukshuks and use them to hide behind. According to established rituals, seal and caribou meat were not to be eaten together, or cooked it in the same pot; and walrus skins were not to be sewn during caribou hunting season.

Noo-le-ah-le-yoon—The Time to Have a Wife

"Before you love, learn to run through the snow leaving no footprints," is an old Inuit saying. As the nights grew longer and the days short, more time was spent inside and this was a natural time to find a mate. The Moon was said to carry people off to the sky in a sled drawn by four black-headed dogs. This could be lucky for a woman, for if the Moon carried her off to his home, he made her fertile and sent her back to Earth. If a woman died giving birth, her soul returned to the Moon and the Moon himself was a protector of the orphan. On the other side of the coin, if a woman did not want to become pregnant, she had to avoid moonbeams.

See-koot-se-roon—The Ice Is Making In the Bays

The seals can still be reached by digging a hole in the ice and standing still for hours before harpooning. If there was one thing the Inuit hunter knew, it was patience. By now the people who had dispersed to smaller groups in the summer have all returned to make a winter camp. Stories will be told of Annigan, the Moon and brother to the Sun, who chases her across the sky in his incestuous lust; and of Irdlirvirisissong, demon cousin of the Moon, who makes people laugh by dancing and clowning. The people must restrain themselves, or they will laugh so hard the demon will dry them and eat their intestines.

Sik-ker-ne-loon—The Sun Disappears

This winter month was also called Siringilang, which meant "without sun." The name sometimes applied to the whole time in winter when the Sun cannot be seen above the horizon. It lasts between two and three months. Though there is darkness all around, there is still a great Moon lighting the way in the frozen North of the Inuit, awaiting the cycle to begin again. And as the elders would say: "May you have warmth in your igloo, oil in your lamp, and peace in your heart."

About the Author

Nancy Bennett has had her work published in various places including Llewellyn's annuals, We'moon, Circle Network, and many mainstream publications. Her pet projects include studying history and creating ethnic dinners to test on her family. She lives near a protected salmon stream, where the deer and the bears often play, in British Columbia, Canada.

Today Is the Day

By April Elliott Kent

The alarm rings at 7:00 am sharp. You stumble to the kitchen, turn on the coffee-maker, and jump in the shower. Yikes— no shampoo! You meant to buy some yesterday—well, soap will have to do. Showered and dried, you rummage through the knot of socks in your dresser drawer and salvage the pair with the fewest holes. Speed to the kitchen, slosh some coffee in a thermal cup—no time for breakfast; you'll grab a Danish at work. Where are your keys, where are your keys—you start your car and a warning light appears on the dashboard: You're almost out of gas. You're going to be late—again!

Life is hectic, and it's tempting to imagine that keeping our busy households in order is a uniquely modern challenge. The truth is, our basic needs for food, clothing, and safe shelter haven't changed over our long history of living together in homes—although our methods of meeting these needs certainly have.

In our modern age of electric lights, coffee-makers, and fast-food restaurants, we're largely disconnected from the normal cycles of seasons, phases of the Moon, and even day and night. Not so long ago, however, daily activities were routinely planned around these familiar cycles. I grew up on a farm in the early 1960s, and my father consulted the *Old Farmers Almanac* before planting his crops to ensure that the phase and sign of the Moon were appropriate. My aunt, who often gave us haircuts, would only wield her scissors when the Moon was in its waxing phase; she claimed this guaranteed faster-growing, healthier hair.

These were not astrologers, just people with a rich tradition of respecting and working with natural cycles. In agricultural societies, cooperation with nature has always been acknowledged as crucial to survival and to a successful harvest. It's only natural that domestic routines came to reflect the same sensibility. The seasons and lunar phases dictated times for planting, fertilizing, and gathering; and the days of the week, with their connection to the Sun, Moon, and five visible planets, suggested a natural system for organizing tasks, such as housework, that are done on a regular basis.

This connection is visible even in the names of the days of the week. Sunday was, of course, named for the Sun, and Monday for the Moon, honoring the rulers of day and night. The other days take their names from Norse gods of antiquity, and are ruled by the planets named for their mythical Roman counterparts. Tuesday was named after Tews, the god of war, and is ruled by Mars. Wednesday (Woeden's Day) derives its name from Odin, the god of wisdom; its ruler is Mercury. "Thor's Day" was named for the god of thunder and protection and is ruled by Jupiter. Friday, named for Freya, goddess of love and fertility, is ruled by Venus. Finally, Saturday takes its name from Saturn, the Roman god of the harvest.

Each day is believed to have a sympathetic connection with tasks that are ruled by the planet for which it was named. So culturally pervasive is this connection that it has found its way into folklore and song. The nursery rhyme "Here We Go 'Round the Mulberry Bush," which is believed to date from the mid-eighteenth century, began as a way for washerwomen to teach their children basic housekeeping. The rhyme details a system for completing the week's chores that not only makes perfect practical sense, but also reflects the traditional planetary rulerships for the days of the week. It's a system that was still being used, in a slightly modified form, by Victorian homemakers:

> Monday (the Moon's day) for laundry;
> Tuesday (Mars' day) for ironing;
> Wednesday (Mercury's day) for mending;
> Thursday (Jupiter's day) for shopping;
> Friday (Venus' day) for housecleaning;
> Saturday (Saturn's day) for baking;
> Sunday (the Sun's day) for rest.

When I grew up in mid-twentieth-century America, this domestic schedule was still deeply entrenched in the culture. I vividly remember my neighbors' "days of the week" aprons, each embroidered with the day's chore! Nor was this tradition confined to America or England. A friend who grew up in Mexico confirms that essentially the same routine was followed on her family's ranch.

But can modern homemakers take our cues from the Victorian housewife or from an eighteenth-century children's rhyme? After all, the landscape of daily life has changed dramatically. These days, dinner in many households is more likely to be a take-out meal from the local fast food restaurant than a pot roast cooked at home. Housecleaning and laundry are done during odd moments stolen between more pressing obligations, and usually only after the family has depleted its store of clean shirts (and in a world devoted to wrinkle-free miracle fabrics, who irons?).

Most modern American families no longer grow their own food, other than what is produced on their small hobby gardens. Unlike the households of the Victorian era, or even the 1950s, few households have a full-time homemaker with time to mend hems and bake her own bread. Have we jettisoned the need for planetary wisdom along with our plows and thimbles?

Considering our estrangement from most of nature's cycles, it's a bit surprising to find that the answer is no. We may buy our food from supermarkets, clothe ourselves in wash-and-wear shirts, and hire someone to clean our house every couple of weeks, but the planets still have plenty of advice about the best days to do these things. All that's needed is a bit of invention to align the chores of modern living with the ageless wisdom of the planets.

Monday: Moon Day

In the traditional home, Monday was the day for laundry, which is Moon-ruled. Before the blessed advent of automatic washing machines, it took the whole of the Sabbath for a homemaker to rest up for what was the most physically punishing of her chores. Now machines do most of the hardest work, and the modern homemaker usually wrestles with the laundry basket on the weekend, leaving Monday free for other lunar chores.

With the Moon's connection to nourishment, Monday is a good day to cook up a large pot of something tasty—soup, say, or spaghetti sauce—that can be frozen and thawed for future dinners. Haul out your old Crock-Pot and fill it with ingredients that can cook slowly while you're at work. When you come home, you'll sit down to a nice, hot bowl of stew and feel as cherished as a child.

Monday, ruled by the nurturing Moon, is also a day for taking care of others. Take a container of your homemade stew to an elderly friend, inscribe a pretty greeting card to a sick relative, or phone your homesick daughter who is away at college.

Tuesday: Mars Day

Mars-ruled Tuesday was set aside for ironing in the traditional home, because Mars has an affinity for heat and metal. If you're like me, you don't iron clothes more than a few times a year. But Mars, the warrior planet, can help you untangle knotty problems requiring confrontation and assertiveness. If you've put off arguing with the phone company over an erroneous charge, or with the neighbors whose tree limbs are damaging your roof, today is the day to put the heat on them; Mars makes warriors of us all!

Sharp objects and cutting are Mars-ruled, so today is the day to cut the grass, trim your cat's claws, get a haircut, or sharpen your cooking knives. Mars, with its abundant energy, rewards physical activity; today is the day to begin an exercise program or enjoy your favorite sport.

Wednesday: Mercury Day

On Wednesday, the traditional housewife mended clothing. Wednesday is Mercury's day, and Mercury rules detailed work requiring manual dexterity. Other than replacing the occasional button, few of us today do any real sewing. But communicative, quick-witted Mercury has other useful tools to share.

The students in your home might find that studying and test-taking go especially well on Mercury's day. In the office, use Wednesday to tackle research, write reports, file paperwork, interview new employees, and schedule meetings.

At home, today is the day to catch up on correspondence —letter-writing, e-mail, phone calls; to write short articles or essays; to balance your checkbook; and to run errands in your neighborhood. And don't forget to fill your gas tank today: Mercury rules cars.

Thursday: Jupiter Day

Thursday was marketing day for the traditional homemaker. Jupiter loves to share its prosperity, so today is the day to shop for your household needs (including new socks to replace the ones you didn't mend yesterday!).

Jupiter compels us to share our thoughts and beliefs, so teaching, lecturing, and writing for publication are favored on this day. Jupiter also represents unfamiliar people, places, and things. Today is the day to try a new kind of ethnic restaurant or go to a gathering, such as a class or club meeting, where you are likely to meet new people.

Jupiter enjoys the outdoors, so try to schedule a walk or bike ride on Thursday. Failing that, eat your lunch outdoors.

Friday: Venus Day

Friday was cleaning day for the traditional homemaker, perhaps in homage to Venus' urge for beautiful and harmonious surroundings. But Venus also describes the ability to attract what you want. Why not combine the two? Often, I perform a simple energy-clearing ritual on Friday. This begins with light cleaning, mostly clearing clutter in anticipation of a major cleaning on Saturday. I smudge with a sage wand, light some candles, open all the windows, and offer a quick request to Venus to bless our home with love, harmony, prosperity, and good friends.

With its connection to beauty, Friday is a good day to indulge in a manicure, pedicure, or facial treatment. Appropriately for Venus' day, Friday is popular for dating. Along with your other pre-date preparations, consider honoring Venus with a quick and simple ritual. Set up a small altar with a flower, a candle, and some sweet offering, such as a cookie. Light your candle, state your intentions for the evening, and visualize a warm, pleasant evening.

Saturday: Saturn Day

The traditional homemaker baked on Saturday so that fresh bread would be available for the Sabbath, when no cooking could be done. I love to bake when the weather is cool, but it does require more Saturnine time and patience than the typical harried home-maker has to spare.

Saturn rewards hard work and stiffens the spine for unappealing chores. That's why I've chosen Saturday for tackling my least-loved tasks, such as washing cars or windows, weeding the garden, and cleaning the refrigerator.

Any kind of hard, physical labor is compatible with Saturn's energy. If you need to move heavy objects, such as furniture, today is the day you will find the strength for it. Clean your fireplace or till the soil in your garden, and watch Saturn smile.

Sunday: Sun Day

Sunday was the traditional "day of rest," set aside for relaxation, recreation, and worship (the Sun rules creation, re-creation, and the Creator). In our household, Sunday tends to be the day we catch up on sleep, errands, and time with each other. Watching favorite TV programs or movies is a favorite Sunday ritual in our home, often shared with friends.

Today is the day for anything that makes you feel rested. It's a day for play, which restores physical and creative energy for the week ahead. "A change is as good as a rest," the old saying goes, and Sundays are often happiest when they are completely different from your usual routine. A trip to a museum, visiting with family, or preparing a special meal are all excellent ways to honor the Sun's day.

A household routine of any kind can help you stay centered. When you know that every task will have its day, you can relax and focus on the day's work without worrying that you've overlooked something important. Instead of rushing around, discovering too late that you've forgotten to buy the shampoo, mend the socks, or fill the gas tank, you can instead enjoy the hearth fires of your well-tended home as they blaze comfortingly, contentedly. Planning your household's activities with the wisdom of planetary tradition is astrology in its most basic and practical form—a way to add a touch of cosmic purpose to a household full of earthly contentment.

About the Author

April Elliott Kent, a professional astrologer since 1990, is a member of NCGR and ISAR, and graduated from San Diego State University with a degree in communication. April's astrological writing has appeared in The Mountain Astrologer *(USA) and* Wholistic Astrologer *(Australia) magazines, the on-line magazines MoonCircles and Beliefnet, and Llewellyn's* Moon Sign Book *(2005, 2006). April specializes in the astrology of choosing wedding dates and the study of eclipses. Her Web site is: http://www.bigskyastrology.com.*

Tattoo by the Moon

By Robin Ivy

Tattoo has evolved over thousands of years. From tribal ritual to a form of torture to a way of identifying the most noble in society, the history and connotations of this kind of body art are complex and will always remain shrouded in a degree of mystery. For much of the twentieth century getting a tattoo was a rebellious act, often distinguishing the wild side of life. In the past decade or two, what was once an act of youthful rebellion, or the result of a night of debauchery, has become a common method of self-expression.

Individuals from all walks of life proudly wear their chosen pictures, symbols, and words permanently. And while some wearers choose one, small, carefully concealed tattoo, others will accumulate a collection of boldly displayed ink designs. In fact, aficionados say the process is addictive, despite any pain involved, and it's easy to spot the living proof at a rock concert, on the beach, or at the basketball court, where arms, legs, and torsos are often covered in dramatic, colorful form!

Once you've decided you want a tattoo of your very own, two decisions await: (1) What your tattoo will look like, and (2) When you'll take the leap. As a form of adornment and a surgery of sorts (the needle pierces the skin to alter the body), considering lunar phase and sign, and common guidelines for health and beauty, can be helpful. Let's explore some astrological indicators to determine favorable dates and designs by Moon signs.

Timing

Tattoo involves altering your appearance, and while it is a generally safe procedure when done in a sterile environment, it is an invasive act. The Moon's phase, sign, and aspects to other planets on your chosen date can have a beneficial or aggravating effect in both the healing process and the overall result of the tattoo artist's work.

As with any other surgery, the first priority is to schedule away from the Full Moon period to minimize swelling or bleeding. The most favorable lunar times for tattoo are in the week following a New Moon, and more than three days past the Full Moon. Timing your appointment during those times will help decrease discomfort and discourage ill effects in the days that follow.

Avoiding the void-of-course Moon times is also a good idea since the judgment of both the artist and the client can be affected, increasing the chance of mistakes!

As with all other permanent decisions, it's best to have the Moon solidly in one sign and in favorable aspect to other planets on the day of your appointment. Check the Moon's last aspect in the sign and look for a beneficial influence from Venus, Jupiter, or the Sun. It's best if the Moon is not in any aspect with Mars, Uranus, Saturn, Neptune, or Pluto on the day you select.

Finally, you may want to consider the sign the Moon is traveling through since some signs are more resilient or receptive to the tattoo process. Paying attention to the body parts governed by each sign will also help, since it's best to avoid undue stress on an area when the Moon is in that body part's ruling sign.

Aries Moon

The Aries Moon is fiery and impulsive, so this may not be your top choice. Tattoo involves heat and can cause inflammation, both of which are more likely during Aries Moon times. A last minute decision to tattoo when the Moon is in Aries could result in regrets! If you must schedule tattoo then, make sure the Aries Moon is in harmony with Venus and clear of any influence from Mars, Saturn, Uranus, Neptune, and Pluto, all of which can tamper with the healing and appearance of your tattoo. Aries rules the head, so scalp, ear, or any facial tattoos should be avoided completely when the Moon travels this sign.

Taurus Moon

Ruled by Venus, planet of beauty, this Moon sign may be a good choice for solid results and lasting color in your design. Taurus takes a careful, thoughtful approach, and is supportive in the healing process. Most body parts are free and clear for tattoo while the Moon is in Taurus, but save neck and throat designs for another date. Check for void-of-course Moon times and planetary aspects to find your best time.

Gemini Moon

Gemini rules the nervous system and is therefore sensitive to pain. This Moon sign makes it hard to sit still and concentrate, making it a challenge for both the artist and you. Gemini rules the hands and arms, which may be wiggly and restless that day. Anxiety and duality characterize the Gemini Moon. It's probably better if you can consider another date.

Cancer Moon

On one hand, the Cancer Moon is creative and intuitive, making it a favorable day for artistic work and selection of your design.

However, it must be considered that the sign ruled by the Moon has some Full Moon qualities, so swelling and bruising may increase during Cancer Moon time. If there are no aspects between the Moon and the "forbidden" planets indicated earlier, this can be a very emotional and powerful day to add a tattoo to the arms, legs, or shoulders, but avoid the chest, stomach, or breasts.

Leo Moon

Leo is a sign of energy and vitality and may contribute to quick healing. It is also a sign that loves adornments of all kinds, so your Leo Moon tattoo is likely to be considered an accessory, worn in an obvious area of the body. The Leo Moon is fixed, indicating permanence of the ink design and confidence in your decision. As long as the other planets are in cooperation, go forth with tattoos on the arms, legs, torso, or buttocks, but avoid the spine and back.

Virgo Moon

Attention to detail is enhanced during the Virgo Moon, so this date is a good choice for perfectionists. This doesn't mean you won't be nervous, though. Virgo is connected to the nervous system, and you may obsess about your decision. The artist works well with these conditions, and this is a good sign if you're considering tattoo with very detailed graphics or fine lines. Since Virgo relates to the intestines, all surfaces of the body are fair game!

Libra Moon

The Libra Moon relates to all forms of beauty and adornment so this is a very attractive time to schedule your tattoo. Adding color to existing tattoos is also a good idea when the Moon is in one of the signs related most to different hues. The lower back is Libra's physical domain though, so if your heart is set on a belt line design, try another sign and avoid the Leo Moon as well.

Scorpio Moon

With the Moon in such a complex sign, one that rules surgery and is co-ruled by Pluto and Mars, it's probably safest to avoid tattooing altogether on these dates. However, this is a deeply emotional and spiritual sign and if your tattoo will have great significance to you, or if you need guidance in selecting a meaningful symbol, Scorpio Moon time may be perfect for making your choices. Shop for your studio and explore your artistic options, but save the appointment for another time.

Sagittarius Moon

If you've wanted a tattoo, but tend to get cold feet, the Sagittarius Moon will give you the nerve to take the plunge. This Moon sign has a sense of adventure, which helps build confidence, and the dry quality of the sign may help in healing. As long as the hip or thigh is not the destination for your design, take advantage of the free-spirited feeling the Sagittarius Moon brings.

Capricorn Moon

On one hand the Moon is in a cardinal sign, which is known for recuperative powers, but on the other, consider that Capricorn is ruled by Saturn, a planet to avoid as you select your appointment time. If you do choose to tattoo when the Moon is in Capricorn, the knees and other bony areas are the spots to avoid.

Aquarius Moon

Aquarius is a fixed air sign, which favors healing. Aquarian rebelliousness and originality do connect this Moon sign to the art of tattoo. Aquarius Moon days are excellent for creating or choosing a distinctive graphic, but this time may be even better for planning the tattoo than for having the work done. If you do schedule for an Aquarius Moon, leave the calves and ankles alone.

Pisces Moon

Pisces is emotional and imaginative, the artist of the zodiac. If you choose to tattoo under a Pisces Moon, the experience is very personal and spiritual. Since Pisces is a water sign, take extra care to keep the area clean and dry during the healing process. The feet are Pisces ruled and will be extra sensitive and vulnerable, so look for another date if a foot or toe design is what you have in mind.

Symbolism

Tattoo choices reflect the individual who wears them, and a design can mark a moment in time, like a rite of passage, or express a deep affiliation, a part of the soul that is constant through life. A young man may tattoo his name or symbol of ethnic heritage as a sign of pride and desire to carry on tradition, while a newly divorced woman in mid-life selects a lightning bolt as she moves into a new and exciting phase. Abstract symbols like Celtic armbands or Asian writing may appeal to many of us, but for different reasons. One person may express family origin while another is drawn to the meaning of the symbol. The symbolism behind a design may be a strong influence even if we don't completely understand it at the time, as our subconscious draws us to the energy we need to express.

Since our natal Moon sign reflects our emotions and dreams, who we are on the inside, and what we feel and value, the body art we choose can be our way of bringing that inner part of our personality to the surface. Whether you're covered in tattoos or are thinking about adorning yourself with ink for the first time, consider some of the symbols connected to your Moon sign. What will your tattoo say about you?

Earth Signs

The earth signs are feminine and receptive and, of course, connected to nature. The number five corresponds with earth, as human beings have five fingers on each hand, five toes on each foot, and five points (including the head, arms, and legs). Pentacle designs may appeal to you; and creatures of the Earth, like lizards, snakes, and other garden dwellers, correspond to Taurus, Virgo, and Capricorn. Flowers and vines are natural reflections of your earth energy, as are any symbol for growth, fertility, or prosperity. From the mythical world, consider fairies, Earth dragons, elves, or gnomes.

Air Signs

Gemini, Libra, and Aquarius are signs of community and friendship, so designs that express affiliation with a group or "tribe" may be very appealing to you. Asian, Native American, Celtic, or any other nation's symbol for peace, harmony, or beauty also reflects the nature of an air sign Moon. Creatures that fly make sense for you, from the delicate dragonfly to the wise hawk, and all birds, butterflies, and fairies, as well. Celestial designs also complement your energy in air.

Water Signs

If your Moon is in Cancer, Scorpio, or Pisces, you're likely to have an emotional connection to your tattoo design. Religious symbols may attract you. The Moon in all her phases connects to water, and all that is nautical or symbolizes the sea carries that same theme of ebb and flow. Mermaids, fish, and other water creatures express your Moon sign, as do symbols for emotion such as hearts, tarot cups, or even teardrops. Abstract characters for love, marriage, family, and loyalty will attract you. Cats carry water sign energy as well.

Fire Signs

Aries, Leo, and Sagittarius may go for the most dramatic designs. Magic wands and other symbols correspond to the fire element. Graphics that integrate the Sun, heat, fire, and arrows connect to fire-sign energy, which is powerful and masculine in nature. Animals of strength and dominance, such as lions, eagles, and horses, represent your Moon sign well. Symbolically, characters for courage, honor, truth, and nobility express your Moon sign best.

About the Author

Robin Ivy is a radio personality, educator, and astrologer in Portland, Maine. She fuses her passion for music and the metaphysical in Robin's Zodiac Zone, a feature on her morning show on 94 WCYY, Portland's new rock alternative. Visit Robin's Web site at www.robinszodiaczone.com.

Million Dollar Empathy

By Robin Antepara

The Lunar Connection Between Clint Eastwood and Hilary Swank

In late 2004, a movie about a scrappy female boxer named Maggie Fitzgerald swaggered into movie theaters, garnering critical acclaim and grabbing four Academy Awards.

It wasn't the fight scenes in *Million Dollar Baby* that packed the biggest punch, but the extraordinary chemistry between actor/director Clint Eastwood and his leading lady Hilary Swank. It was this chemistry (keyed astrologically by Cancer) that gave the movie its unique power.

On the surface, the focus of the film is Maggie's rise to fame. On a deeper level, though, the film is about how the relationship between Maggie (Swank) and her trainer Frankie (Eastwood) fueled her transformation from poor white trash to boxing champ. Such is the power of their relationship that Frankie also undergoes a metamorphosis from gruff, macho man to empathetic father figure and mentor.

More important for the purposes of this article is how Frankie's metamorphosis mirrors Eastwood's real-life transformation: from playing gunslingers in spaghetti Westerns to being an internationally acclaimed film director, who has directed and starred in some of this decade's finest films

In this article we'll view these transformations, and the encounter with the Feminine that Maggie symbolizes, through an astrological lens. At the heart of the chemistry between the two actors is a strong Cancer link that, although not involving the Sun sign in either chart, connects the pair in profound ways. We'll examine the Cancer connection as it manifests both through their cinematic relationship and in their personal lives.

Maggie's dramatic rise from the trailer park in which she was raised begins when she approaches Frankie and asks him to train her. He refuses, saying he doesn't train girls. Frankie has spent his career coaching top-ranking heavyweights. He certainly isn't going to waste his time on a nobody—and a female nobody at that—from the wrong side of the tracks.

The tough guy that Eastwood portrayed in the film was not just a role. Astrologically, it can be seen in his natal Sun and Moon (in air and fire signs, respectively). Fire and air are the two "masculine," outgoing elements of the zodiac and, in their pure form, not prone to empathy. Even more revealing is that his Mars, the god of war, is in Aries: the quintessential symbol of the warrior. This is macho impulse, energy, and drive with a capital M.

It's hard to find precise correlates for this macho energy in Eastwood's personal life, in part because he has been so reticent about discussing it. However, we do know that he has been married twice and has fathered seven children, both in and out of wedlock. Befitting the martial energy in his chart, he once informed his first wife that he would do as he pleased, a perquisite that included "nooners" with various starlets. One such tryst, with an exotic dancer who worked with a big snake, produced a child who would later become an actress.

We can see myriad examples of the alpha male in Eastwood's earlier films, from the authority-baiting Harry Callahan of the *Dirty Harry* series to the rowdy trail hands he portrayed in 1950s-era TV westerns. These macho men took on a darker cast in later films such as *Play Misty for Me* and *The French Connection*.

In *Million Dollar Baby*, the tough, gruff Frankie is transformed into a loving mentor, largely as a result of Maggie's doggedness. However, this does not happen without a struggle. In the beginning, the hardened trainer dismisses her out of hand, telling her she's too old to fight and pathetic for even trying. But this does not deter our girl. She shows up at his gym every morning to work out and pays dues by waiting tables at neighborhood dives.

However, it's not only Maggie's persistence that melts Frankie's heart but her *sweetness:* her wide-eyed wonder as she watches a prize fighter in the ring, and her gentleness with Frankie's best friend Scrap.

It's here, in Maggie's gentleness, that we catch our first glimpse of the Cancer connection. While every Mars-driven microfiber in Frankie's being mitigates against training her, something else irrevocably pulls him in.

That something else is Venus in Cancer, a placement that combines the goddess of love with the soft, watery realm of the fourth sign of the zodiac—Cancer. What's fascinating is that both Swank and Eastwood have Venus in Cancer, and at just about the same degree (Eastwood's Venus is at 8 degrees, Swank's is at 11). Before examining the way the two charts interact, let's look more closely at the Cancer energy.

Cancer, a water sign ruled by the Moon, is the archetypal mother. More than any other sign it is associated with nurturing and sensitivity. It denotes a woman's way of knowing: not through hardheaded logic and analysis but through instinct and intuition. In short, through connection and empathy with the Other.

This pliant feminine energy is enhanced by the presence of Venus. Another archetypal symbol of the feminine, Venus is more associated with aesthetics and pleasure than with the rooted, maternal instincts of the Moon. In Greek and Roman mythology, Venus/Aphrodite can often be found dallying with Mars, Adonis, or Anchises, among others, straying far from hearth and home. Although promiscuous on the surface, at base Venus is about relation—fickle though that relatedness may be.

Into this feminine love-fest creeps one of the bad guys of the zodiac: Saturn. Here again we see synchronicity, for both Swank and Eastwood have Saturn closely aspecting Venus in their natal charts (Swank has a tight conjunction, Eastwood a tight opposition with Saturn in ruling Capricorn).

You couldn't find a more antithetical impulse to the feminine than Saturn. Unlike the relational tendencies of Venus or the nurturing instincts of Cancer and the Moon, Saturn is a strict taskmaster. His tools are restriction, limitation, and ultimately, pain. Everything that contracts, constricts, or controls has a Saturn base, whether it's granules of salt or the proverbial Zen master's stick.

What we see in the synastric picture between Eastwood/Swank-Frankie/Maggie are two sweet, gentle people with a strong need to *nurture* and *connect* with others, hunted by the astrological equivalent of the grim reaper.

One manifestation of Saturn's limitation is want and frugality, something that both Eastwood and Swank experienced in their lives. Like Maggie, Swank was raised in a trailer park. Her parents had little money and Hilary sometimes found herself the victim of bullies at school as a result.

Born nearly half a century before Swank, Eastwood was a Depression-era kid. Eastwood's father was always scouting around for work, and the actor grew up learning that ". . . nothing comes from nothing, you've got to work for what you get." Like Swank, Eastwood was introverted and self-sufficient as a child.

Another manifestation of Saturn-Venus is thwarted intimacy. This was true for Swank, who admits to being lonely as a child. That loneliness was amplified after her parents divorced when she was just fifteen; the same year, her mother was fired from her job. "She was at a crossroads in her life and knew I wanted to act," Swank recalled in a *Newsweek* interview. "So she said, '"Let's go to Hollywood."' Befitting Saturn's energy in Swank's chart, the pair lived in the car for several weeks. But Swank also has her Sun in resilient Leo and could alchemize the hardship. "It wasn't a negative thing," she said. "It was kind of like an adventure— like: Wow, we're in Hollywood."

Let's return to the film and see how Venus-Saturn-Cancer plays out in the relationship between Maggie and Frankie. This can best be viewed through Frankie's transformation from an emotion-phobic trainer to a man in touch with his lunar, feminine side. In Jungian terms, one could say that *Million Dollar Baby* tells the story of how Frankie connected to his anima.

At the outset, not only is Frankie coldly unreceptive to Maggie's pleas, but we learn he is estranged from his daughter. He writes her regularly, but to no avail. His letters are always returned marked "return to sender." Some big rupture has occurred—one too big for mending, it would seem. Frankie must have said or done something *really* bad, thinks the viewer, to have precipitated such a break.

Frankie clearly wants to make amends. In addition to all the letters (which he keeps in a shoebox in the closet), he attends mass every morning and prays for forgiveness every night before he goes to sleep.

"You know what I want," he says, kneeling beside his bed. "There's no use me repeating myself."

God works in mysterious ways—this we know. In the movie, Spirit does not respond directly to Frankie's prayers. Indeed, even at the story's end, Frankie and his daughter have not reconciled. However, God does send anima in the form of Maggie. And once Maggie decides it's Frankie she wants for a trainer, she does not take no for an answer.

She does, however, endure some hard Saturn knocks before their connection is solidified. After reluctantly agreeing to train Maggie, Frankie proceeds to unload her on another trainer just before her first fight. Maggie is devastated but wants to fight so she agrees. However, with Venus in Cancer, Frankie can't stay away the night of the match; he can see from the first round it is a disaster. Not able to stand it any longer, he steps in and gives her the pointers she needs in order to subdue her opponent. It is at this stage, after all the Saturn trials and rites of passage, that Frankie really commits to the relationship—and to the feminine within himself.

After the fight, as Maggie decompresses, she throws him a sharp left hook. "You gave me away. Are you going to leave me again?" she says to Frankie.

"Never," he says. And this time we know he means it.

What unfolds in the unlikely pairing between girly boxer and macho trainer is not only Cancerian empathy but both the dark and the light of Saturn. For many people Saturn is a daunting planet, harbinger of pain and disillusion. This is particularly true when it aspects sensitive places in our charts. It's one thing for Saturn to square the Sun or oppose Mercury: those are hard-nosed, masculine archetypes that can handle it. But empathetic Moon or Venus? Saturn surely has no business there.

But Saturn goes where he will go, and the cosmos often leads him to those very vulnerable places in our psyches. Although those contacts often bring searing pain, what we learn from Maggie and Frankie is their stunning potential—*if* we can endure that pain. Indeed, Saturn brings a depth of commitment that would be hard to achieve without him.

Having endured these Saturn trials, Maggie and Frankie become an unbeatable team. He coaches her on footwork and teaches her how to control her breathing. He goes beyond giving mere technical advice, though, paying money under the table when he can't find any managers willing to put their fighters in the ring with Maggie.

But as the Cancer energy suggests, Frankie and Maggie are more than just a team; they become family. Frankie encourages Maggie to save money. He surreptitiously peeks into her checkbook to see how she's doing and tries to prevent her from making mistakes he has made. For all his gruffness, he is much the same way with his friend Scrap: fretting over holes in his socks, chastising him for wasting money.

Maggie exhibits the same nurturing tendencies. She saves her pennies (just as Frankie had advised), and then surprises her mother with a new house. Alas, once again Saturn rears its head when Maggie's mother brutally rejects her daughter's generosity. Realizing how alone she is in the world, Maggie later tells Frankie he's all she's got.

"Well, you've got me," he says. "At least, that is, until we find you a new manager."

In this moment, in the joke we know is a joke, we know that the bond between Maggie and Frankie is rock solid, not to be torn asunder by any force in the universe. This Cancer bond, forged by Saturn, is there to stay.

In *Million Dollar Baby*, Frankie and Maggie share a similar pain: alienation from their families. This is Saturn-Cancer to the core. Because it is so perfectly mirrored in their natal charts, there is a strong suggestion that these are wounds that both Eastwood and

Swank carry in their personal lives as well. Just as Saturn provided a vehicle of healing in the screenplay, it might be that the playing of those roles provided real-life redemption for these two sensitive and gifted Souls.

About the Author

Robin Antepara is an astrologer and freelance writer who has lived in Japan for over fifteen years. She is available for consultations and may be reached by e-mail at robina@gol.com.

Entertaining by the Signs

By Lynn Gordon Sellon

J ust as it influences the tides of the ocean, the Moon can also affect the mood or atmosphere on a daily basis. Astrologers who elect favorable dates for events, such as weddings or important business meetings, will consider the transiting Moon when determining these dates. When it is not possible to select the perfect time for a special occasion, simply knowing the Moon's sign on any given date offers unique information.

Each day the Moon's affiliation with a sign of the zodiac is like an emotional weather report for the day that can be used to plan for or to create an atmosphere for those special occasions. Each sign colors the influence of the Moon, and offers clues about the undercurrent to expect during an event on any given day.

You do not need to be an astrologer to learn how to work with the Moon's regular rhythm. In order to prepare for an event, all you need is a daily lunar table indicating what astrological sign the Moon passes through each day. Moon to planet aspects do influence the Moon's energy, but generally the sign the Moon is in will give a great deal of information about how people will react in different situations. The day's Moon sign also describes the kind of atmosphere people will feel comfortable in, the types of events that resonate with people, and even the topics of conversation that will most likely spark interest.

Each sign the Moon passes through is listed on the following pages with a description of the general tone to expect, the types of events to plan, the décor to have, and even the foods to serve when the Moon is in that sign. Keep these in mind when planning your next special occasion.

Knowing the sign of the Moon is not only helpful in planning, but also in providing information when attending an event. Before you go out next time, take note of the Moon's sign and see if you can sense the subtle differences in the crowd.

Aries Moon

When the Moon is in Aries, people will be adventurous, talkative, and willing to explore new areas of interest. It is important to be open to different points of view and to be prepared for others to have strong opinions, because they will. People may lose interest in a topic and quickly move on to another. Sports, exercise, woodworking, and camping are all great topics for conversation. Aries is a great sign for brainstorming. Guests may enjoy unplanned activities and be willing to take action without much notice. If there is a tedious task to be completed, guests may become restless, so physical movement should be included in planned activities.

Types of Events: "Dancing on the rooftop" is a great theme for an Aries Moon event. The best time for a party is later in the evening. Include activities like dancing, sports, or playing games. Introduce new concepts, work toward a goal, or build something. Be aware that projects started under the Aries Moon may not be completed in the course of an event.

Décor: Warm atmosphere with a fire in the fireplace or candles. A red or brightly colored centrepiece, highlighted by Birds of Paradise, adds flair. Serving pieces or party favors made of carved wood also add a great touch.

Food: Italian, hot foods (not spicy), or lamb.

Taurus Moon

When the Moon is in Taurus, people gravitate toward anything involving the arts, music, and acting. People may be very opinionated during conversations, but common ground can be found when an appreciation for the finer things in life is expressed; and, discussing the latest movie, theatre production, or the best bargains is exciting. When the Moon is in Taurus, people are willing to work hard as long as they feel comfortable. Multiple food breaks will ensure better productivity.

Types of Events: Themes around artistic expression and creativity are perfect. April is a great month for Taurus-influenced occasions. Activities should involve acting, charades, or musical entertainment. Guests will enjoy seeing things that are very beautiful, and they'll *truly* appreciate good food. An event held at a retail store will also attract people.

Décor: Create an atmosphere that appeals to the senses with pastel colors, daisies, music—especially piano—and scented candles. Handcrafted serving pieces will be admired. Small sculptures, copper-crafted party favors, or hostess gifts are great finishing touches.

Food: Greek or Spanish.

Gemini Moon

Sharing information under a Gemini Moon feels very natural. People are interested in a wide variety of subjects and have a great need to communicate. However, conversations will be brief, and books, cars, radio, or computers are great topics to spark interest. Learning new information and collecting facts will intrigue people. If an activity is planned which requires people to sit and listen for any length of time, they might enjoy taking notes.

Types of Events: People will enjoy book group meetings, family reunions, automotive shows, running, lectures, technology demonstrations, and story telling; and trivia games will be a big hit. Gemini events held in a library, bookstore, or even a school, are perfect.

Décor: A travel theme with paper decorations will incite great interest. Muted earth-tones highlighted with shades of violet will resonate with guests under the Gemini Moon. A party favor or hostess gift of personalized notepaper will be treasured.

Food: Egyptian or African.

Cancer Moon

An intimate gathering at home provides the most comfortable setting under the Cancer Moon. People will be interested in issues that are related to family life—the accomplishments of family members and any recent family outings—as well as improvements that can be made to their homes. People may enjoy talking about home repair, real estate, or the local economy. If the event involves people who are not familiar with one another, finding common interest through past experiences is a great way to break the ice.

Types of Events: Housewarming parties, pot luck suppers, Mother's Day, or a sunset sail are all great ways to celebrate under a Cancer Moon. A mother/daughter event would be a big hit; and, if someone is in need, guests will show compassion for others and pitch in to help those less fortunate than themselves.

Décor: A relaxed atmosphere will help people feel at home. Iridescent colors and pearl whites set a great tone. Glassware on the table along with a simple bouquet of white roses portrays a sense of calm. A beautifully wrapped baked item makes a wonderful hostess gift or party favor.

Food: Locally grown meats and vegetables.

Leo Moon

Romance is the perfect word to describe an evening under the Leo Moon. An elegant grand ballroom and an intimate romantic dinner for two will feel right. Leo brings out the child inside, giving people the ability to view things with hope, enthusiasm, and a willingness to take on new challenges. People are interested in enjoying themselves, their surroundings, and conversations about the latest movie, the lives of the rich and famous, or childhood milestones.

Types of Events: A romantic dinner, galas, club meetings, a night of theater, a Father's Day celebration, an awards banquet, or a baby shower are great Leo occasions. The tone of an event can range from being very joyful and childlike to romantic. People also thrive on recognition.

Décor: Any decorations which create a sense of drama capture the Leo energy. A grand room with elegant décor, a small intimate table for two with candlelight, or a brightly colored children's party are themes that work well. A full spectrum of colors used on the table topped off with a large Sunflower centerpiece makes a great statement. A small jeweled box or a bag of gourmet almonds makes a wonderful hostess gift or party favor.

Food: French or Italian.

Virgo Moon

When the Moon is in Virgo, people will be interested in making improvements, serving others, or creating order out of chaos. During your conversations, find out what the other person's expertise is. This will help serve two purposes: you will learn more about a subject you may not have known anything about before, and the other person gets an opportunity to fill his/her need to serve. If you are at a loss for words, diet, exercise, and health are natural topics for Virgo.

Types of Events: An event that serves a purpose—raising money for charities, a book group, or a public health forum—

work well. Any event happening under the Virgo Moon requires attention to detail, and guests will need to feel useful so involve them in helping to make the event a success.

Décor: Navy and white or pale pinks and violet make a simple but elegant statement. A finely stitched tablecloth will draw a lot of attention. For a centrepiece, try a bouquet of fruit that can also serve as dessert. A selection of gourmet cheeses or a handy little tool work well as either a party favor or a hostess gift.

Food: A taste of Paris or beautifully prepared food.

Libra Moon

The Libra influence encourages a sense of cooperation. People *want* to find common ground and get along harmoniously. Topics of conversation that revolve around fashion, decorating style, or works of art will definitely generate interest. Politics and issues governing legal rights may also prove to be very lively topics. When the Moon is in Libra, people are generally interested in anything that creates symmetry or beauty. The arts, entertainment, and music have great appeal.

Types of Events: Weddings, fashion shows, garden tours, poetry readings, and artistic programs are great themes for an event ruled by Libra. Libra's influence heightens the visual and auditory senses, so the addition of soft music in the background or interesting works of art will be quickly noticed.

Décor: Create an atmosphere that soothes the senses with symmetry. A floral theme fits any occasion. Use soft colors complemented by white roses to fill a need for balance. Complement floral arrangements with white china. Beautifully potted violets or a bouquet of flowers will be received graciously as a hostess gift or party favor.

Food: Danish.

Scorpio Moon

A Scorpio Moon brings out great intensity and commitment in people. When the Moon is in Scorpio ask someone what is really important to them and be prepared for an in-depth answer and to be moved by their response.

When trying to create an atmosphere that is in tune with the nature of Scorpio, be aware of an intense underlying drive to be understood by others and that great passion provides the fuel to create something new. Capturing the innate determination of the crowd can be revolutionary.

Types of Events: Celebrate promotions or milestones in life, hold a tag sale to get rid of old junk. A magic show will generate interest. Activities that relay information which can change someone's outlook or way of life, even in a seemingly insignificant way, is in keeping with the true nature of Scorpio.

Décor: Bright red and fiery colors suit a Scorpion mood. Candles floating in a water-filled clear glass bowl, centered on a table covered with a richly colored table cloth, make a very dramatic statement. Any unique decorations add a great touch. A fun magic book or interesting sculptures made out of recycled materials are a great hostess gift or party favor.

Food: Norwegian cuisine, Bavarian chocolate.

Sagittarius Moon

When the Moon is in Sagittarius, people are interested in new concepts and philosophy. When you're participating in a conversation, people may want to talk more than they want to listen because they are anxious to share their own wealth of knowledge. Religion, philosophy, and travel are topics that will be met with great enthusiasm.

When influenced by Sagittarius, people are willing to take things to an extreme, move out of their comfort zone, and explore new areas of thought as well as new places. Most importantly, people really want to have a good time!

Types of Events: College activities, "meet the author" sessions, writing forums, religious ceremonies, and travel are all very Sagittarian occasions. People will feel most at ease attending events held at a financial institution, university, or church. November is a great month to plan a Sagittarius Moon event.

Décor: Compliment a travel theme with travel posters, and specialty foods. Rich colors, turquoise, and pale green should be incorporated into the décor. A prayer or famous literary quote prominently placed will promote discussion. Any type of book given as a party favor or hostess gift will be received with great appreciation.

Food: Spanish cuisine.

Capricorn Moon

The Capricorn influence sets a serious "no nonsense" tone. People are goal-oriented, efficient, and interested in seeing results for hard work. Most people feel compelled to make a contribution, and they need to be heard when involved in a conversation. Enter a discussion with the purpose of finding out what the other person's accomplishments are. Interactions usually revolve around work, what needs to be done, and what the best ways are to get something done. Great discussion topics include business matters, organizational techniques, antiques, and time.

Types of Events: December is a great month to hold a Capricorn event. Business-related activities, office parties, auctions, and gatherings that are not overly fussy create an atmosphere in tune with the Capricorn nature. Ceremonies and rituals are also perfect. A work party that requires everyone to pitch in is a great idea. If guests are given assignments, they will take their responsibilities seriously.

Décor: The simple elegance of black and white creates a neat and orderly impression. A stunning ice sculpture will draw extra attention. Pine branches arranged in beautiful pottery create an interesting centrepiece. Leather accessories or a timepiece make a great hostess gift or party favor.

Food: Greek or Mexican.

Aquarius Moon

A group of friends or colleagues working together toward broader social change is a great example of the influence of Aquarius. People are compelled to engage in activities that promote the betterment of society in general. People are very interested in meeting new friends and sharing their knowledge. This is a great time for people to brainstorm or share their hopes and wishes. They may tend to be very talkative. Computers, technology, astrology, or even the latest television program are great conversation starters.

Types of Events: Surprise parties, friendly gatherings, science symposiums, even telethons are events ruled by Aquarius. Raising public awareness for a special cause is also a great way to use this energy. Do not be surprised if there are sudden changes in the flow of an event. Perhaps it will start later or last longer than expected.

Décor: Electric blue and bright colors. Special lighting creates an atmosphere that resonates with people. A sleek look fashioned by a white tablecloth and brightly colored candles, and accented by modern tableware, gives a very fresh clean feeling. Any item that has modern design qualities makes a great party favor or hostess gift.

Food: Swedish cuisine.

Pisces Moon

The Pisces Moon creates a need for completion and serenity. People need time to think about what they have accomplished and contemplate future goals. They are very sensitive to the world around them and receptive to learning about charitable opportunities. They may hold back their true feelings and be easily hurt by words that might not have bothered them on other days, too. Discussing animals, poetry, or the theatre are great conversation starters.

Types of Events: Church services, art gallery openings, spa retreats, swimming parties, or meditation classes are great examples of events that are in sync with the nature of Pisces. People will want to escape from life's everyday activities. Create a mini-vacation from the world with soft music to provide a welcome rest.

Décor: A dream-like quality to the décor soothes the senses. Try shades of white on the table for everything, including the tablecloth, dishes, and floral arrangements. The subtle sound of a fountain gives the illusion of being outside by a quiet stream. A lovely little painting or a box of assorted tea make a wonderful hostess gift or party favor.

Food: Portuguese cuisine.

About the Author

Lynn Gordon Sellon has incorporated astrology into her life since childhood. She holds degrees in sociology and education. She is a professional member of the American Federation of Astrologers, and a Level IV consulting astrologer through the National Council for Geocosmic Research (C.A. NCGR). Lynn is the coauthor of Simply Math: A Comprehensive Guide to Easy & Accurate Chart Calculation, *and a contributor to Llewellyn's 2006 Moon Sign Book. In addition to writing, she maintains a professional astrological practice in Connecticut. She can be reached through her Web site at www.celestialguidance.com.*

Green Living:
We're All Connected

By Cathy Combs

The color green symbolizes growth, life, and hope in many of our worldwide traditions. In Mother Nature's brilliant, alive tapestry, the crops are good and there is hope for the future. I have always been an optimist, and I treasure the myriad expressions of natural beauty in life: sunrises, sunsets, rainbows, mountains, oceans, and deserts. I am touched by the small and huge acts of generosity and kindness I have experienced and witnessed because these acts speak to me of our incomparably fragile and beautiful connectedness. I recognize that we are all vitally connected!

Be Kind

I will never forget the response from a woman in a shopping mall, when I simply opened the door for her. She looked depressed and preoccupied as she walked toward me, and when I held the door open for her, she smiled and softly said, "Thank you." I smiled and said, "My pleasure." She stopped dead in her tracks, turned around, and backed up to look me. The look on her face was incredulous. It was like she'd never experienced an act of kindness before.

Be Kind to Our Environment

In our physical environment, green living expresses values such as:

- Recycle
- Use environmentally friendly, biodegradable products
- Eat locally grown organic foods
- Help to keep our air and water clean
- Don't litter
- Keep our local, national and international parks safe, clean, and beautiful
- Be mindful of Mother Nature's natural resources
- Use public transportation as much as possible
- Buy automobiles that get at least 35 miles per gallon
- Be mindful that all of our actions have immediate—and distant—consequences

Some time ago I read about a mind-boggling example of the impact our actions do have. In the U.S. it is our routine practice to load tons of garbage onto barges and dump this garbage in the ocean off the coast of Africa. I can only say I hope we're not still doing that anywhere! The way we live our lives makes a difference! We are delicately, intricately interconnected with everything and everyone in our universe!

I'm reminded of the beautiful motto of the Iroquois Confederacy: "In our every deliberation, we must consider the impact of our decisions on the next seven generations." This beautiful motto reminds us that our thoughts, words, and actions are powerful. What we think, say, and do literally come into manifestation. With our thoughts, words, and actions we create our lives, so it is in our best interests to mindful and to pay attention to the world we're creating.

Research done in the field of psychology over the last thirty years revealed some powerful and fascinating examples of how green-living values—recognizing our connectedness—affect our emotional environment. Some research efforts have now switched to a focus on what is called positive psychology, spearheaded by Dr. Martin Seligman. Rather than the illness focus of the last 150 years, his research focuses on "exploring and enhancing virtues such as creativity, courage, integrity, self-control, leadership, wisdom, and spirituality." The three pillars of positive psychology are: (1) positive subjective well-being, (2) positive character, and (3) positive groups, communities, and cultures.

This research adds a new dimension to the medical and psychological research of the past. It clearly indicates that people with optimistic attitudes and outlooks have fewer illnesses and outlive their pessimistic counterparts. Now we can literally see the results of our attitudes through the imaging capabilities of the PET scan as it shows us where the different areas of the brain register the impact of our acts of kindness, generosity, and anger. Our inner and outer environments mirror the impact of our actions!

The many levels of our vibrant interconnectedness are being expressed in the training and practices going on in our medical schools. The age-old practice of working seventy-two hours straight with no sleep is being discontinued as the body-mind-spirit interconnectedness is more widely recognized. Research clearly indicates a marked reduction in our capacity to function when we are sleep deprived. Sleep is restorative, and we need to sleep on a regular basis.

Current statistics show that over 60 percent of our medical schools now teach the blending of spirituality and medicine. Holistic healing, "hands on" healing, preventative medicine that focuses on maintaining wellness, and learning how to listen and communicate compassionately and effectively, are all part of the teaching curriculum in Western medical schools. Even the impact of prayer on patients' speed of recovery is being researched in carefully controlled scientific studies. It is felt that prayer changes not only our attitudes of hopefulness or despair; prayer changes us at a cellular level!

We have come to realize that when the body or mind is ill or well, it is a function of our connectedness with our spirit. When we feel uplifted and hopeful we heal faster. We are reaping the benefits of recognizing and treasuring our vibrant interconnectedness as a unified body-mind-spirit wholeness. This change recognizes our body-mind-spirit connectedness and our connectedness to each other as we work together to bring an attitude of wholeness to how we live and work together.

Be Kind to Your Neighbors Everywhere

Green living also extends into our physical, emotional, political, and spiritual understanding of our neighborhood, and it extends far beyond our immediate surroundings. We are invited to extend the concept of green living far beyond our immediate personal concerns to vibrantly engage in the healing of our precious planet Earth on every level.

I am so encouraged by the global efforts I see moving us in the direction of a generous, passionate, hope-filled effort to help and heal our entire world. By our choices we can either regard each other or we can destroy each other. Einstein movingly tells us of his reaction to this choice when he said, "If I had known what they were going to do with this knowledge I would've become a carpenter." Einstein made this statement after the atomic bomb was used for the first time.

As we move toward global recognition of our interconnectedness it seems we are invited to consider how far our hearts and minds and spirits can take us. Perhaps we feel invited to consider if, when, and how the fields of religion and science intersect:

never, always, or sometimes. With the advent of the information flowing from the fields of quantum physics and beyond, it seems we stand on the threshold of a dynamically pulsating new vision of who we are. These advancements make me wonder how much more intelligent our hearts will become! What other boundaries will we be meeting, considering and crossing? What other dynamic blends of body-mind-spirit connectedness will we be discovering? What questions will our discoveries compel us to ask and answer? With our seeming technological advancements the key question for us might be what will we discover about the power and necessity of love? It is no secret that love is transformative. It is no secret that love is healing. Can we teach people to love? What other biological connections to love will we discover? People who seem to have no capacity or will to love, what are the boundaries there for intervention? Is there more to it than changing attitudes and beliefs; more to it than healthy, peaceful social relationships and structures; more to it than political systems based on cooperation and mutual respect? Where will this cosmic love take us? Is that our next threshold to explore?

It seems to me that the boundaries and horizons of green living values are as far reaching as our hearts, minds and spirits can take us. As we continue to explore our conscious living capacity, our oneness with the natural rhythms and cycles of nature and each other, we step out into a flexibility, strength, resilience, and transformative love that is beyond anything we presently imagine. From this loving, wholehearted, generous vantage point I propose that there is room for everyone and everything in our precious Universe. There is room to embrace our heritage as caretakers. There is room to move beyond war and violence and fear. There is room to embrace a worldview that cherishes the old and the new. There is room to embrace and cherish a worldview that teaches us we do not have to destroy a culture in order to progress. We are generous enough to embrace and cherish paradox and cultivate the lessons and blessings we need to learn. I propose that there is more than enough room to lovingly embrace, encourage and cherish each other in our vibrantly, interconnected, shared Universe! I know this is true because I have experienced this level of loving generosity so many times in my lifetime. One such example is a man I had the great honor and joy of meeting in the 1980s. He was internationally known psychologist and writer Dr. Leo Buscaglia. Known to many as Dr. Love, Buscaglia radiantly epitomized the living spirit of love and generosity. The huge auditorium where he spoke was completely filled. People waited for hours to be hugged by him. He had said it was always his practice to hug everyone who wanted to be hugged wherever he spoke because he so believed in the power of loving people. I waited for my turn to hug him and to be hugged by him. When our eyes met I was thunderstruck. I "knew" he most definitely walked his talk. I could feel the love emanating from his presence. It was like looking into the eyes and heart of infinity. It was like we had known each other for all of eternity. This transformative example and many more like it are why I am so passionately devoted to green living; to living an optimistic, joy-filled, generous, caring, hope-filled life. Blessings to you, fellow traveler! I recognize my connection with you!

About the Author

Cathy Combs is a freelance writer and workshop architect specializing in personal empowerment and spiritual community leadership development. Cathy lives in Kansas City, MO. For more detailed information visit her Web site: www.cathycombs.com

The Mood Enhancer

By Cerridwen Iris Shea

You've heard it before: there's a lady in the Moon, or a man in the Moon; the Moon is made of cheese; werewolves transform in the light of the Full Moon. The Moon has cast a spell of fascination on mankind since humans evolved enough to recognize that there was such an object hanging in the sky. Many of the legends and lore deal with madness and loss of control, and so many generations have been exposed to the folklore that the negative response is almost reflexive. But is it possible to look to the Moon to enhance your moods in a practical and forthright way?

Farmers, who know that the lives of plants are enhanced by the movement of the Moon, have planted by the Moon for centuries. Tides are affected by the Moon, and since over half the human body is comprised of water (60 percent, according to most of the medical research, though it varies by individual, gender, age, and body type), why not use the Moon to enhance our own personal tides?

On a psychological level, darkness represents a part of ourselves that we either don't like, are unaware of ("in the dark"), or don't want to know. The more we deny it, the more we repress it, the more we pretend it doesn't exist, the more it will cause disruption and destruction in our lives. By enjoying "the light of the Moon," we can stop being at war with ourselves and lead healthier, more balanced lives.

At the simplest level, the Moon can enhance your mood simply via acknowledgement. The next time you are out at night, look up into the sky. Find the Moon (if you're driving, wait until you're at your destination or pull over—safety first!) Enjoy the shape of it—crescent or sphere—and the color of it. Depending upon the time of year and the atmospheric conditions in your region, there are huge variations in color, from the pale bluish-white Wolf Moon in January, to the summer yellow, to the bright orange globe that hangs low in the sky, to the Blood or Harvest Moon of October. Let the natural beauty of the night sky fill you and lift your spirits.

The three phases of the Moon—waxing, full, and waning—also have practical application. Farmers know that there are planting days and harvesting days.

The waxing Moon is the time from the New Moon to the Full Moon. It is a time for fresh starts, new projects, and growth. A glance each night at the growing Moon reminds you to reflect on how your current project grows, and to take delight in its progress. Instead of muttering over all the things you didn't get done on your to-do list, take a few minutes by the light of the Moon to congratulate yourself for all the things you got done. The Moon becomes a tool to practice self-encouragement. And the more you feel encouraged, the more you actually get done, and the balance tips in favor of your accomplishments.

The Full Moon is the time of fulfillment, accomplishment, achievement, ripeness, and maturity. It's a good time to reap the rewards of your hard work. It's also a time to be generous to those around you, to celebrate, and to communicate a sense of joy about what's good in the world. We live in frightening times, times when thousands of lives are extinguished in an instant via a terrorist's bomb or a major storm. Taking time during the Full Moon to celebrate what is right with the world renews and refreshes us. It gives us the strength and courage to keep working for a better, a stronger, a more compassionate, and a more loving world. If we only focus on the problems, we drain ourselves and are unable to take positive action. We must find ways to celebrate the positive. Taking a few moments to stand at the window or outside, enjoying the beauty of the full Moon, replenishes our own souls.

Waning Moon, when the Moon grows smaller and seems to vanish before its next cycle of growth, is a time to reflect, create quiet time, complete projects, and cut out of your life what you no longer need. It's not a time to fear loss. It's a time to rejoice in removing old, worn-out, useless habits to make way for something new at the New Moon. Each night, as you look up at the shrinking crescent, remind yourself how far you've come since the last New Moon. Reflect upon the goals you set for yourself. What was achieved? What fell by the wayside? What do you no longer need that you thought was so important earlier in the month?

We are fortunate because we have the opportunity for a fresh start thirteen times a year—each time the Moon begins its next journey. We can rearrange our priorities as our lives change. We can build on the foundation of the previous months. Instead of feeling locked in and trapped by our circumstances, we can use the Moon's day-to-day growth and change as inspiration for our own.

Feeling down? Wait until it's dark. Go outside and stare up at the Moon. Let the joy and the beauty, and, most importantly, the hope and possibility of positive change fill you. Hope and possibility are the first steps to action. The Moon is active every night. Use it to motivate the change you desire in your own life. Begin to define "lunacy" as "positive choice" rather than "lack of control."

About the Author

Cerridwen Iris Shea is a writer and teacher, and she loves ice hockey and horse racing.

Dining with the Stars

By Nancy Bennett

If Aries is such a strong sign, should an Aries food be strong too? Would you serve airy *hors-d'oeuvres* to an Aquarian? Is fish for a Pisces a no no? Whether it's a first date, a meal for one, or an astrological party, it is good to know which signs like which foods. Take this advice into consideration when you are dining with the stars.

Aries

For Aries, variety is not only the spice of life, it belongs in the kitchen too! Serving lots of small courses, buffet style, will win favor with the Rams in your life. Ethnic foods, especially European ones, are high on the list of favorites. Most Aries love meat (except the vegetarians). Barbecued ribs with fettuccini pasta, lamb Souvlaki with lemon potatoes, and a Greek salad on the side was a favorite meal my Aries friends all agreed on.

Not that they don't like desserts. Aries Jackie Chan, when in Toronto filming *The Tuxedo*, devoured a cake (called an Oreo Smash Cake) made by one cooking crew because he loved it so much. Chocolate covered almonds also favored high with Aries for a quick pick me up.

For starters, here is a soup recipe that is sure to please the Aries in your life.

Greek Red Lentil, Lemon, Rosemary and Feta Cheese Soup

2 cups red lentils
2 tablespoons olive oil
1 large onion, diced
2 teaspoons salt
8 garlic cloves, minced
2 carrots, diced
1 teaspoon cracked pepper
¼ teaspoon red chili flakes
1 tablespoon minced rosemary
2 tablespoons minced oregano
2 bay leaves
8 cups vegetable stock
Zest of lemon
Juice of 2 lemons
1 ¼ cup Feta cheese, crumbled
2 teaspoons minced rosemary
Cracked pepper to taste

1. Rinse lentils thoroughly in a colander under cold running water. Set aside to drain.
2. Heat oil in soup pot over medium-high heat and saute onion with 1 teaspoon salt until translucent. Add garlic, carrots, pepper, chile flakes, herbs, bay leaves, and remaining salt. Stir well; saute until the carrots are just tender.
3. Add rinsed lentils and stock; bring to a boil. Reduce heat to simmer and cook, partially covered, until the lentils are soft and falling apart.

4. Stir in 1 cup of crumbled Feta cheese.

5. Season soup with lemon zest, lemon juice; add more salt and pepper to taste. Combine the remaining Feta cheese, rosemary, and pepper. Sprinkle over the hot bowls of soup, and enjoy.

Taurus

You won't find many Taurus folk in fast food places. They like to savor their meals at home, served up with good wine and good company. Fish or shellfish such as lobster figure prominently for special occasions. If they are in a hurry (and Taurus hates to rush a meal) you may find them having pasta (George Clooney's favorite is Newman's Marinara Sauce on fresh pasta), or going all out on a monster burger.

When they want something sweet, they lean toward comfort food. A chocolate cake with mint ice cream is sure to satisfy the Bull. Taurus has a tendency to overindulge and pay the price later. If they keep up their activity level, all is well. You might suggest a nice brisk hike before that steak and lobster barbecue. Alongside that why not serve potatoes!

Double-Baked Stuffed Yukon Potatoes

4 medium Yukon gold potatoes
1 cup cooked crab
1 cup green onion, chopped
¼ cup sweet red pepper, diced
1 teaspoon garlic, minced
¼ cup olive oil
1 cup grated Parmesan cheese

Scrub potatoes and cook in large pot of salted water for 15 minutes or until almost tender. Drain.

1. Allow to cool to the touch. Slice potatoes in half lengthwise and take a small slice off the skin side of each half to make a flat surface. Use a small spoon to hollow out the middle of

each half, leaving a one inch "wall" to make a potato "boat." Reserve insides of potato for stuffing.

3. Remove any bits of shell and cartilage from crab meat. In a small bowl stir together crab, potato insides, green onion, red pepper, garlic, and 2 tablespoons olive oil. Add salt and pepper to taste.

4. Carefully spoon stuffing into each potato boat, packing firmly. Cover with plastic wrap, and refrigerate until ready to grill.

5. Prepare grill and preheat to medium. Brush bottom (flat side) of potatoes with remaining olive oil. Grill on top rack for 10 minutes or until bottoms are crisp and stuffing is heated through.

Gemini

Geminis like food, but make it snappy! They are folks on the go and don't want to spend hours in the kitchen. Geminis love pasta in different combinations. Seafood fettuccine drew twin applause, and Gemini Drew Carey likes a chicken tequila pasta. Geminis like fast food, but they can also appreciate the finer things. They may shock you with their eating habits. Sometimes they like to dress up or down for a meal just to have fun. For instance, Gemini Marilyn Monroe's favorite dessert was Miss Milton's Lovely Fudge Pie, and she'd eat it wearing nothing but Chanel No. 5 and a raincoat!

Geminis tend to have stomach problems, so they need to be careful of what they eat. If you can, slow them down! It'll help their digestion if they just take more time. Try this smoked salmon pasta recipe, but make sure to twin it with a good bottle of dry white wine.

Smoked Salmon Caper Pasta

l lb. penne pasta
2 tablespoons butter
1 small onion, finely chopped
5 ounces smoked salmon, coarsely chopped

1 cup heavy cream
2 teaspoons capers
Salt and freshly ground black pepper to taste

1. Cook the pasta in a large pot of boiling water. Meanwhile, prepare sauce.
2. Melt the butter in a heavy pan. Saute the chopped onion until it is soft and transparent. Add half the chopped smoked salmon and the cream. Warm the mixture gently, blending thoroughly with a wooden spoon. Keep warm but not boiling.
3. Once pasta has cooked (about 8 to 10 minutes), drain it well and pour it into a warm serving bowl. Add the sauce. Stir thoroughly and add a little freshly ground black pepper. Gently stir in the remaining salmon. Sprinkle with the capers and serve at once.

Cancer

People born under the sign of Cancer like to stay in their shell. Home-cooked meals, comfort food, and comfortable surroundings make them smile. Italian food is favored by this sign, especially pasta, chicken dishes, or lasagne with wine. Another Cancer favorite is the traditional turkey dinner with all the fixings. Indian food such as curries and samosas are Cancer pleasers.

Though some Cancers hate dessert, others go for decadence. Princess Diana's favorite dessert was pears in port wine sauce with cinnamon ice cream. Yum! For culinary Cancers try:

Prosciutto Turkey Marsala

6 tablespoons butter
8 thick slices cooked turkey breast
8 thin slices Prosciutto
8 slices mozzarella cheese
1 cup Marsala wine
Chopped parsley

1. Heat butter in skillet. Saute turkey slices until golden on each side. Remove and keep warm.

2. Place a turkey slice, mozzarella slice, and prosciuto slice back in pan, slightly overlapping. Continue in this order until all 8 pieces are in the skillet. Pour Marsala wine over all.

3. Cook covered 3 to 5 minutes, until it is heated through and the cheese is melted. Serve from the skillet, garnished with parsley.

Leo

Think warm foods when you think of Leo. Most of them *love* meat—the redder the better. Wild meat appeals to Leos, so if you have access to moose or venison, they will be sure to come for dinner. Cheese is a big favorite, as are curries, grilled salmon, baked potatoes and lots of raw salads.

Leos tend to overindulge at times, as you can see by Leo Sandra Bullock's special meal remembrance: "My favorite birthday meal was when a friend took me to the Kentucky Fried Chicken drive-through. We ate it all in the car, the extra crispy chicken, the biscuits, and the gravy. Then we hit the Dairy Queen. Going down, it was the best meal I've ever had."

Leo's weak spot is the heart, so the Lion's diet should include lean meats and veggies. Avoiding fat will keep a Leo in trim condition, though it's hard with all that tempting good food out there! Try this on your favorite Lion.

Steak and Blue Cheese Salad

3 tablespoons red wine vinegar
2 tablespoons olive oil
1 clove garlic, minced
1 teaspoon salt
1 teaspoon pepper
1 boneless beef sirloin steak, cut 1-inch thick (about 12 ounces)
1 tablespoon fresh chives, snipped
2 teaspoons fresh rosemary, snipped
4 thick slices red onion
6 cups lightly packed torn mixed salad greens
4 Roma tomatoes, sliced
1 tablespoon almond slices
2 tablespoons Blue cheese, crumbled

1. Combine vinegar, oil, garlic, salt, and pepper in a jar. Mix well.
2. Trim fat from steak. Remove 1 tablespoon of vinegarette and brush evenly onto both sides of the steak. Press herbs onto both sides of the steak. Coat both sides of onion slices with some of the remaining vinaigrette, reserving the rest.
3. Grill steak until meat is at desired doneness, turning once halfway through grilling. While the steak is grilling, add onion slices to grill and cook until tender and slightly browned, turning once halfway through cooking.
4. Divide the greens among four dinner plates. To serve, thinly slice the steak across the grain. Separate onion slices into rings. Arrange warm steak slices and onion rings on top of salad. Drizzle with the reserved vinaigrette. Top with tomatoes, cheese, and sliced almonds.

Virgo

Virgos demand order, especially in the kitchen. They like balanced foods, and can suffer from upset stomachs if they get nervous. Unfortunately some Virgos turn to food for comfort, or try fad diets to lose weight. Others don't really care what they eat, as they are too busy with life to pay attention to their diets.

Shania Twain is a vegetarian whose favorite food is pasta. Her favorite dessert is peach pie. Ed Begley, Jr.'s favorite snack is Avocado Veggie Sushi. Other Virgos like prawns with lemon butter, spring rolls, rice, and a seared Brie.

When cooking for a Virgo, fresh herbs such as mint, chives, and parsley should always be used, and vanilla ice cream should be made with real vanilla. Virgos want the best if it is going into their mouths! For a fresh starter for a Virgo try:

Walnut, Herb, and Gorgonzola Crostini

1 cup butter at room temperature
18 ¼-inch thick baguette bread slices, cut diagonally
6 tablespoons toasted walnuts, chopped

4 ounces Gorgonzola cheese, crumbled

3 teaspoons fresh thyme leaves

3 teaspoons fresh parsley, chopped

1 teaspoon fresh chives, chopped

1. Preheat oven to 400°F. Spread butter over one side of each baguette slice. Arrange slices on a baking sheet, butter side up, and bake until golden. Remove bread and let cool.

2. Reduce oven temperature to 350°F.

3. Meanwhile mix walnuts, Gorgonzola, and herbs in a medium bowl. Spoon nut mixture evenly on top of baguette toasts, pressing it in slightly. Bake toasts until cheese melts, about 6 minutes. Cool crostini slightly before serving.

Libra

If the scales are balanced, then Libras are happy. This can mean having two servings of everything, so plan on lots of little things, not large helpings! Libras love lots of savories, mini-desserts, and finger foods.

Libra Sarah Ferguson loves pasta, and for a treat, chocolate chip scones. (She has created a low calorie version of this through Weight Watchers.) Libras love fresh fruit, including blueberries, strawberries, and cherries.

Savory curries and chunks of cheese with good French bread make a great meal. For dessert, pumpkin cheesecake and apple pie tip the scales in your favor. Just make sure you have enough for seconds! For starters try:

Cheese and Chive Pillows

2 cups flour

¼ teaspoon salt

4 teaspoons baking powder

3 tablespoons unsalted butter

½ to ⅔ cup milk

2 cups strong cheddar cheese, grated

3 tablespoons chives, chopped
oil for deep frying

1. Combine flour, salt, and baking powder. Cut in butter. Add milk a little at a time to make a dough. Cover dough while you combine cheese and chives.
2. Roll the dough out very thin and cut into 2-inch squares.
3. Brush edges of each square with water, and put a dollop of filling in the center. Cover with another square, and press down edges.
4. Deep fry a few of the pillows at a time until golden and crisp. Serve warm with sweet and sour sauce.

Scorpio

Those born under the sign of Scorpio are passionate about their food and like it bold in flavor. They also love food that reminds them of home, so if you're dating a Scorpio, find out their Mom's standby recipes.

Prince Charles, a royal Scorpio, likes scrambled eggs and a good whiskey—though not together! Other Scorpios like a thick meaty stew with fresh baked bread, or Mexican food with lots of salsa and sour cream. French onion soup with lots of cheese also tops the Scorpio chart. For something zesty, try this on your Scorpio buddies at your next barbecue:

South of the Border Corn

Soak unhusked corn on the cob for half an hour, then cook on the grill until done (about 20 to 30 minutes). Meanwhile, prepare a mixture of:
    1 cup butter, softened
    1 cup mayonnaise
    1 cup Parmesan cheese
    2 tablespoons pico de gallo (or other Mexican spice)

Spread mixture on hot corn, and serve. Alternately husk corn after soaking and apply mixture liberally to it. Wrap in foil and cook on grill for 20 to 30 minutes, turning occasionally.

Sagittarius

Most Sagittarians *love* their food, but they don't always like to wait for it! Sandwiches, pizza, and Italian food hit the spot with this crowd. Spicy foods are in, as are hot wings and bowls of chili. They also go in for nuts, mushrooms, and great breads. For Sagittarian Dick Clark, chicken seems to figure high on his charts. If you check out the menu at his Bandstand Restaurant, a great sandwich he favors is the chicken, Portobello mushroom, and spinach on sourdough bread.

With all this decadence, Sagittarians have to watch that their love of great food and good wine does not interfere with their health. For your favorite archer try:

Pizza Chicken

4 skinless boned chicken breast halves
1 jar spaghetti sauce
4 slices Mozzarella cheese
¼ cup Parmesan cheese
Italian seasoning

1. Preheat oven to 350°F. Place breast halves in a casserole dish. Top with one jar spaghetti sauce (we like the Classico brand) Mozzarella, and Parmesan cheese with a generous shake of Italian seasoning.
2. Bake for 30 to 40 minutes. Cut into chicken to confirm doneness, as it will depend on the thickness of the breast.
3. Serve with a Caesar salad and garlic bread. Enjoy!

Capricorn

Don't try any haute cuisine on a Capricorn. This earthy sign likes simple foods, ones that fill them up and keep them going. Shrimp dishes, oyster stew, and pound cakes made with cloves or nutmeg are favorites. So are dark rich breads like pumpernickel or Boston brown.

The meal Capricorn Tiger Woods chose for the championship dinner at the Masters in 2002 included Porterhouse steak and chicken, with a sushi appetizer. (In case you didn't know, the year's winner gets to pick the menu, and pick up the tab!) From Capricorn Eileen K comes this recipe for the goat in your life:

Oyster Stew

    1 pint oysters, drain, strain and reserve liquid
    4 tablespoons butter
    Salt and pepper to taste
    1 teaspoon paprika
    1 teaspoon Worcestershire sauce
    1 quart whole milk
    1 cup sherry

1. Put cleaned oysters, strained oyster liquor, butter, and seasoning into a saucepan and simmer gently until oysters curl at the edges.
2. Add the milk and sherry and bring quickly to the simmering point. Serve hot with whole wheat bread.

Aquarius

Some foods they love, some they hate. Some they can't get enough of, and then all of a sudden don't want anymore. Aquarians crave adventure in their meals, and love to find new restaurants and new cuisines. For them, diet is *die* with a *t*, and they have a hard time always eating what is good for them. They need to temper the rich foods they love with fruit and fresh veggies in order to put order into their disorder.

Favorite foods include popcorn shrimp, spaghetti and meatballs, and mashed potatoes with gravy. When visiting the Tuscany II Ristorante, Aquarian Tom Selleck's favorite meal is liver and onions, a good steak, or the Dover sole. Being an Aquarian myself, I tend toward the ethnic. Ethiopian red lentils with Injera bread is a wonderful Ethiopian menu I use for wowing company. You will be amazed at how filling it is!

Ethiopian Red Lentils

  2 cups dried red lentils, washed
  6 cups water
  1 teaspoon turmeric
  1 teaspoon ground cardamon
  1½ teaspoon cinnamon
  1 teaspoon nutmeg
  1 teaspoon ground cloves
  3 tablespoons garlic, chopped
  red onion, chopped.
  ¾ cup red or orange peppers, seeded & chopped

1. Boil the lentils in water for five minutes, then drain, reserving liquid.
2. In a large pot melt ½ cup butter. Saute the peppers, spices, garlic, and chopped onions until they are tender. Add the lentils and 4 cups of the reserved liquid. Simmer, covered, over low heat 35 to 40 minutes, stirring occasionally to prevent sticking.

Injera Bread

  3 cups warm water
  2 cups self-rising flour
  3 tablespoons club soda

1. Add warm water slowly to the flour, stirring to make a thick batter (about pancake batter consistency). Add the club soda.
2. Cook half of the batter at a time in a non-stick pan. The bread is done when bubbles are on the surface and it is no longer wet. Turn it over for a brief searing when almost dry. Remove it to a plate and keep the breads separated with kitchen towels. Can be made up to three hours ahead, and it freezes well.

Pisces

This sign is big on seafood and natural foods. Some favorites include garlic prawns with lemon, crabcakes, and calamari. Pisceans tend to diet one day and binge the next. Self-control equals self-denial for this fish, and cheesecake, strawberry shortcake, and crunchy cereals make them feel comforted.

Caesar salad, especially with anchovies and organic greens, is a good healthy favorite among the Pisces lunch crowd. Actress Drew Barrymore likes sushi. She favors the spicy, crunchy tuna when eating out at En Sushi in California. Here is a favorite recipe I serve to my fishy friends.

Coquilles St. Jacques

    1 cup dry bread crumbs
    5 tablespoons butter, melted
    6 ounces grated Gruyere cheese
    1 cup mayonnaise
    ¼ cup dry white wine
    1 tablespoon fresh parsley, chopped
    1 pound sea scallops, quartered
    1 pound button mushrooms, sliced
    1 cup onion, chopped
    1 cup Parmesan cheese, grated

1. In a small mixing bowl, toss the bread crumbs with 1 tablespoon of melted butter and set aside.
2. In another small bowl, combine the cheese, mayonnaise, wine, and parsley; mix thoroughly and set aside.
3. Saute the scallops in 2 tablespoons of melted butter over medium heat until opaque. Remove from pan.
4. Reheat the pan over medium heat, and cook the mushrooms and onion in 2 tablespoons of melted butter until tender. Add the cheese mixture, and return the scallops to the pan. Cook until heated through and the cheese is melted.

5. Preheat broiler to medium/high. Spoon the mixture into individual sea shells. (Buy these at a cooking store.) Sprinkle the top with the bread crumb mixture and grated Parmesan.

6. Broil in preheated broiler 2 to 4 minutes or until browned and cheese is bubbly.

Whatever sign you are born under, make sure you enjoy your dining experience. Search out new recipes and interesting companions, or take comfort in familiar foods and warm surroundings. Bon Appétit!

About the Author

Nancy Bennett has had her work published in various Llewellyn's annuals, We'moon, Circle Network, and many mainstream publications. Her pet projects include studying history and creating ethnic dinners to test on her family. She lives near a protected salmon stream, where the deer and the bears often play, in British Columbia, Canada.

Who Rules the Moon?

By J. Lee Lehman, Ph.D.

Years ago, I noticed an odd phenomenon. In the modern astrology literature, it's almost impossible to avoid books that give lists of planets by sign, or planets by house, and so forth. These have been dubbed the cookbooks: they contain generally a paragraph or two to help the beginner try to understand the mixed concept of planet plus sign, or whatever combination. Before 1800 this is almost impossible to find. Why should there be this difference?

At first, I thought it was merely a difference in how astrology was being taught. A. J. Pearce was one of the nineteenth-century authors who itemized the planets by sign. But as I re-examined this, I realized that the publication of the cookbook list actually represented a shift in approach to the understanding of the planets.

Consider, for example, what William Lilly (1647) had to say about what the Moon rules:

Abscess, Apoplexy, Bartenders, Baths, Belly Fluxes, Bladder, Bogs, Brain, Brewers, Careless, Charwomen, Cold Rheumatic Disease, Cold Stomach, Common People, Convulsions, Drunkards, Edema, Epilepsy, Eye, Fish-Mongers, Fishponds, Fountains, Giddiness, Hates Work, Ladies, Lead Poisoning, Left Side Diseases, Measles, Menstruation, Messengers, Midwives, Navigation, Night Owl, No Concern for Future, Nurses, Obstructions, Pilgrims, Prodigal, Queens, Rheums in the Eyes, Rivers, Sailors, Silver, Soft, Stomachaches, Surfeits, Timorous, Vagabonds.

To update some of the terminology, a "belly flux" is a stomachache, and "surfeit" is eating or drinking too much.

Compare this idea to Alan Leo (1927) on the Moon:

> "The Moon acts as the vehicle, or link of communication between the Sun and each living thing. In Astrology the Moon is the representation of the Personality, the portion of the individual that is manifested during the one life period, and as such the Moon's position and aspects become the most important when judging a nativity."

—From *How to Judge a Nativity*

Notice how simplistic Leo's definition is by comparison. On the other hand, Lilly's list is clearly oriented toward horary, and only partially usable in natal. The implication is certainly there that the Moon rules certain professions, like brewers or sailors, but this doesn't look much like our modern conception of the Moon.

Let's take this up to the present time, with a definition of the Moon from StarIQ.com (www.stariq.com).

> "The Moon symbolizes emotions, instincts, habits and routine. It describes the ways in which we feel most nurtured and secure. The Moon also reflects the public mood as it changes signs every two to two and half days. The Moon shows how we were nurtured as children and the kind of caring we received from mother (or mother figure). We feel most at home with the Moon according to its sign, house, phase and aspects in the natal chart. It is a key planet of security and intimacy."

By this modern definition, we have the kind of encapsulated view of the Moon that we are used to seeing: key concepts like habits or security. Here, the psychological function of the Moon is dominant. So the obvious question is: What happened between Lilly and StarIQ?

To read Lilly's sample natal delineation, the answer is: a lot. Lilly describes the person's life, emphasizing what and when. The modern style is to primarily discuss who: the kind of person, not the things that happen to the person. It is virtually the difference between noun and verb.

But there are bigger changes still. The modern tendency is to equate planets, signs, and houses: the so-called twelve letter alphabet. There was less of a tendency to do this in earlier times, but the question remains: How much of a planet, or "Light's," meaning is derived from its sign rulership, and how much is not?

I would add a further question: How much has the meaning of a planet shifted in order to accommodate it to the twelve letter zodiac idea?

To begin to answer this first question, let's compare the three sources on their description of Cancer, the sign ruled by the Moon. Then, we can see just how much the overlap is in words between the planet (or in this case, Light) and the sign.

Cancer, according to William Lilly, overlaps with the Moon are underlined:

Algiers, Amsterdam, Belly: Upper, Breast Cancer, Breast Pains, Breasts, Brooks, <u>Cancer Disease</u>, Cellars, Cisterns, <u>Cold & Moist</u>, Digestion, Digestion Poor, Ditches with Rushes, Green & Russet, Holland, Milan, Mucus Salt Phlegm, Nipples, North, Prussia, <u>Rivers</u>: Great, Rushes, Scotland, Sea, Sea Banks, Sedges, Ship's Bottom, Springs, <u>Stomach, Stomach Absesses, Swelling: Watery</u>, Trenches, Tuberculosis, Variable, Washhouses, Waters: Navigable, Wells

The two overlap based on quality (cold and wet), the stomach, edema (the watery swellings here), and in association with rivers. This is not a huge overlap.

Cancer-rising Alan Leo:

"You have a strong domestic and social nature, warm affections, and are fond of home life. You are easily influenced by those whom you love or admire, but are apt to be cold, reserved, and distrustful to those you do not know well, or whom you dislike. You have an active imagination and fancy, and often live the past over again in your mind and anticipate the future. You have much prudence and forethought, are careful and cautious, and have a good deal of tenacity and firmness. You have some natural ability for trade and business management and might gain success in this direction, as you have a sense of value and economy."

Here there is no overlap at all, although this might be understated because Leo was applying Cancer to the Ascendant:

"Cancer is a water sign that nurtures and protects. It is the nest builder who provides emotional support and structure.Cancer is associated with the Moon, mother, home and family. It is highly responsive to the environment and is sometimes considered moody. This sign is often a collector of objects and memories. It appreciates the past, tradition and history. Cancer energy can pull a group together through its responsiveness to need and focus of emotional attention."

Here there is a greater overlap. "Mother" is an overlapping quality, as well as nurturance, as well as other emotional qualities. There is not a complete overlap; for example, both Lilly and StarIQ noted the use of the Moon for the common people, and there is no echoing of that idea in the sign of Cancer.

One of the principal components of the definition of Moon sign as it was understood was certainly the ruler of the Moon. Thus, it would be wise to consider how Mars affects the meaning of the Moon in Aries or Scorpio. The purpose of this chapter will be to review this effect.

However, before we can figure out how the rulerships affect the meaning of the Moon, we have to first understand what the Moon itself means. What do we understand as the bottom-line meaning of the Moon, apart from whatever houses it rules in a particular chart?

A Soul Connection

Historically, the Moon was understood as one of the two principal indicators of the Soul. The other was Mercury, but to understand this, we need to also understand Aristotle, whose writings exerted a profound influence upon all philosophical developments touching upon soul for centuries, including astrological developments.

First, we should be clear that Aristotle's understanding of soul was not the later Christian one. One could justifiably say that the greatest horsepower of medieval intellectual activity went into attempting to reconcile the Philosopher with Christian teaching. In the case of the Soul, the biggest inconsistency was that Aristotle did not believe in the immortality of the individual soul, although he left room for an impersonal soul. He believed that the individual soul was too inextricably wrapped up with the body to be able to survive the body's death. However, what he did say about soul was still important:

> "It therefore seems that all the affections of soul involve a body-passion, gentleness, fear, pity, courage, joy, loving, and hating; in all these there is a concurrent affection of the body. Consequently their definitions ought to correspond, e.g. anger should be defined as a certain mode of movement of such and such a body (or part or faculty of a body) by this or that cause and for this or that end. That is precisely why the study of the soul must fall within the science of Nature, at least so far as in its affections it manifests this double character."

Aristotle defined movement and sensation as the two qualities that indicated the presence of soul. In other words, living beings have soul (i.e., they move and experience sensation); nonliving things do not. The soul forms a composite with the physical mind: "Thinking, loving, and hating are affections not of mind, but of that which has mind, so far as it has it." Movement was a much more general concept to Aristotle than what we would define; it could include such things as thinking or feeling, or any other changes of state.

How do we understand this astrologically? The soul was understood as a nonphysical entity that was enmeshed in a body, that somehow moved and affected the body. This is why Aristotle believed that the (individual) soul did not survive death: that it was so entwined in the body, that separating from it would literally kill it.

The soul, however, experiences passions, what we would call emotions. These passions "move" the soul, and hence the body. Thus, we could understand this function of soul astrologically as showing what passions are likely to move the soul, and hence, the body. Practically, this indicates what passions, emotions, or processes are necessary for you to feel satisfied with life. This is, in the words of Joseph Campbell, the path by which you "follow your bliss."

So, what rules the Moon's passions? We can see this in part through the ruler of the Moon's sign.

Moon in Aries

Mars rules the Moon's passions. Mars, being hot and dry itself, expressing through a hot and dry sign (Aries) gives the passions what used to be called a choleric character: quick to anger, quick to love, acting in haste and repenting at leisure. Impetuous is a pretty good word, because Mars would always rather act than not act, so rashness is an issue here. You have an aspiring imagination, but are rarely fortunate for extended periods of time. Don't worry, your fortunes have a tendency to be always changing! .

Mars as the ruler of passion demands attention, demands solutions, demands action. Mars is not subtle, and Mars prefers the direct path to the indirect one. Mars as a guide to passion requires courage and conviction, but not necessarily forethought. And if you don't find a place in your life to exercise this action-orientation, you will be unhappy, frustrated and angry.

The effectiveness of this passion depends on the condition of Mars in the natal chart. Mars in its own signs Aries and Scorpio, and its exaltation Capricorn, tends to be better behaved. Mars in Libra, Taurus, and Cancer tends to be more demanding. Also, Mars in easy aspect to the Moon will tend to be more functional; the hard aspects of Moon-Mars very likely take their frustrations out on someone else's hide.

Moon in Taurus

Here Venus is the ruler. Venus is naturally cold and wet, and Taurus is cold and dry. The dryness of Taurus is mostly likely why the ancients did not consider Taurus to be a fertile sign, although I have found it to be so. Both Venus and the Moon have an immediacy to their passion, an "in the moment" quality. Venus is the planet of passion, but this passion is more than sexual, although that represents a component (Taurus was, after all, classified as a bestial sign, and bestial signs were thought to lack control). Venus needs proof of adoration, and that is what the Moon in Taurus craves. But, being an earth sign, Taurus recognizes the proof not so much through words as deeds. The Moon must feel valued to feel happy.

How well this works depends on the condition of Venus in the natal chart. Venus in Taurus, Libra, or Pisces, her ruling signs and exaltation, will reinforce the positive qualities of the Moon here. Natives are of ". . . gentle disposition, and obliging temper, a sober carriage and deportment, just in all his Actions, and consequently gains respect from all . . ."

But a Venus without such dignity, such as in Aries, Scorpio or Virgo, can mean that the Native comes across in ways unintended, such as bold, when that's not the best circumstance.

Moon in Gemini

Even in the seventeenth century, Gemini was known for gossip! This Moon has a distinct lack of tact, combined with the tendency to spread tales. The Moon's ruler, Mercury, takes on the qualities of what it is with, which emphasizes Mercury's tendencies to bounce back and forth between people, places, and things. The good news (and news is really Mercury's business), is that this can result in some really fabulous, if occasionally off-the-wall, trivia. The bad news is this is also "an ingenious subtile Person, notably crafty, yet generally unfortunate, unless other testimonies assist."

How well this works depends on the condition of Mercury in the natal chart. Mercury in Gemini or Virgo, his ruling signs and exaltation, will reinforce the positive qualities of the Moon here. This person is curious, and probably a bit of a busy-body. Interested, in other words. In the signs of its Detriment and Fall, Sagittarius and Pisces, the information gathered doesn't quite fit the free-for-all pattern of Mercury, but with a greater tendency to funnel the information into patterns where it may or may not fit.

Even if you don't want to be Gossip Central of your group, with this Moon placement you must find a place in your life to let Mercury do its thing, this place being perhaps related to either the houses that Mercury rules, or its house placement.

Moon in Cancer

Cancer is one of the signs that is interpreted strongly through its element, with the Moon in Cancer often coming across as rather moody, an interpretation obtained by combining the strong emotional nature of the water signs with the starts and stops of the cardinal signs. This is not the ancient idea. Coley referred to the Moon in Cancer as flexible, jocular, and pleasant, perhaps too much addicted to others' company.

So where did he get that?

The Moon in all definitions rules change, but this is going to be true whether the Moon is in Cancer or not. The cardinal signs would be expected to have the most swings, but by choosing the word "flexible," Coley had added a nuance to the strength of the Moon in its own sign: flexible implies the ability to adapt ñ but not the necessity. The rest of Coley's definition shows the strength of the Moon here: but he also emphasizes the social side. The soul does not exist well in a vacuum: otherwise, why be born into this teeming mass? Emotions are not taking place within a vacuum, but in relation to others; and with the Moon in Cancer, this can really work, if other chart indicators don't preclude it.

Moon in Leo

The Moon in Leo takes on the qualities of the Sun, its ruler; thus, Coley refers to it as "lofty, proud and aspiring Person, very ambitious of honour." Honor is a huge issue in the traditional meaning of the Sun; and its negative side, vainglory, needs to be understood as well.

The problem we have in understanding these concepts is that the modern conception of honor has gotten mostly subsumed under the term ego or egotistical, and in the wake of Freud, ego is a very loaded word. In traditional culture, one of the most important measures of a man (and hopefully a woman as well) is that one's word is one's bond—the ability to conduct oneself in a truthful and honorable fashion. This is the proper function of the Sun, and this linkage to the Moon in Leo is that the soul craves living by a code of honor. When honor is replaced by ego, then we get vainglory, and the negative side of the Sun. Without a place or a plan for honor, all that's left to this Moon placement is standing on ceremony. And that's what the tendency will be if the Sun is weakly placed in the chart, whether by being in Libra or Aquarius, or through aspect to the malefics.

Moon in Virgo

Here we arrive at the first "duplicate" sign (i.e., both Gemini and Virgo are ruled by Mercury, so just what is the difference, anyway?). The major difference classically is that Virgo is an earth sign and Gemini is an air sign, and this radically changes the interpretation. Thus, Coley refers to the Moon in Virgo as ingenious, melancholy, and well-reserved, with some covetous tendencies, not to mention "guilty of few commendable actions."

Let's sort these pieces out. The "ingenious" bit is simply a function of Mercury. "Melancholy" is a general function of earth signs. The modern understanding of melancholy tends to look a bit too much like Laurence Olivier playing a brooding Hamlet. A better description of this function was the brain revving on idle: the inability to turn off the mind, and the moodiness produced by thinking about something too much. And as for covetousness (not to mention the "few commendable actions"), Mercury is, after all, the thief. The Moon in Virgo shows a soul very much embodied and in the material word, able to manipulate it, and miserable, if there is no opportunity to do this.

How well this works depends on the condition of Mercury in the natal chart. Mercury in Gemini or Virgo, his ruling signs and exaltation, will reinforce the positive qualities of the Moon here. This person tends more toward the ingenious. In the signs of its Detriment and Fall, Sagittarius and Pisces, the covetous side may predominate.

Moon in Libra

Libra is the second sign of Venus, and like Mercury, the two signs of these inferior bodies are placed in air and earth. The interpretation of air astrologically has been radically altered by Jungian astrology, which has emphasized air's "thinking" function. What we have to sort out is the difference in "thinking" associated with the Moon, Mercury and Air, the three astrological components that relate to this word.

Historically, Mercury related to the rational soul; the Moon related more to the passions, although not completely. These could be understood not as active processes, but as faculties, or abilities: the ability to be rational, not necessarily steps one through ten of the actual sequence. The word that most characterizes the ancient idea of air is "rarefied." Air lacks the grosser dross of water and earth, and thus, represents not being in the body, but the essences extracted therefrom. Air is like the beginning of the purification which is the essence of the alchemical process: the extraction of essence.

How does this idea fit with Venus, the ruler of Libra? Coley says of the Moon in Libra that Natives are pleasant, jocund, and lovers of mirth and recreation, well-respected, and admired by women. The earthiness of Taurus is gone (unless, for example, the Native's Venus is in Taurus). The qualities of Venus emphasized are the aesthetic, which is Venus purified of its earthly dross.

How well this works depends on the condition of Venus in the natal chart. Venus in Taurus, Libra, or Pisces, her ruling signs and exaltation, will reinforce the positive qualities of the Moon here. An easy Venus makes this purification easy, and so you become a beacon for the positive side of the pleasure principle. But a Venus without such dignity, such as in Aries, Scorpio, or Virgo, can mean that the purification is problematic, and you may focus on the dross instead of the essence, unless and until you can train yourself to do otherwise. Either way, an aesthetic outlet is necessary for the Moon's satisfaction.

Moon in Scorpio

The two signs where the Moon is considered to be in debility are Scorpio and Capricorn, signs of the two malefics, Mars and Saturn. The Mars flavor malefic quality to the Moon is that Mars is hot and dry, while the Moon is cold and wet. These simply don't match! Curiously, though, it is not the Moon in Aries, where the sign itself is hot and dry, which was considered malefic. The Moon in Aries simply blew off steam and got it over with. It was the colder Moon in Scorpio, with the sign of the same nature as the Moon, which was classified as the malefic one. Why?

This is the Moon placement that reminds one that too much of a good thing can be a bad idea! The Moon is cold and wet, and so is Scorpio. Cold is actually a more dangerous quality to living things than Hot is. Cold is the quality of poison, and too much cold is the quality of death. But this is not the sense one gets with the Moon in either Cancer or Pisces: here it is the coldness of water combined with Mars' quality of cutting things off, abscission, as it's called in botany. The fixed quality of Scorpio also has a way of freezing the natural "fluxion" of the Moon, which by itself can make the Moon uncomfortable.

Coley says that Natives with this Moon placement can be very malicious and treacherous.

However, Coley emphasizes that the Native nonetheless chooses to be that way, and so may choose not to be that way as well, especially when alternatives can be pointed out by others. The qualities Coley mentioned are due to a direct clash of the Moon with Mars. Moodiness results from any unresolved conflict. Maliciousness and treachery are qualities of both a negative Mars and a negative Moon.

How well the possibility of choice may reign is dependent on the condition of Mars in the natal chart. Mars in its own signs Aries and Scorpio, and its exaltation Capricorn, tends to be better behaved. Mars in Libra, Taurus, and Cancer tends to be more demanding. Also, Mars in easy aspect to other planets will play more easily with others; the hard aspects make Mars very likely to take its frustrations out on someone else. And this is going to be especially true if Mars isn't given a forum. An idle Mars is a dangerous thing!

Moon in Sagittarius

Jupiter is the greater benefic, and the meaning of the Moon here shows it. Coley says that these Natives are generous, free-spirited, and passionate, although in the latter case, the passion wanes easily and quickly. But the Moon in Sagittarius is ambitious, aiming at great things.

The Natives are so obliging, they have a chance to achieve their goals because of the respect they generate. Constructive goal-setting is a vital activity for this Moon.

Ambition can be the dark side of Jupiter. Ambition for the right reasons can be a goal, and this can be the path when the Native's Jupiter is well dignified, especially in Sagittarius, Pisces, or Cancer. But ambition combined with pride is the path of an ill-dignified Jupiter, such as in Gemini, Virgo, or Capricorn, or afflicted by malefics; unless the Native steps off the path of least resistance and decides to take personal control.

Moon in Capricorn

The two signs where the Moon is considered to be in debility are Scorpio and Capricorn, signs of the two malefics, Mars and Saturn. Saturn's influence is much different than Mars, in that Saturn's intrinsic influence is cold and dry, just like the earth sign Capricorn. While cold is also a quality of the Moon itself, the effect is way too much cold, as Capricorn is the most extreme of the earth signs. (In classical astrology, the three signs of an element are considered to be increasingly extreme in their qualities as one progresses from Aries, and each sign gets more extreme, the higher the degree number of the placement.) Thus, one could argue that the melancholy qualities of Virgo are redoubled in Capricorn, and this may reflect on a critical difference between the Moon in Virgo (which has Triplicity there) and the Moon in Capricorn (which may have Triplicity, but also has Detriment). The inability to shut down the mind from idling in Virgo, which on a positive note can result in ingenuity, goes into overdrive in Capricorn, as well as turning in upon itself, resulting in a massive case of self-criticism. Here the quality of Saturn to see the cup half empty rather than half full has full reign.

In my opinion, Coley's comment that the Native is not inclined to high activity or thought, except when it comes to debauchery, is only referring to one component of the Capricorn Moon complex, namely, that Capricorn is a bestial sign. But for consistency's sake, one should say the same thing about Moon in Aries, Taurus, and half of Sagittarius as well!

What can help the Capricorn Moon is a well-placed Saturn in Capricorn, Aquarius, or especially Libra, as the malefics seem to work better in their exaltations compared to their rulerships.

What can also help, according to Coley, is a beneficial aspect from Jupiter, the Sun, or Venus. At least the illusion of permanency about something in the environment is critical to this Native's sense of well-being. An ill-placed Saturn in Cancer, Leo, or Aries can make this placement even more difficult, because it serves to emphasize the self-criticism.

Moon in Aquarius

One would think that Saturn's other sign would have as bad a classical reputation as the Moon in Capricorn, but that's not really so. In the Capricorn-Cancer axis, Saturn is the enemy of the Moon; on the Aquarius-Leo axis, Saturn is the enemy of the Sun. But more than that, it's clear that the old description of the sanguine or air temperament was the want-to-be type: the upbeat, sociable type who knows how to party. There is something distinctly pleasant about these air souls, because, despite the Saturn rulership, Coley could say of the Moon in Aquarius that Natives are ingenious, affable, and courteous, inoffensive to all, loving puzzles and recreations, and having an aptitude for invention.

If there seems to be a little Mercury in this definition, this clearly shows the Mercury nighttime rulership of the air Triplicity.

While this package doesn't have the down side of Saturn's other sign to the same degree, the utility of this Moon is still partly dependent on Saturn's placement: in Capricorn, Aquarius, or especially Libra, as the malefics seem to work better in their exaltations compared to their rulerships.

Moon in Pisces

Everyone has to not like some planet and sign combination, and this was not on Coley's short list of beloved combinations. Coley implied that this Native would be "unfortunate in most undertakings, neither good for himself or others."

Oh well! Apart from prejudice, why did he say this?

At first, it's rather surprising, because one would expect Pisces to be the best of all possible worlds: Jupiter-ruled, with Venus exalted here and the Moon one of the three Triplicity rulers. Is this just too much of a good thing? This might be the case, with Pisces being the coldest and wettest of the signs, perhaps there's just too much inertia (phlegm?) to overcome. Coley does say that a good placement in the chart, and good aspect patterns, will ameliorate these effects.

Coley ends his section on the signs with a very odd phrasing, given his seventeenth-century setting. In referring to the importance of aspects of the Moon in Pisces to "good and adjuvant," Planets, he says, "which must also be considered in all the Planets in their particular significations (especially of the disposition and qualities of the mind)."

About the Author

J. Lee Lehman has a Ph.D. in botany from Rutgers University. She is the author of several books, including Classical Astrology for Modern Living *and* The Martial Art of Horary Astrology. *She teaches classes in Amsterdam, and she is a professor and academic dean at Kepler College. In her spare time she studies herbalism and Chang-Hon-style tae kwon do.*

Resources Used in Lunar Gardening Guide

Page 21: http://agfacts.tamu.edu

Page 23: http://www.jacksonandperkins.com

Page 25, 38, 49: *Jude's Herbal Home Remedies* by Jude C. Todd (Llewellyn, 2005)

Page 27: http://maple.dnr.cornell.edu

Page 29, 30: *Gardening for Life The Biodynamic Way* by Maria Thun (Hawthorn, 1999)

Page 31: http://www.bcpl.net/~tross/by/house.html

Page 33: *Rodale's Successful Organic Gardening: Companion Planting* (Rodale, 1994)

Page 34: *Urban Gardens* by Sue Phillips and Neil Sutherland (CLB Publishing, 1995)

Page 35: www.sciencedaily.com

Page 36: *Backyard Almanac* by Larry Weber (Pfeifer-Hamilton Publishers, 1996)

Page 40: http://www.pawtuckawaybeekeepers.org/seedcatalog.htm

Page 44: http://faq.gardenweb.com

Page 45, 50, 59: *A Field Guide to Buying Organic* by Luddene Perry and Dan Schultz (Bantum Dell, 2005)

Page 56: *Let It Rot: The Home Gardener's Guide to Composting* by Stu Campbell (Garden Way Publishing, 1975)

Page 57: *Fields of Plenty: A Farmer's Journey in Search of Real Food and the People Who Grow It* by Michael Ableman (Chronicle Books, 2005)

Page 61: *Mushroom Pocket Field Guide* by Howard E. Bigelow (MacMillan, 1974)

Notes: